QUALITATIVE METHODS IN SOCIAL WORK RESEARCH Second Edition

Sandy Mahoney

QUALITATIVE METHODS IN SOCIAL WORK RESEARCH

Second Edition

Deborah K. Padgett

New York University, New York

Sage Sourcebooks for

the Human Services

Los Angeles • London • New Delhi • Singapore

For information:

Sage Publications, Inc.
2455 Teller Road
Thousand Oaks, California 91320
E-mail: order@sagepub.com

Sage Publications India Pvt. Ltd.
B 1/I 1 Mohan Cooperative
    Industrial Area
Mathura Road, New Delhi 110 044
India

Sage Publications Ltd.
1 Oliver's Yard
55 City Road
London EC1Y 1SP
United Kingdom

Sage Publications Asia-Pacific
    Pte. Ltd.
33 Pekin Street #02-01
Far East Square
Singapore 048763

Printed in the United States of America

Library of Congress Cataloging-in-Publication Data

Padgett, Deborah.
Qualitative methods in social work research/Deborah K. Padgett.—2nd ed.
    p. cm.
(Sage sourcebooks for the human services; v. 36)
Includes bibliographical references and index.
ISBN 978-1-4129-5192-0 (cloth)
ISBN 978-1-4129-5193-7 (pbk.)
    1. Social service–Research–Methodology. I. Title.

HV11.P24 2008
361.3072—dc22   2008011023

This book is printed on acid-free paper.

08   09   10   11   12   10   9   8   7   6   5   4   3   2   1

Acquisitions Editor:	Kassie Graves
Editorial Assistant:	Veronica K. Novak
Production Editor:	Kristen Gibson
Copy Editor:	Annette Pagliaro Sweeney
Typesetter:	C&M Digitals (P) Ltd.
Proofreader:	Sue Irwin
Indexer:	Terri Corry
Cover Designer:	Candice Harman
Marketing Manager:	Carmel Schrire

Contents

List of Tables, Figures, and Boxes

Preface

What a difference a decade makes! The first edition of this book was neither highly technical nor laden with details. Through its brevity and style of writing, I hoped that the book would be as engaging as the methods themselves. The interim decade has brought an unprecedented rise in the level of sophistication and diversification in qualitative methods. It has also witnessed an explosion in their popularity, attracting the attention of even the most diehard of quantitative researchers. From their origins in the social sciences to their rapid expansion in education, nursing, and social work, qualitative methods have never been more powerful or appreciated as they are today.

These days the challenges for qualitative inquiry are as much internal as external. Differences within the qualitative methods "family" range from paradigmatic allegiances to definitional issues to the lack of consensus about standards for quality. The first edition of this book opted for a generic approach, focusing on the common ground shared by these methods. However, events of the ensuing decade along with reader suggestions (including the helpful reviewers of the first edition of this book) have opened the door to this expanded, more comprehensive second edition.

What's New in This Edition

- Detailed description of six of the most commonly used qualitative methods (ethnography, grounded theory, case studies, narrative analysis, phenomenological analysis, and community-based participatory research)
- Inclusion of specific illustrative examples from the literature as well as from my own research
- Expanded discussion of the epistemological debates that continue among leading qualitative researchers
- A broad, multidisciplinary perspective that is rooted in social work but also applicable to public health, nursing, and other service-oriented professions

- An appreciation for the global nature of research problems and methods
- Expanded discussion of participatory action research as well as the role of social responsibility in all forms of research
- Greater emphasis on the specifics of coding and thematic development
- Detailed guidelines on writing a qualitative research proposal in the Appendix
- Exercises at the end of every chapter that can be done either individually or in a classroom setting
- Updated and expanded lists of recommended reading

Continuities From the Earlier Edition

- Conversational style
- Pragmatism rather than ideology with regard to "what works"
- Emphasis on observation as well as interviewing
- The importance of strategies for rigor in qualitative methods

Background to This Edition

The past decade has been a time of professional growth for me as a qualitative researcher. Having a doctorate in anthropology, subsequent postdoctoral training in public health, and federally funded mixed method research on breast cancer and mammography set the stage for this book's first edition. This second edition comes on the heels of several new personal and professional developments.

First, I edited a reader titled "The Qualitative Research Experience" (Padgett, 2004a) that afforded an opportunity to showcase the work of social work colleagues who had conducted exemplary qualitative studies. Second, all of the planets aligned so that I could fully practice what I preach. In 2004, I was able to secure funding for a four-year, all-qualitative R01 grant from the National Institute of Mental Health. Although hardly the first person to succeed at such an accomplishment (and definitely not the last), I found it deeply gratifying to obtain funding for an advocacy-friendly yet theoretically grounded study of homeless mentally ill adults in New York City. The project, titled the "New York Services Study," will be cited throughout this edition to illustrate a number of points. Lastly, New York University instituted a Global Masters in Public Health Program in Fall 2006 in which I was fortunate enough to play a key role. Involvement in this program has given me license to redevelop my anthropological and public health knowledge by teaching about community-based participatory research and sociobehavioral health issues from a global perspective. These influences are reflected in this revised edition.

Much has happened in the world of research to give impetus to a "qualitative revolution." The National Institutes of Health and the National Science Foundation have offered guidelines for qualitative research proposals along with specialized training programs and workshops. Although still of minority status in the United States (where the dominance of science and technology holds sway), qualitative methods have become increasingly visible in the scientific journals and conference programs of the professions—education, nursing, social work, public health, occupational therapy, and so on. The methods have also become a multidisciplinary meeting ground for researchers in the social sciences, humanities, and applied professions who eschew the scientific mainstream in favor of constructivist, postmodern approaches. Meanwhile, in the United Kingdom and Western Europe, qualitative methods have achieved parity or even a majority status in the social sciences and social work.

The upward trajectory in the popularity of qualitative methods in social work mirrors earlier trends in education and nursing. Nowhere is this popularity more evident than in the annual conference program of the Society for Social Work and Research (SSWR), an organization whose rapid growth has transformed the profession and endowed it as the preeminent place for knowledge development and professional pride.

The momentum of the "qualitative revolution" is strong and expansive. Qualitative methods, decidedly low-tech for much of their existence, have ridden the wave of technology development with the rise of analytic software programs such as ATLAS/ti and NVivo, digital audio and video recording, and the creative use of what the Internet has to offer in online data collection and file sharing. The creativity and commitment of qualitative researchers ensure that the methods will stay current with the pace of technological change.

I have taken the liberty in this new edition of occasionally pointing out weaknesses in quantitative methods based on my experience in conducting large-scale, multivariate analyses and teaching quantitative methods for 10 years. This is neither motivated by epistemological objections nor is it done gratuitously out of some deep-seated animus toward quantification. Instead, such targeted criticism is offered as a way of being more even-handed when discussing the limitations inherent in all types of methods. For too long qualitative researchers have been put on the defensive without getting the chance to turn the tables. This is my chance.

Last but certainly not least, events in the world have brought home the need for research that is relevant to human experience, which encompasses a broad range of problems from deeply embedded structural inequalities (poverty and discrimination) to acute but multiplying world crises such as wars and natural disasters. Researchers who aspire to be socially responsible have work to do. Broad-based aggregate data and quantitative analyses are needed to address social problems; grass-roots perspectives from (and involvement with) those most deeply affected are essential to understanding and acting to resolve these problems. Qualitative methods provide essential techniques for doing this.

Such real-world considerations sometimes get lost in the paradigm debates that continue within qualitative methods, particularly in academic circles. In a recent work (Padgett, 2004a), I described joining others in finding a home in philosophical pragmatism, that uniquely American phenomenon owing its existence to early 20th-century thinkers such as John Dewey, Charles Peirce, and Jane Addams (the latter of whom took seriously pragmatism's bent for social activism). Pragmatism was the philosophical foundation for much of the Chicago School's contributions to the social sciences, and it has undergone a revival in recent times. What Cornell West calls "prophetic pragmatism" (1989) and Howard Becker calls "practical epistemology" (1996) places a premium on the social relevance of research as its main claim to credibility rather than allegiance to one or another philosophical argument about the nature of reality.

Scope and Organization of the Book

This revised edition continues to emphasize the how-to aspects of qualitative inquiry. As the reader will see in Chapter 1 and beyond, the term "qualitative methods" covers a wide variety of techniques and approaches. These diverse approaches coexist as a loosely connected family—a bit contentious at times, but always interesting and lively.

The chapters are roughly organized around the sequential steps involved in carrying out a qualitative study—even though the reader is cautioned that qualitative inquiry is rarely if ever a linear process. Instead, it is recursive, going back and forth between data and analyses and between analyses and write-up until findings become consolidated into a form of representation that "fits" the phenomenon being studied.

Chapter 1 gives a brief history of the theoretical and disciplinary origins of qualitative methods, grounds the reader in epistemological and other sources of diversity within the qualitative methods family, and sets the stage for what follows. Chapter 2 has been reconfigured to include a description of six of the most commonly used qualitative approaches (ethnography, case studies, grounded theory, narrative, phenomenological, and community-based participatory action) to give the reader an overview of options from which to choose. Chapters 3 through 7 take the reader through the various stages of carrying out qualitative research: study design and sampling (Chapter 3), ethical issues (Chapter 4), entering the field and conducting observation (Chapter 5), interviewing and use of documents (Chapter 6), and data analysis and interpretation (Chapter 7). Chapter 8 is devoted to rigor in qualitative research, addressing what is often considered its Achilles heel. Chapter 9 provides guidelines for writing up the study and telling the story. Chapter 10 is devoted to mixed method studies, whose various iterations represent one of the fastest growing types of research. Finally, the Appendix presents the basics of writing a qualitative methods proposal based on my experiences and the experiences of others.

A Few Words on Writing and Terminology

This Preface seems the best place to make a few points about writing style and use of terminology. First, I have tried to incorporate sensitivity to gender, ethnic, and other forms of diversity throughout the text. Second, the awkwardness of nonsexist usage has led me to alternate use of masculine and feminine pronouns and to use plural pronouns on other occasions. Finally, I bring to this new edition a preference for the term "study participant" with occasional substitutions of "respondent," "interviewee," or "informant," depending on the context of the discussion. The researcher is also a "study participant," so this choice is not perfect but it seems most suited to the interactive dimension of qualitative research.

The reader has probably already noted my liberal use of the first person. This more informal style of expression has become commonplace in research and is a natural consequence of the trend toward greater self-disclosure and transparency. After years of being confined by the restrictive writing of quantitative reports, I am pleased to be able to write more informally and playfully. By the same token, I have tried to avoid unnecessary jargon and have highlighted key terms with italics to underscore what is important.

Although considerably longer, more comprehensive, and (I hope) more sophisticated, this revised edition is still an introductory text designed to complement specialized works and classroom instruction in qualitative methods. I have included examples and citations of these works throughout to aid the reader seeking more in-depth understanding of specific approaches and techniques.

One overarching goal of this second edition is to promote greater methodological transparency as well as rigor. Paying attention to what happens during a qualitative study—and meticulously documenting decisions and procedures even and especially when they change—ensures that others can understand how the findings were produced. There will always be an element of "trust me" in qualitative inquiry (compared to "trust the methods" in quantitative studies) due to its reliance on the researcher-as-instrument. But it is incumbent on qualitative researchers to minimize this tendency and demystify their methods as much as possible. This book is intended to help move us farther along in that direction.

When all is said and done, textbooks and coursework are necessary but never sufficient—mastery in qualitative methods requires hands-on experience. With this in mind, I invite you on a journey of discovery that I hope will keep you engaged and informed.

The Audience for This Second Edition

This book has its origins in the rapidly growing enthusiasm for qualitative methods in recent years. While rooted in the proud tradition of social work research, the chapters take an ecumenical approach and can be useful to a variety of practitioners and researchers in applied fields. Intended for graduate students, faculty, and other professional researchers, this book provides a solid foundation for carrying out rigorous and relevant research.

Acknowledgments

The many students and colleagues I have encountered as a member and former President of the Society for Social Work and Research (SSWR) have provided me with ideas and encouragement over the past 10 years for which I am deeply grateful. I offer my deep gratitude to the research team and study participants of the New York Services Study, the former including Andrew Davis, Ana Stefancic, Courtney Abrams, Ben Henwood, Kim Hopper, Colleen Gillespie, Michael Fung, Kristen Kang, Tazuko

Shibusawa, Cheryl Harris Sharman, and Rebecca Lopatin. The study, funded by the National Institute of Mental Health (#R01 MH69865), provided many of the examples used herein. My esteemed colleagues Daniel Gardner, Karra Bikson, and Debbie Gioia offered helpful comments along the way. Finally, I sincerely appreciate Kassie Graves at Sage Publications and the reviewers (including Section Editor Charles Garvin) whose comments and support made this revised edition possible.

1

The Qualitative Methods Family

A colleague once astutely remarked that virtually anyone can read and appreciate qualitative research—its narrative reporting style makes it appear deceptively easy to carry out. By comparison, a quantitative study relies on complicated statistical analyses that require prior knowledge to decode their meaning. Yet the appealing end product of a qualitative study represents the culmination of intense involvement and intellectual labor.

This, in a nutshell, is what this book is all about.

What exactly do we mean by qualitative methods? The term is a relative latecomer to the methodological lexicon, coming long after ethnography and other forms of naturalistic inquiry had been on the scene. There is no "one size fits all" qualitative method to make the definitional task easier; these methods are not always sharply distinct from quantitative methods. The tendency to dichotomize—"a mile wide and an inch deep" versus "a mile deep and an inch wide"—is useful heuristically but is sometimes misleading.

Nowadays, qualitative research can be referred to as a family of methods in which some members are more compatible than others. Some members have been around for a long time (e.g., ethnography, case studies, and grounded theory). Others such as narrative analysis, constructivism, and phenomenological approaches are newer on the scene.

Whether one celebrates its internal diversity or bemoans its fragmentation, the qualitative methods family is vibrant and appealing to researchers.

Differences From and Similarities With Quantitative Methods

Use of the phrase qualitative methods implies far more than the logistics of how data are collected and analyzed. To varying degrees, qualitative methods entail assumptions and approaches that set them apart from quantitative research as practiced in the sciences. At the risk of over-simplifying, the common denominators are:

- Insider rather than outsider perspectives
- Person-centered rather than variable-centered
- Holistic rather than particularistic
- Contextual rather than decontextual
- Depth rather than breadth

Qualitative methods emphasize being inductive over being deductive. They favor naturalistic observation and interviewing over the decontextualizing approaches of quantitative research. As such, they imply a degree of closeness and an absence of controlled conditions that stand in contrast to the distance and control of traditional scientific studies. Qualitative research is predicated on an "open systems" assumption where the observational context (and the observer) is part of the study itself (Manicas & Secord, 1982). In contrast, quantitative research favors a closed (or controlled) system approach in which every effort is made to neutralize the effects of the observational context (including the observer).

Qualitative studies seek to represent the complex worlds of respondents in a holistic, on-the-ground manner. They emphasize subjective meanings and question the existence of a single objective reality. Furthermore, they assume a dynamic reality, a state of flux that can only be captured via intensive engagement. Whereas the heart of a quantitative report is its statistical findings, a qualitative report is a bricolage, a pieced-together, tightly woven whole greater than the sum of its parts.

Doing qualitative research requires an unparalleled degree of immersion by the researcher as the instrument of data collection. Unlike the pre-coded standardized questionnaire, the qualitative researcher must be a sensitive instrument of observation, capable of flexibility and on-the-spot decision making about following promising leads.

Drawing these contrasts between quantitative and qualitative methods is a necessary heuristic device to highlight what makes qualitative methods unique. There are also similarities between the two methods; some believe that the differences are more stylistic than epistemological (Flaherty, 2002, p. 513). Among their shared characteristics, both quantitative and qualitative approaches are empirical, relying heavily on firsthand observation and data collection to guide findings and conclusions. Second, both are systematic. Contrary to some misperceptions, qualitative research is not haphazard or unfocused, nor is it prescriptive or predictable. This dynamic tension between flexibility and serendipity on the one hand and methodological rigor on the other makes qualitative research exciting and challenging. Qualitative studies start out as inductive but need not remain exclusively so; such studies often alternate between induction and deduction (Morgan, 2007).

The Intellectual Life Course of Qualitative Methods

The Formative Years

The scope and purpose of this book do not allow an in-depth treatment of the long and complex lineage of qualitative methods. Nevertheless, it is useful to provide an overview of their "donor disciplines" such as anthropology, sociology, philosophy, and linguistics (McCracken, 1988), as well as the next-generation disciplines that have embraced and extended the methodologies known collectively as "qualitative." The latter include (in rough chronological order): education, nursing, and social work.

The longest tradition of qualitative inquiry belongs to anthropology, originating with late 19th-century ethnographies of non-Western peoples and cultures and continuing today, albeit in much different form. The era of the Lone Ethnographer (Rosaldo, 1989), which extended until World War II, introduced many of the defining characteristics of qualitative methods as they are known today. Interestingly, the leading anthropologists of their day—Boas, Kluckoln, Malinowski, Lowie, Benedict, Mead—offered minimal guidance in the how-to aspects of ethnographic fieldwork. Instead, oral traditions and learning-by-doing constituted methods training.

By the mid-20th century, the Chicago School of sociologists had begun to produce a rich and varied body of qualitative research based on observations closer to home, including studies of medical students

(Becker, Geer, Hughes, & Strauss, 1961) and entire towns and communities (Lynd & Lynd, 1937, 1956). Based at the University of Chicago, the sociology department pioneered an approach that became systematized as a unique methodology, beginning with the early leadership of Robert Park, Ernest Burgess, and W. I. Thomas, and culminating with the publication of *The Discovery of Grounded Theory* by Barney Glaser and Anselm Strauss (1967). Glaser and Strauss's vision of inductively derived midrange theories was set against two intellectual traditions dominating 20th-century social science in the United States—on the one hand, a fascination with the nomothetic (i.e., the grand theorizing of Sigmund Freud, Karl Marx, and B.F. Skinner), and on the other hand, a commitment to anthropology's trademark emphasis on localized idiographic description.

A number of exemplary qualitative studies of American life were produced by social scientists during this golden era, including *Whyte's Street Corner Society* (1955), Goffman's Asylums (1961), Powdermaker's *Stranger and Friend* (1966), Liebow's *Talley's Corner* (1967), and Stack's *All Our Kin* (1974). These works endure as classic examples of *verstehen*—understanding of human interactions and societal structures via participant observation.

An unprecedented move toward elucidating and codifying qualitative methods began in the 1970s, heavily influenced by Glaser and Strauss's grounded theory (Charmaz, 2006; Glaser & Strauss, 1967; Strauss & Corbin, 1990), but also by the works of anthropologically trained researchers in the field of education such as George and Louise Spindler, Jules Henry, and Harry Wolcott. Much of what is the received wisdom about qualitative methodology today was developed by members of this second generation of researchers, including Yvonna Lincoln, Egon Guba, Madeline Leininger, Michael Q. Patton, Janice Morse, Margarete Sandelowski, Matthew Miles, Michael Huberman, and John W. Creswell. In sociology, the new generation included, *intera alia*, Norman Denzin, Paul Atkinson, Kathy Charmaz, Jaber Gubrium, and David Silverman and in anthropology Pertti and Gretel Pelto, Michael Agar, H. Russell Bernard, Gery Ryan, and Jeanne Schensul. Psychology arrived on the scene somewhat later (Rennie, Watson, & Monteiro, 2002) as did social work (Padgett, 2004a; Riessman, 1994).

The Rise of Quantification and Operationalism

The life course of qualitative methods was profoundly affected by the rise of statistics and survey research beginning in the 1930s. Quantification was developed decades after field observation and ethnography had become popular in the biological and social sciences. (Consider the 19th-century contributions of Charles Darwin and Bronislaw Malinowski.) The dominance of quantitative methods was not foreordained but nevertheless became a reality by the mid-20th century.

Two converging trends made this dominance of quantitative methods possible. First, mathematicians (Fisher, Pearson, and colleagues) began to develop formulas for correlating numerically measured phenomena to assist in agricultural research on fertilizers and crop yields. Second, an interest in business and marketing took root in sociology that represented a distinct alternative to the Chicago School's focus on immigrants and communities. Paul Lazarsfeld and colleagues at Columbia University's sociology department were leading proponents of this shift toward survey research, opinion polls, and mathematically driven sampling.

The post–World War II economic boom, the Cold War arms race, and the U.S.–U.S.S.R. competition in outer space led to an unprecedented degree of interest in scientific research just as statistical methods and computer systems were being developed that could accommodate large datasets and multivariate analyses. This rise and dominance of *operationalism* (i.e., measuring things in order to study them) effected a dramatic change in the social and behavioral sciences, coinciding with (and contributing to) a decline in the popularity of ethnographic and case study approaches. Nowhere was this more apparent than in the nascent discipline of psychology, where measures derived from psychodynamic and behaviorist theories became the order of the day. In academia, psychology experiments became a standard part of undergraduate education. In education, business, and the military, psychological testing and measurement were considered the most reliable means of screening and detecting the troubled as well as the more "intelligent" or capable.

Among the social sciences, sociology, economics, and political science became heavily quantitative by the 1970s. This shift had the side effect (whether intentional or not) of aligning some of these disciplines with the well-funded "hard" sciences of biomedicine and technology. History and anthropology also joined in the popularity of quantification but retained a strong allegiance to qualitative methods.

According to sociologist Andrew Abbott (1997), a troubling turning point in the era of quantification came when social scientists began to move from correlations to causation, an ambitious undertaking made possible by sophisticated statistical modeling procedures such as path analyses. Problems arose when the popularity of causal modeling outpaced researchers' willingness or ability to meet its daunting assumptions. For example, one of these assumptions—temporal antecedence of the presumed cause—was routinely violated by use of cross-sectional (non-longitudinal) data. Other assumptions—normal distributions of variables, reliable and valid measures, lack of multi-collinearity—were neglected or inadequately addressed. Finally, the randomized experiment, considered the "gold standard" for establishing causation, was infrequently used compared to quasi- or non-experimental designs and a reliance on statistically controlling intervening variables. Moreover, many experiments were beset by high rates of attrition, and their narrow sampling criteria made generalizing problematic.

Quantitative researchers can be forthright in admitting that such problems exist. Leading methodologist Donald Campbell expressed his own doubts about the unassailability of quantitative designs and his previous dismissal of case studies (1979). However, most tend to overlook problems or view them as solvable by further refinement of statistical methods and designs. Laudable as these efforts may be, they are often absent from the vast research literature in which non-probability sampling is common, experimental designs are rare or flawed, and measures have questionable validity.

A quantitative study can excel in meeting all demands for internal and external validity and still offer a frustratingly incomplete and decontextualized portrayal. The quantitative investigation of a phenomenon requires breaking it down into observable parts, thereby severing the ties that bind them in order to measure each one separately before recombining them for statistical testing of relationships and causal predictions. This extraction and reduction produces a curious situation in which the ubiquitous aspects of human lives—messy, interconnected, and ever-changing—are considered little more than "methodological nuisance"(Abbott, 1997, p. 1162). The statistical solutions to these challenges—testing interaction effects, "censoring" outliers, and constructing structural equation models—are flawed approximations at best.

Since the 1960s, an abiding faith in science and technology caused the scales to tip heavily toward quantification. Quantitative methods have undoubtedly brought new knowledge, ranging from sophisticated opinion polling to mapping the human genome. No one wants to turn back the clock when it comes to life-saving medications and surgical techniques made available by rigorous experimentation. However, problems arise when one approach, quantitative or qualitative, is presented as having all of the answers (or raising the only questions worth asking). Thankfully, greater balance is evident these days.

Paradigmatic "Camps" in Qualitative Methods

Positivist reasoning and quantification came under withering criticism from academic thinkers in the latter part of the 20th century. This broad-based critique drew on 20th-century philosophy (particularly phenomenology) but owes most of its impetus to the post-1960s upheaval among French intellectuals including Jacques Derrida, Michel Foucault, and Pierre Bourdieu. A number of philosophers and social scientists in Europe and the United States joined a burgeoning postmodern movement (Harding, 1987; Rabinow & Sullivan, 1979). In anthropology, Geertz (1973, 1988) and Clifford and Marcus (1986) inspired a profound re-examination of ethnography in light of previous assumptions of "naïve realism." In sociology, Berger and Luckmann's treatise on the social construction of reality (1967) provided a revelatory counterpoint to positivism. Last but by no means least, Lincoln and Guba's landmark book *Naturalistic Inquiry* (1985) and their subsequent collaborations with Norman Denzin set definitional boundaries around "qualitative methods" as separate from and largely in opposition to positivism and quantitative methods. Invoking Kuhn's (1970) observations on paradigm shifts, these proponents argued that epistemology was paramount and positivism was incommensurable with the nascent approach of constructivism. By the late 1980s, disciplinary boundaries were becoming blurred as social scientists embraced the humanities—philosophy, literature, and the arts—and produced works such as poetry, dance, and autobiography

Interestingly, the epistemological debates were heating up at roughly the same time that qualitative methods were gaining a secure foothold in the practice-based professions of education and nursing; social work was a bit later on the scene but no less enthusiastic (Chambon & Irving, 1994; Rodwell, 1998). Learning about qualitative methods meant being drawn into paradigm arguments in which one was urged to declare allegiance (with the "side" considered superior championed by the leading methodologists of the day). For opponents of positivism, the label given to this resistance—postmodern, anti-foundational, post-structural, constructivist, interpretivist—mattered less than the message being promulgated. Rather than softening, this stance became more solidified in the successive editions of the *Handbook of Qualitative Research* (Denzin & Lincoln, 1994, 2000, 2005).

Constructivism—a belief that human phenomena are socially constructed rather than objectively "real"—proved to be a liberating force for many researchers (Charmaz, 2006; Denzin & Lincoln, 2005). It has led to re-examination and reflexive critiques of what is meant by "race," "gender," "deviance," and "mental illness" among many other social "facts." Exposing the ways that such concepts are invented and reified has been a prime source of new understanding in the social sciences. The rub comes from taking this point of view to mean that there is no reality attached to concepts such as "race" or "gender." Although few would argue that "race" is one of humanity's most troubling inventions, it has an objective existence manifested in the discriminatory treatment of individuals with darker skin common to so many societies. Similarly, "poverty" has multiple meanings—absolute and relative—and all have consequences for health and well-being (Link & Phelan, 1995).

A third epistemological camp is explicitly devoted to research on inequalities as an ideological and moral imperative. Critical approaches such as feminist, Marxist, race, and queer theories (Harding, 1987; Ladson-Billings, 2000; Madison, 2005; Olesen, 2000; Swigonski, 1994) are united in their commitment to the disempowered. Critical theorists point to inequalities based on gender, race, social class, and sexual orientation as hidden (and not-so-hidden) subtexts of much of the knowledge produced by Western science. Left unchallenged, these inequalities are reinforced through power differentials that are virtually self-perpetuating. Of the three camps, critical theory probably has the narrowest base within qualitative methods, more often associated with discursive critiques in law and cultural studies than with empirical research.

Whether by default or deliberate intent, postmodern critiques embraced qualitative methods as the "answer" to the flaws and reductionism of positivist research, and the constructivist and critical theory camps became aligned with the postmodern movement (although some individual members kept their distance). Their hortatory language and indictment of all things positivist set the stage for a mild counter-rebellion by pragmatists and others unwilling to accept the conflation of methods with epistemology.

The resistance to postmodernism came from several quarters. In a book on critical ethnography, Thomas accused its followers of being "armchair radicals" (1993, p. 23). Concerned about the characterization of ethnography as caught up in a "crisis of representation" (Denzin & Lincoln, 1994), the *Journal of Contemporary Ethnography* featured articles in which leading ethnographers rejected this notion along with calls that "science in any of its revisionist postpositivist forms" be rejected in favor of "post-Marxism and communitarian feminism" (Denzin, 2002, p. 484). Snow asserted that the postmodern elevation of texts reversed the proper order of things (i.e., interpretations have to come from somewhere and the nitty-gritty work of observation makes them possible; 2002). Flaherty decried the "endless cycle of advocacy and exegesis" (2002, p. 509) that favors form over content and text over context. Finally, in an essay reviewing postmodern texts in qualitative research, Travers states that postmodernism has been passé since the 1990s, remaining "in vogue only in certain sub-fields of qualitative research and in cultural studies" (2006, p. 267).

The Pragmatic Middle Ground

Whether its time has passed or not, few would question the enthusiasm and dedication of postmodernism's adherents as they seek a moral high ground in research using qualitative methods as the best (and only) means to that end. However, it is possible to appreciate aspects of the critiques (especially those focused on the privileges of power) without endorsing the whole paradigmatic package. After all, ethnographers and grounded theorists were practicing "interpretivism" long before it became part of a postmodern agenda, and they continued to do so using symbolic interaction theory, phenomenological approaches, and social constructivism without declaring allegiance to a particular camp. Similarly, doubts about quantification and traditional research designs have emerged from within the positivist camp (Campbell, 1979) as well as from without (Abbott, 1997)—most scientists these days accept that knowledge is provisional and research is value-laden.

The stubbornly independent thinking that characterizes the qualitative family ensures its intellectual vitality regardless of which (or how many) camps seek to hold sway. Indeed, the paradigm debates have always had more traction in intellectual circles and methods texts than in the day-to-day world of qualitative researchers. Whether acknowledged or hidden, the foundation laid by the Chicago School's symbolic interactionism and pragmatism continues to undergird much of what is now called qualitative research (Snow, 2002).

Several qualitative researchers (Becker, 1996; Creswell, 2007; Patton, 2002; Tashakkori & Teddlie, 2003) have gone on record favoring pragmatic philosophy. A uniquely American phenomenon developed by John Dewey, Charles Peirce, and Jane Addams (among others), pragmatism was a reaction to metaphysical arguments on the nature of Truth and Reality (Cherryholmes, 1992; Menand, 2001; Rorty, 1998; West, 1989). Rather than take a stand on such philosophical conundrums, pragmatists accept the fallibility of knowledge development, elevating utility over ideology or philosophy. Thus, one can be comfortable with the notion that there are occasions when reality claims can and should be made ("geno-cide in Rwanda"), when a presumed reality practically cries out to be deconstructed ("deviant behavior"), and when multiple subjective mean-ings can produce a broader understanding of something ("chronic back pain"). Put another way, all concepts are human inventions, but some are more socially contrived and consequential than others.

Anthropologist Nancy Scheper-Hughes argued in favor of a "strong scientific and moral imperative to get it right" (1996, p. 891). Thus, "while reality is always more complex, contradictory and elusive than our lim-ited theories and methods can possibly encompass, some things remain incontestably 'factual'" (italics in original; 1996, p. 891). Scheper-Hughes goes on to discuss the need to boldly report acts of genocide and violence that beset many of the world's poor and displaced.

Evidence-Based Practice and Qualitative Methods

Coming directly out of a positivist framework, evidence-based practice (EBP) became a powerful movement sweeping through health care in the late 20th century (Gibbs & Gambrill, 2002; Morse, 2006). Rooted in biomedicine, EBP presents a standing challenge to the practicing profes-sions to offer "evidence-based" interventions and abandon those found to be ineffective or harmful. Determinations of effectiveness are made using a "hierarchy of evidence" that places randomized experiments at the top.

With the rise of EBP, meta-analyses and systematic reviews have gained favor as a means of synthesizing extant research. The Cochrane and Campbell Collaborations (the former dedicated to health and the latter to social welfare, education, and criminal justice) have generated numerous reports from such syntheses showing the effectiveness (or lack thereof) of interventions ranging from breast cancer screening to anti-psychotic medi-cations (see www.cochrane.org and www.campbellcollaboration.org).

It is perhaps not surprising that Cochrane reviews have multiplied while the Campbell initiative has been slowed by the complexities of social welfare research as well as the scarcity of experimental trials. Even when available and amenable to meta-analysis, the evidence remains problematic given the dynamic, often-changing conditions of social work, human services, educational, and criminal justice systems.

Overarching concerns about EBP center on the narrowness implied by scientific definitions of "evidence" and the methods deemed adequate for its determination. From a qualitative research standpoint, the elevation of experimental evidence from "gold standard" to "only standard" is worrisome because it leaves little or no room for the creativity and flexibility of qualitative studies (Morse, 2006). Practitioners' responses in some quarters were to embrace the reflective practitioner approach as an alternative (Schön, 1983). Schoen's work has proponents within social work given its emphasis on a type of self-evaluation that avoids the empiricism and external validation implied by traditional research (Butler, Ford, & Tregakis, 2007; Yip, 2006). Although some proponents of EBP have expressed interest in accommodating qualitative methods, progress has been slow and understandably hobbled by the distinctive nature of qualitative studies.

The EBP movement clearly has its limitations, although its underlying premise is difficult to repudiate. Who, if anyone, would want to use a surgeon who ignores the latest research findings and prefers to rely solely on personal experience? In retrospect, empirical research on Bruno Bettelheim's "cold mother" explanation for autism might have prevented the damage it caused to parents and families of autistic children.

At the same time, acceptance of what EBP has to offer need not lead to devaluing other forms of knowledge (e.g., subjective meanings, cultural beliefs, and discursive revelations). EBP advocates must take qualitative methods seriously or risk becoming narrow and losing relevance. A step in the right direction has been taken by some leading quantitative researchers who have gone on record favoring qualitative methods as a "touchstone of reality" in community-based interventions (Hohmann & Shear, 2002, p. 205). The survival of the EBP movement (or some newer iteration such as "best practices") depends on fostering appreciation for multiple methods.

Theoretical and Conceptual Frameworks in Qualitative Inquiry

Some Are a Better Fit Than Others

The relationship between qualitative research and theory is complex and subject to varied opinions (Anfara & Mertz, 2006). On the one hand, allowing one or more theories to drive the inquiry deprives a study of what qualitative methods do best—explore the unknown or find new ways of understanding what is known. On the other hand, qualitative studies do not take place in a conceptual vacuum.

It is helpful to distinguish among several versions of what is meant by "theory" in the social and behavioral sciences. This variety in meaning of "theory" is due to differing degrees of explanatory ambition, conceptual abstraction, and openness to multiple interpretations. These differing meanings include: 1) grand theories having a sweeping scope and high level of abstraction (e.g., Freudian or Marxist theory); 2) somewhat less ambitious theories in psychology and sociology, of which some are more amenable to being operationalized and tested than others (an example of the former is Bandura's Self-Efficacy Theory and of the latter is Bowlby's Attachment Theory); 3) critical theories (feminist, race, queer, etc.) that address societal inequalities; 4) theories that operate as an "open system" and are not deterministic (e.g., Blumer's Symbolic Interaction Theory or Bronfenbrenner's Social Ecology Theory). Falling short of full status as a "theory" are: 5) conceptual frameworks that offer organizing principles and evocative concepts for research without being strongly predictive (e.g., the Health Belief Model and the Andersen and Newman model of service utilization); and 6) inductively derived "mid-range" theories that have been the foundation of grounded theory methodology.

Perhaps not surprisingly, Versions 1 and 2 are least suited for qualitative studies to the extent that they are determining rather than orienting in their intent and use. Psychological and biomedical theories present a distinct challenge because they are focused on identifying and solving problems of an intra-psychic or physical nature. As such, their underlying propositions are less open to non-pathologizing interpretations. Critical theories (Version 3) have been adopted by many qualitative researchers as a one-to-one fit but are less about methodology than ideology. In contrast, Versions 4 and 5 are a closer fit for qualitative research given their openness to inductive reasoning. Version 6 is only possible with qualitative research.

Qualitative researchers often use a variety of theories and conceptual frameworks to mine relevant concepts for use (known as "sensitizing concepts" in grounded theory). Here again, some theories and frameworks are a better fit than others. The concepts of "mastery" and "sense of control," for example, could be borrowed from self-efficacy theory because of their versatility and interpretive latitude. On the other hand, the importation of "transference" from psychodynamic theory is problematic because it is a clinical label for an unconscious process not amenable to empirical verification.

Concepts not deeply enmeshed in theoretical frameworks can also be useful. Recent interest in "social capital" is an example (Szreter & Woolcock, 2004), as are "stigma," "identity," and "fatalism." As Barney

Glaser aptly noted, concepts have staying power and the capacity for representation and evocation that transcends vivid description (2002). Their contribution to a qualitative study is never guaranteed, but without conceptual frameworks coming before (and most importantly from) data analysis, the study's contribution is severely diminished.

The Place and Timing of Theories in Qualitative Studies

In contemplating the role of theories in qualitative research, a few questions arise:

- What (if any) theoretical ideas and concepts are to be used?
- When do they inform the study?
- How are they incorporated into the study?

Answering these questions can depend on the study's epistemological foundation as well as its approach and methodology. If epistemology is viewed as occurring "upstream" and methods "downstream," theories and conceptual frameworks operate somewhere in between. Figure 1.1 depicts this flow from the abstract to the concrete, with examples given for each phase indicated by Roman numerals. It is fair to say that many qualitative studies start at Phase IV and bypass the earlier three phases altogether.

The "what" question builds on this discussion with the additional point that qualitative researchers may simultaneously draw on several theoretical frameworks and concepts as "lenses" through which the study's data and ideas are refracted. This is a good reason for adopting a multidisciplinary perspective, because an openness to ideas from a variety of sources lends freshness and creativity to a qualitative study. However, it also entails making decisions and taking risks.

How might this work? A study of family caregivers of schizophrenia patients might draw on concepts from social exchange theory (such as reciprocity), from the research literature (such as burden and stigma), and from the researcher's practice orientation (such as resilience and recovery). These represent a place to start but hopefully not to finish, their survival dependent on whether they earn their way into the findings (Charmaz, 2006). The study's potential is fully realized when its findings invite the reader to understand caregiving in a deeper, more nuanced, and even surprising way.

The "when" question about theories refers to timing (i.e., whether theories influence the study from the beginning or are held in abeyance

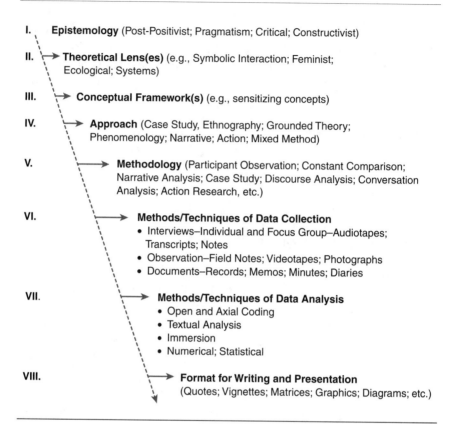

Figure 1.1   The Foundations and Processes of a Qualitative Study

until the data analysis and interpretation phase). The latter approach is often used in phenomenological research, which favors immersion and fresh insights. Most qualitative approaches, however, involve some theoretical ideas and concepts early on in the process; these ideas and concepts may remain during the analyses and some new ones may be incorporated as well. In a sense, Phase II in Figure 1.1 can be seen as cascading down over subsequent phases, although it should never lay a heavy hand or crowd out serendipitous and inductive findings.

The how question is the most challenging (and least discussed) question pertaining to the role of theory in qualitative research. As a rule, theories are imported but not necessarily incorporated into qualitative studies (i.e., they are held lightly and discarded easily). In the early stages of a study, theories provide leads and directions in formulating study questions. There are few guidelines to follow; each researcher must decide how much (or how little) to do this.

The importation of theoretical ideas becomes more complicated in the data analysis stage because by this time emergent ideas begin to support or supplant previous concepts and ideas. As will be discussed further in Chapter 7, the interpretive latitude exercised by the qualitative researcher is considerable. Qualitative researchers are obliged to be careful when making the "how" decision (i.e., going where the data lead rather than following their own personal predilections).

Reasons for Doing Qualitative Research

What kinds of research interests are best suited for qualitative research? There are several scenarios possible. These are not mutually exclusive, nor are they exhaustive, but they do provide some of the more common arguments for using qualitative methods.

1. You are exploring a topic about which little is known—especially from the "inside" perspective. This approach is the hallmark of qualitative methods. The following list of dissertation topics pursued by doctoral students I have worked with is one indication of this:

- Young women who self-mutilate their bodies (Susan Conte).
- South Asian women's experiences with arranged marriage (Reji Mathew).
- "Gender-queer" young adults who refuse to be labeled by their biological sex or sexual orientation (Jennifer Lewis).
- Adolescents who run away from their Orthodox Jewish homes (Patricia Attia).
- Male batterers' relationships with their partners before and after violent episodes (Christine Theuma-Wilkins)

There are many fascinating research topics (e.g., risky sex among men "on the down low" who proclaim themselves heterosexual, women who are impregnated by rape and decide to keep the child, parents who adopt disabled children from foreign countries, family members who participate in assisted suicide). Such topics need not be left pristinely untouched. What is important is that too little is known about them and an in-depth understanding is sought.

2. You are pursuing a topic of sensitivity and emotional depth. Social workers and other human service professionals routinely encounter human crises and dilemmas that require empathy and understanding. These professional experiences provide a wellspring of ideas for research

and the use of a standardized, close-ended interview would be inappropriate or insensitive.

For researchers interested in behaviors considered taboo or stigmatized, qualitative methods may be the only plausible approach. Ethnographic studies of cocaine dealers, gang members, sex workers, and car thieves portray the lives of individuals who are not likely to cooperate with the usual forms of survey research. Moreover, studies of sensitive topics need not be confined to the fringes of polite society—one can "study up" as well as "study down" (e.g., community leaders after a natural disaster, business executives with gambling addiction, doctors who abuse prescription drugs). Of course, members of an elite target population are often the hardest to study, capable of using their power to limit access in ways that the poor cannot (Hertz & Imber, 1995).

3. You wish to capture the "lived experience" from the perspectives of those who live it and create meaning from it. When researchers seek *verstehen* (deep understanding), they pursue studies that are *emic* (i.e., focused on the insider point of view, rather than *etic* [the outsider's perspective]). Examples include studies of the lives of older homeless women, the experiences of chronic pain patients, or the day-to-day dilemmas of caseworkers in a child welfare agency.

4. You wish to get inside the "black box" of practice, programs, and interventions. Perhaps not surprisingly given the push for accountability in social services, program evaluations have become heavily focused on quantitative outcomes. Yet qualitative methods have a secure place in evaluation research (Padgett, 2005). They are a natural fit with formative evaluation given their capacity to identify unforeseen effects of a new program that may hamper (or pave the way to) its implementation. Likewise, qualitative methods in process evaluation shed light on how (not whether) a program succeeds or fails.

Of course, so much of professional practice plays out in messy, unbounded ways that do not lend themselves to preformed standardized measurement. The deeply communicative aspects of practitioner–client relationships are fertile ground for narrative analysis, the daily hubbub of an agency or clinic practically cries out for ethnographic observation (Hall & White, 2005), and that rare but successful pairing of program theory and staffing can set the stage for a case study of best practices. Qualitative studies do not yield "hard" outcomes, but their naturalism and agility can produce a description that emerges organically from the practice setting.

5. You are a quantitative researcher who has reached an impasse in explaining or understanding. It is striking how often unanswered questions emerge during quantitative studies that call for qualitative research. My earlier quantitative research on ethnic differences in mental health services help-seeking frequently led me to fall back on a "cultural" explanation calling for more in-depth examinations of how members of ethnic groups perceive mental illness and the service delivery system (Padgett, Patrick, Burns, & Schlesinger, 1994). The insurance claims database we used was of no use for such a purpose.

6. You are seeking to merge advocacy with research. Broadly interpreted, this reason underlies much if not all of social work research. When merged with overt activism, *action* and *participatory research* are devoted to countering the effects of oppression and social injustice (Fals-Borda & Rahman, 1991; Freire, 1973; Reason & Bradbury, 2001). Rooted in the efforts of community activists, feminists, and Third World liberation movements of the 1960s and 1970s, action research seeks to fuse knowledge building with advocacy. Although the nature of the researcher–community partnership varies considerably, an overall goal is to use research methods on behalf of social change. Although both qualitative and quantitative methods can be used, the central premises of action research are closely aligned to the relationships common to qualitative research.

In summary, there are many sound reasons to do qualitative research— some or all of the aforementioned scenarios may underlie a particular study. There are also reasons not to pursue qualitative research. Foremost among these is that the topic of interest is better served by quantitative designs such as experiments or surveys. Second, anyone seeking qualitative methods as "the easy way" should be forewarned—the intensive labor and immersion required of the qualitative researcher are reason enough to think twice.

Desirable Qualities and Skills in the Qualitative Researcher-as-Instrument

The abilities needed to successfully carry out qualitative research draw on a number of talents, traits, and skills. The researcher's unique position as the instrument of data collection imposes special burdens as well as opportunities. By comparison, quantitative researchers rely on preset standardized questionnaires and measures. Assuming the instructions are followed carefully, they yield quantitative data that do not vary according to the abilities and personal qualities of the researcher. Quantitative research designs also provide a degree of structure that guides the process and reduces ambiguity and uncertainty.

A qualitative study's success depends heavily on the researcher's personal qualities as well as intellectual capacity. When carried out by a collaborative team, these qualities need to be present within the group. The absence of structure allows wide latitude—to reach creative heights as well as the depths of intellectual paralysis and/or disturbing biases. A few qualities that an individual can have or cultivate make the conduct of qualitative research more successful. These include: flexibility, self-reflection (reflexivity), and an ability to multitask in an iterative, nonlinear way.

Flexibility is a state of mind and of behavior (Ely, Anzul, Friedman, Garner, & Steinmetz, 1991) well-suited to the unpredictable, ever-changing landscape of naturalistic inquiry. This happens on a number of fronts. Respondents may suddenly refuse to cooperate with an interview, put off being interviewed, or not show up at all. They may divulge shocking information, make sexual overtures, or suddenly turn the questioning around to put the interviewer on the spot. Data analysis may (and often does) lead to new directions and new study participants. One's favorite ideas or theories may not be borne out and, as a result, may have to be cast aside. The strength and success of qualitative research lie in the researcher's ability to go with the flow rather than always try to control it.

Reflexivity, the ability to examine one's self, is a central preoccupation in qualitative research. As noted by Michael Agar (1980), "the problem is not whether the ethnographer is biased; the problem is what kinds of biases exist and how can their operation be documented" (p. 42). Examining one's biases is not a one-time thing, but requires ongoing vigilance throughout the course of the study.

Finally, a qualitative study is guaranteed to produce vast amounts of raw data awaiting management and analysis from its earliest stages. The ability to multitask on a number of levels (i.e., to simultaneously collect and analyze data, keep track of what is happening via memos, and remain open to new insights and the bigger picture) must be present and constantly nurtured in the researcher-as-instrument.

In addition to personal capabilities, certain skills are essential to the qualitative research enterprise. Among these are the skills of observation and interpersonal communication. Both of these are common elements of a practitioner's training, but their application in qualitative research follows a different track. When teaching qualitative methods, I ask my students to carry out an exercise in participant observation. They must go to the public place of their choice (a park, subway station, street fair, playground, etc.), observe the action for one hour, and write up field notes describing what they have seen. What a departure this is for them! Trained to actively engage clients and focus on problem resolution, they must be passive observers of all they can take in. The open-ended nature of qualitative observation can be awkward and even painful for individuals who are more comfortable with the "filters" of clinical theories and the authority to guide what happens.

The interpersonal skills of empathy and sensitivity, so important in clinical practice, are put to somewhat different ends in qualitative research. Rather than foster engagement with clients for treatment purposes, these skills enable listening as part of the pursuit of knowledge and understanding. This requires a degree of humility and subordination of self that takes some getting used to.

Finally, two of the most essential skills needed in qualitative research are the interrelated abilities to think conceptually and write well. The need to think abstractly and create new perspectives is the sine qua non of qualitative methods. Termed *theoretical sensitivity* by Glaser (1978), this refers to the ability to give interpretive meaning to data, to separate the wheat from the chaff.

Formulating ideas and developing concepts and theories depend on the ability to write. Experienced qualitative researchers often remark that the act of writing (i.e., recording memos and writing up preliminary ideas) is central to the success of a study. Quantitative researchers also need to think conceptually, but mostly at the beginning rather than throughout the study. And the writing of quantitative findings is largely formulaic, leaving comparably little room for discretion and creativity.

A well-developed sense of humor helps enormously in qualitative research, particularly the ability to laugh at oneself. One's vulnerability and inexperience when entering the field almost guarantee that there will be mistakes; some of them will be funny in the eyes of others. (Anthropologists invariably have stories of abject humiliation and about jokes made at their expense.)

Finally, there is the capacity for collaboration. With the exception of doctoral dissertations, the days of the lone investigator are fading fast. Although individuals can and still do carry out qualitative studies with little outside assistance, the scope and sophistication of research makes teamwork and collaboration increasingly the norm. Multidisciplinary participation is especially welcome in a qualitative study in which the richness of insight is enhanced by differing perspectives.

Studying the Familiar Versus the Unfamiliar

It is useful to consider the social, cultural, and psychological distance to be traveled when embarking on qualitative research. There are so many potential topics of study that the choices can seem endless. The physical setting can be nearby or halfway around the world. The topic can arise from a number of places, including personal and professional interests as well as sheer intellectual curiosity about some aspect of the human condition as yet unknown. This distinction between studying the familiar versus the unfamiliar (Ely et al., 1991) has far-reaching implications.

The temptation to stay with the familiar can be powerful. Many a valuable study has had its origins in personal biography: Irving Zola's (1983) struggle with physical disability, Catherine Riessman's (1990) exploration of divorcing couples, and Arlie Hochshild's (1989) study of working mothers are a few examples. Among doctoral students I have known, studies of single fathers, interracial couples, and breast cancer survivors were motivated by personal concerns.

Professional interests and accessibility often converge. Hence, teachers carry out studies in schools, nurses conduct research with patients, and psychologists study their undergraduate students. For social workers, research usually involves what is familiar—social service agencies and their clients. Studying practice settings is quite natural for many professions because the pursuit of knowledge has an ultimate goal of improving practice.

There are two main advantages to studying the familiar:

1. Easier development of rapport: With the familiar, the path to acceptance and cooperation is usually smoother and comfort levels are higher. This is no small benefit, as gaining access to a research site and to respondents can be very demanding for the qualitative researcher.

2. A head start in knowledge about the topic: Studying the familiar presumes prior knowledge about the subject, either through personal or professional experience.

There are also disadvantages. Perhaps most obvious are the risks of being too close. For example, let us say that you are an AIDS counselor and have chosen to study support groups for persons with AIDS. In an interview, one of the study participants reveals that he refuses to take his antiretroviral medications because of the side effects. You are appalled, because you have seen firsthand how these drugs can prolong life. The temptation to overstep bounds is strong when one is on familiar turf.

Consider another example of an agency supervisor interested in studying her own program. What happens if/when the staff find it difficult to accept her in this new (and considerably humbler) role as a qualitative researcher? Those who cooperate might give prepared answers, worried that they might be judged harshly. The remedy for these dilemmas is straightforward but far from easy: find a way to make the familiar unfamiliar (Ely et al., 1991).

Fascination with the unfamiliar, a longstanding motivation in qualitative research, offers its own advantages. Starting with the vantage point of an outsider means having the distance needed to discover tacit cultural rules and norms. In this instance, role confusion is less problematic because one enters the field with the identity of a researcher.

Of course, studying the unfamiliar can be risky. Just as knowing too much creates blinders, knowing too little can lead to prejudice and stereotyping and "filling in the blanks" prematurely. Accessibility and acceptance are more demanding when entering unfamiliar territory. One must negotiate with formal gatekeepers as well as individual respondents to enlist their cooperation and trust. Reversing the process—making the unfamiliar familiar—requires patience and persistence (Ely et al., 1991).

Values and Social Responsibility in Qualitative Research

Qualitative methods have an inherent appeal to social workers and other practitioner-researchers because they are rapport-driven and do not strive for value-free (or value-minimized) inquiry. Their low-tech "go where the participant is" approach is also an attraction.

However, qualitative methods are not inherently morally or ethically superior. Anthropologists have long been accused of supplying "insider" information to European colonial authorities as well as the U.S. Bureau of Indian Affairs. One of the most egregious examples of complicity was the 1960s revelation that anthropologists were deeply involved in the CIA's Project Camelot, a counter-insurgency campaign designed to suppress populist movements in South America. Although this led to a decades-long boycott of intelligence work by ethnographers, some have recently returned to government work by giving counter-insurgency advice to the American military in the "war on terror" (Packer, 2006).

Clearly, qualitative methods can be used for questionable, even unethical, ends. Yet the vast majority of qualitative studies not only "do no harm" but have quasi-therapeutic effects on the study participants. This is largely attributable to the way that qualitative research is carried out (e.g., the reversing of power differentials to ensure that participants are the experts and the ethos of sharing study findings).

Social work research is change-oriented, regardless of methodology. As such, it is unapologetically committed to improving peoples' lives by contributing to more effective and humane practices and policies. One means of expressing these values is to stress human agency and a strengths perspective as a counterbalance to the pathological approach borrowed from medicine and underlying much of clinical practice as it has historically developed (Saleebey, 2005; Schein, 1987). Another related track is to infuse one's research with a consciousness of diversity and of "insider" perspectives (Rosario, 2007). In qualitative research, a concern for human agency is manifested in the ways that human actions are observed and interpreted, in the questions asked and in the interpretation and presentation of the findings. One does not manufacture strengths if they do not appear to exist. Similarly, the temptation should be resisted to portray study participants solely as victims to draw attention to their plight.

How does a socially conscious researcher maintain this balancing act? One way to do this is by distinguishing between personal strengths and larger structural forces. Consider, for example, a hypothetical study of mentally disabled persons confronted with cutbacks in their government benefits. When writing up the study (assuming the data go there), we emphasize their resilience (i.e., how they seek assistance from family and friends amidst tremendous financial stress). But their families have economic burdens of their own and the costs of housing and food already exceed the monthly government check. Thus, the message of the study is one of perseverance in overwhelming circumstances. This could be illustrated using case histories of individuals living in fear of eviction, their mental fragility worsening and their informal resources depleted. In this way, the report can become part of public advocacy without sacrificing the nuance and detail that the methods provide.

What happens if the findings directly conflict with goals supporting social advocacy? It is highly unlikely that a study's results would directly contribute to or worsen misfortune in people's lives (regrettably, few studies are taken seriously enough at the practice or policy level in the first place). However, the temptation to distort or mislead, even for noble purposes, should be resisted at all costs.

Choosing the Topic and Making the "Argument"

Explicitly or implicitly, scholarly work is built around making an argument and using rhetorical devices to support it (Charmaz, 2006). Researchers must anticipate (and internalize) the "so what?" question because their interest in a topic may not resonate beyond their immediate circle of friends and family (if at all). I have witnessed many a doctoral student whose research interests stemmed from personal experience (e.g., single parenthood, infertility, a patient's suicide, and cancer survivorship). As discussed earlier, studying the familiar has both advantages and disadvantages. When it comes to making the argument, the burden of proof falls heavily on those studying the familiar. The more personal the interest, the greater the risk of sounding and being self-absorbed rather than scholarly. Of course, the topic may be unfamiliar to the researcher but written about extensively by others. Here, the "so what?" question compels an explanation for why the new study is needed.

Researchers interested in exploring unknown (or relatively unknown) terrain have a distinct advantage (anthropology made its reputation in this way). However, an esoteric or narrowly defined "unknown" topic can erode this advantage. Patricia Attia, a doctoral advisee of mine, chose to study Orthodox Jewish runaway adolescents—a problem virtually unknown even within the Orthodox community. Such a study clearly had practice implications and appealed to Patricia as a social worker. It also had utility insofar as it addressed the needs of a small but growing religious community in Brooklyn, New York. But the dissertation's scholarly impact depended on its broader applicability—to understanding adolescents and family dynamics, to exploring boundary maintenance among ethno-religious communities, and to examining the differential impact of acculturation across generations of immigrants. Only the researcher can make these connections through well-honed arguments and interpretations (which Patricia was able to do).

Research topics are usually familiar and previously studied but nonetheless raise intriguing questions. These also require compelling arguments to counter the "so what?" question lying in wait. For researchers seeking external funding, the stakes are the highest. As will be discussed in greater detail in the Appendix, one's powers of persuasion and rhetorical grab are fully put to the test.

Introducing the New York Services Study (NYSS): A Qualitative Study of Homeless Mentally Ill Adults in New York City

Being fortunate enough to receive a four-year, all-qualitative grant from the National Institute of Mental Health (NIMH) in 2004 was, for me, the culmination of longstanding personal and professional interests. A post-doctoral-funded professional re-tooling at Columbia University's School of Public Health in the mid-1980s provided training in quantitative methods and opportunities to collaborate with senior researchers analyzing data from a survey of New York City's homeless shelters at the height of the homelessness crisis. Serendipitously, a fellow researcher, psychologist Sam Tsemberis, decided to return to clinical work and conduct homeless outreach for a public hospital in New York City. This position ultimately led Dr. Tsemberis to start the first-ever "housing first" program for the homeless mentally ill in 1992. Four years later, I gladly accepted Sam's invitation to serve on the Pathways to Housing Board of Directors. The values of the Pathways program—offering independent housing and services without requiring abstinence and medication compliance first—fit with my own views regarding consumer empowerment and choice.

During my period of Board service, Pathways to Housing became part of a federally funded study that compared the Pathways model to the dominant "continuum" approach (in which the homeless mentally ill must become clean and sober and live in congregate care with accompanying rules and requirements). The New York Housing Study was a randomized experiment that examined housing stability and other quantitative outcomes from 1997 to 2001. As it happened, few meaningful group differences were found at the study's end beyond that of greater housing stability for the Pathways subjects. This raised questions about the impact of housing first but also about whether the quantitative measures were capturing what was really happening. (Anecdotal reports by the study's interviewers and interviewees pointed to greater dissatisfaction and life problems among the control group participants who remained either in congregate care or on the streets.).

Intrigued by this discrepancy, I drew on my previous quantitative research on homelessness and my self-proclaimed expertise in qualitative methodology to prepare an all-qualitative R01 grant proposal for submission to the National Institute of Mental Health. Success in obtaining funding took a revised submission that ultimately garnered strongly positive reviews.

The New York Services Study (NYSS) began in September 2004 with staff consisting of a full-time project director (Andrew Davis), several interviewers (Ana Stefancic, Courtney Abrams, Ben Henwood, Kristin Kang, and Rebecca Lopatin), and two part-time transcribers. The NYSS had three specific aims that revolved around identifying what worked and did not work in the service delivery system intended for homeless persons with serious mental illness and co-occurring substance abuse. Specific examples from the NYSS will be used throughout this book to illustrate various facets of a qualitative study.

Summary and Concluding Thoughts

The qualitative methods family is a robust and occasionally rambunctious group. At times, it seems that its members' only commonality is their resistance to the primacy and dominance of quantitative methods. Beginning with a rich historic background synonymous with ethnography (and, later, grounded theory), these methods grew ever more diverse and multidisciplinary. Modern influences ranging from mid-20th-century phenomenology to late 20th-century postmodern criticism brought variety in epistemology and methods. Beginning in the 1970s, the various non-quantitative methods that became known collectively as "qualitative" came into full flower—with phenomenological and narrative approaches joining ethnography, grounded theory, and case studies.

The flourishing of qualitative methods took place despite (and because of) the well-established dominance of quantification in Western science. Made possible by the development of statistical analyses and the post–World War II arms and space races, this dominance has eroded in recent years as the limits of operationalism have become apparent. Recent calls for evidence-based practice have renewed interest in aggregate (and aggregated) findings, but have also raised further questions about the nature of evidence and the methods used to determine its existence.

In addition to tracing its history, this chapter introduced key topics that cut across the landscape of qualitative inquiry, including the role of theories and concepts, reasons for using qualitative methods, the advantages and disadvantages of studying the familiar versus the unfamiliar, and social responsibility in research. Addressing each of these orients the reader to the complex and discretionary aspects of qualitative methods—all of which will be in evidence in the chapters to come.

This chapter ended with an introduction to the New York Services Study (NYSS), the NIMH-funded project that has afforded me the unprecedented opportunity to carry out qualitative research with few resource constraints. The NYSS has opened my eyes as never before to the challenges and rewards attending the use of qualitative methods. Examples from the NYSS will be used throughout this book to bring the reader as closely as possible to the nitty-gritty reality that defines what qualitative inquiry is all about.

Exercises

In the classroom, break into small work groups. (This can also be done individually.) Choose a research topic of interest and discuss:

1. The various epistemological positions or "camps" described in this chapter. How might your topic be framed in terms of these paradigms (post-positivist, constructivist, critical)?

2. What advantages do qualitative methods bring to the study?

3. Is the topic familiar to one or more group members? How is familiarity both an advantage and disadvantage in carrying out the study? What are some ways to make the "familiar" become "unfamiliar"?

4. Are there theoretical frameworks or concepts that could be brought to bear on the chosen topic of study? If yes, discuss how this might happen.

5. What (if any) are the ways that social responsibility is reflected in the chosen topic?

Additional Readings

Becker, H. (1998). *Tricks of the trade: How to think about your research while you're doing it.* Chicago: University of Chicago Press.

Bodgan, R., & Taylor, S. J. (1998). *Introduction to qualitative research methods* (3rd ed.). New York: John Wiley & Sons.

Crabtree, B. F., & Miller, W. L. (1999). *Doing qualitative research* (2nd ed.). Thousand Oaks, CA: Sage.

Creswell, J. W. (2007). *Qualitative inquiry and research design* (2nd ed.). Thousand Oaks, CA: Sage.

Denzin, N. L., & Lincoln, Y. S. (Eds.). (2005). *Handbook of qualitative research.* Thousand Oaks, CA: Sage.

Flick, U. (1998). *An introduction to qualitative research.* Thousand Oaks, CA: Sage.

Flick, U., von Kardorff, E., & Steinke, I. (Eds.). (2004). *A companion to qualitative research.* London: Sage.

Huberman, A. M., & Miles, M. B. (Eds.). (2002). *The qualitative researcher's companion.* Thousand Oaks, CA: Sage.

Marshall, C., & Rossman, G. B. (2006). *Designing qualitative research* (4th ed.). Thousand Oaks, CA: Sage.

Merriam, S. (2002). *Qualitative research in practice: Examples for discussion and analysis*. New York: J. Wiley & Sons.

Miles, M. B., & Huberman, A. M. (1994). *Qualitative data analysis* (2nd ed.). Thousand Oaks, CA: Sage.

Morse, J. M. (Ed.). (1994). *Critical issues in qualitative research methods*. Thousand Oaks, CA: Sage.

Padgett, D. K. (Ed.). (2004a). *The qualitative research experience*. Belmont, CA: Thomson.

Patton, M. Q. (2002). *Qualitative research and evaluation methods* (3rd ed.). Thousand Oaks, CA: Sage.

Rossman, G. B., & Rallis, S. F. (2003). *Learning in the field* (2nd ed.). Thousand Oaks, CA: Sage.

Silverman, D. (2005). *Doing qualitative research* (2nd ed.). London: Sage.

Tolman, D. L., & Brydon-Miller, M. (Eds.). (2001). *From subjects to subjectivities: A handbook of interpretive and participatory methods*. New York: New York University Press.

A SELECTION OF JOURNALS THAT FEATURE QUALITATIVE STUDIES

American Anthropologist

Culture, Medicine & Psychiatry

Field Methods

Forum: Qualitative Social Research (FQSR)

Human Organization

International Journal of Qualitative Methods

Journal of Contemporary Ethnography

Journal of Phenomenological Psychology

Qualitative Health Research

Qualitative Inquiry

Qualitative Research

Qualitative Social Work

Qualitative Sociology

Social Science & Medicine

The Qualitative Report

WEB SITES FOR QUALITATIVE METHODS

http://www.nsf.gov/pubs/2004/nsf04219/start.htm (excellent proceedings from workshop on qualitative methods at the National Science Foundation)

http://www.uofaweb.ualberta.ca/iiqm/Conferences.cfm (comprehensive site from the University of Alberta in Canada, who sponsors the leading international conference annually)

http://www.scolari.com (information and downloadable software demos for Atlas/ti, Nud*ist, The Ethnograph, etc.)

http://www.nova.edu/ssss/QR (online journal "The Qualitative Report")

http://www.quarc.de (German–English online resource)

http://qualitative-research.net (German–English–Spanish site with online journal)

http://www.coe.uga.edu/quig (multidisciplinary interest group at the University of Georgia—sponsors national research meeting annually)

http://ejournals.library.ualberta.ca/index.php/IJQM/index (International Journal of Qualitative Methods)

www.researchtalk.com (training/workshop company on Long Island)

2

Choosing the Right Qualitative Approach(es)

Qualitative methods represent different things to different people. The explosive growth in books and articles on qualitative methods attests to their popularity and increasing heterogeneity. Following is a partial listing illustrating the latter:

Perspectives/Approaches:	Analytic methods:
• Grounded theory	• Thematic analysis
• Ethnography	• Content analysis
• Case study	• Case study analysis
• Symbolic interactionist	• Grounded theory analysis
• Narrative	• Narrative analysis
• Constructivist	• Phenomenological analysis
• Hermeneutic	• Conversation analysis
• Phenomenologic/life world	• Discourse analysis
• Life course	• Participatory action
	• Feminist

There are a few caveats about this listing. First, the listed items are neither exhaustive nor mutually exclusive—changes in terminology and general intellectual ferment ensure that any such lists are a work in progress. Second, researchers often mix and match approaches and analytic methods. Some pairings are historically intertwined (e.g., symbolic interactionism and grounded theory), some match up well (e.g., life course perspective and case study analysis), some are more recent mergers (e.g., constructivism and grounded theory), and others are incompatible (e.g., hermeneutic approaches and content analysis). Finally, a few of these analytic methods have a tradition of incorporating quantitative data along with qualitative data (e.g., content analysis, case studies, and ethnography).

This chapter is devoted to six of the most commonly used qualitative approaches: ethnography, grounded theory, case studies, narrative, phenomenological, and action research approaches. Because there are detailed how-to books on each of these, this overview is designed primarily to assist in deciding which approach to use. The choice is neither formulaic (i.e., if your topic is x, then the qualitative approach must be y) nor is it necessarily confined to one approach. After perusing this chapter, readers are urged to research additional literature on specific methods (see the end of this and subsequent chapters) before making a final decision about which approach to use.

Six Primary Approaches in Qualitative Research

Ethnography

Ethnographic research, the most senior of the "elders" in the qualitative family, has been enshrined as a method, a theoretical orientation, and even a philosophical paradigm (Tedlock, 2000). Although its popularity has ebbed and flowed over the years, ethnography has maintained its central position as the quintessential qualitative method. Its reliance on direct observation and *emic* (or insider) perspective sets a high standard for commitment that stands in contrast to the *etic* (or outsider) perspective assumed by many researchers. Leaders in explicating the method include a number of anthropological couples: the Peltos (Pertti & Gretel), the DeWalts (Kathleen & Billie), the Tedlocks (Barbara & Dennis), and the Schensuls (Jean & Steven) as well as individuals such as Michael Agar and H. Russell Bernard.

In addition to requiring skills in gaining rapport, engaging in intense and ongoing observation, and taking field notes, ethnography implies an attitude or stance. Specifically, it means that one adopts a *holistic perspective*, viewing all aspects of the phenomenon under study as parts of an interrelated whole. Ethnography also embraces *cultural relativism*, a perspective holding that cultures must be understood on their own terms, not judged by the beliefs and values of other, more powerful cultures (Fetterman, 1989). Although intolerable if taken to the extreme (e.g., considering the Holocaust to be a manifestation of German cultural values that should not be judged by "outsiders"), cultural relativism has value as a challenge to *ethnocentrism*, or the denigration of cultures other than one's own.

Despite its trademark approach of participant observation, ethnography does not preclude quantitative data and analyses. Anthropologists have for a long time incorporated measures and statistical analyses in their work (e.g., changes in caloric intake or group differences in social networks).

Heavily influenced by criticism from native peoples and postmodernist self doubt, ethnography has undergone tremendous change in recent decades. Two distinct trends are notable. First, ethnography became more self-reflexive and intellectually adventurous. Thus, straightforward description of an assumed reality in a faraway culture (with the investigator remaining invisible in the telling) gave rise to deeper interpretations and multiple realities conducted closer to home. Along the way, ethnography evolved in new directions: on the one hand introspective (giving rise to *auto-ethnography*), and, on the other hand experimenting with new forms of representation (*performance ethnography*). A second trend in ethnography took place on the margins of academia and centered largely in public health and community development. Variously referred to as *applied ethnography* (Chambers, 2000) and rapid *ethnographic assessment* (REA; Manderson & Aaby, 1998), this iteration of the method rendered it time sensitive and resource conserving. REA proved especially useful in global health, in which initiating improvements in sanitation, nutrition, and disease prevention depended on quick turnaround and a respectful interface with local beliefs and practices. Examples include research on nutritional and dietary deficiencies (Scrimshaw & Gleason, 1992) and social and cultural factors influencing the spread of HIV/AIDS (Scrimshaw, Carballo, Ramos, & Blair, 1991). In each of these, the researchers relied on knowledge of the local culture in combination with time-sensitive methods to assess the nature and scope of the problem and its possible resolution.

Doing ethnography means focusing on a cultural system with identifiable features. The boundaries may be physical such as the walls of a hospital or the perimeters of a neighborhood, or they may be defined mostly by shared identities (e.g., gang members, a professional football team, runaway adolescents). Ethnographic inquiry means operating on several levels simultaneously to infer the tacit rules of the culture or subculture from the myriad of actions and interactions being witnessed.

Ethnography clearly has its demands, most notably the amount of time and effort required. Due in part to this intensity, it is less frequently used compared to other options. Nevertheless, ethnography is the progenitor of qualitative methods; its place in the toolkit is secure.

Grounded Theory

Grounded theory (GT) has emerged as one of the most well-known approaches in qualitative research since its debut in the late 1960s (Glaser & Strauss, 1967). Closely aligned with symbolic interactionism and ethnographic sociology at the Chicago School, GT sparked broad interest that led to its becoming the most popular of qualitative methods (McKibbon & Gadd, 2004).

GT's systematic demystifying of methods has made it accessible to researchers across a wide range of disciplines. It has evolved significantly over the years, surviving a dispute between Glaser and Strauss (the latter of whom was joined by Juliet Corbin in subsequent works) and more recently adapted to fit constructivism (Charmaz, 2006) and postmodernism (Clarke, 2005). The popularity and accessibility of GT have undoubtedly led to the wider acceptance of qualitative methods over the past three decades.

Although subject to variations in practice and in use of terminology (Walker & Myrick, 2006), GT entails inductive coding from the data, memo writing to document analytic decisions, and weaving in theoretical ideas and concepts without permitting them to drive or constrain the study's emergent findings. In an elegant inversion of the theory-driven deduction common to quantitative research, GT has made the pursuit of mid-range theories a respectable, even desirable outcome of qualitative research.

Studies using GT typically involve interviews with a moderately sized sample of carefully selected persons (20 to 30 is about right, but sample sizes can be smaller or larger). Cycling between data collection and analysis, GT begins with *open coding* of interview transcripts. The process of coding may use *sensitizing concepts* drawn from the literature, extant theories, and previous research, but its primary goal is inductive. Coding proceeds to axial and selective phases, gradually creating a parsimonious conceptual framework. Along the way, the researcher employs constant comparative analysis to examine contrasts across respondents, situations, and settings. As will be seen in Chapter 7, the procedures of GT are well-explicated. Although terminology varies, all forms of GT require a great deal of intellectual heavy-lifting.

Case Study Analysis

Case studies have a long and honorable history in qualitative research (Feagin, Orum, & Sjoberg, 1991; Stake, 2005; Yin, 2003) and the term is used to refer to approach, method, and product. As studies of "bounded systems of action" (Snow & Anderson, 1991, p. 152), case studies draw on the ability of the qualitative researcher to extract depth and meaning in context. A psychiatric ward, a religious cult, a rural village, or a modern corporation can be the focus of a case study. Its goals may be description and analysis of the ethnographic present or of the historic past. The Lynds' sociological studies of Middletown (1937, 1956) are case studies of a community before and after the Great Depression that remain classics in the social science literature.

Case studies often play an important role in program evaluation (Greene, 2000). A study of an exemplary hospice program, for example, can offer insights into best practices. Noteworthy events can provide an opportunity to explore historical and social changes (e.g., the 1962 Cuban Missile Crisis or the 1992 Rodney King riots in Los Angeles; Yin, 2004). Eric Klinenberg's *Heat Wave* (2002) used media reports, documents, and interviews to provide a "social autopsy" case study of the disastrous effects of Chicago's 1994 heat wave on the elderly poor.

Regardless of its subject matter, the case study draws on multiple per-spectives and data sources to produce contextually rich and meaningful interpretation. In this regard, it is important to distinguish case studies in qualitative research from their counterparts in clinical education. The lat-ter type of case studies—a commonly used pedagogical tool for training students in psychiatry, psychology, nursing, and social work—helps illus-trate the application of clinical theories in individual cases. In qualitative research, the case study is a method of inquiry for knowledge develop-ment that necessitates systematic processes of data collection and analysis (Donmoyer, 1990).

Case study methods are not as explicitly described as other methods such as grounded theory and thus leave more analytic discretion to the researcher. This is especially true of multiple case studies in which the challenge is one of aggregating across cases while maintaining the distinctive nature of each case (Campbell & Arens, 1998; Ragin, 1987; Stake, 2005; Yin, 2004). However, when the object(s) of inquiry requires holism over disaggregation, case study analysis is most likely the route to take.

Narrative Approaches

Narrative approaches (NA) have tremendous intuitive appeal given their emphasis on the power of the spoken word (Mishler, 1986; Polkinghorne, 1988). Indeed, their popularity and widespread invocation have led to an indiscriminate use of the term "narrative" for virtually any human utterance (Riessman & Quinney, 2005), extending into therapeutic and self-help domains in which clients are asked to "re-story" their lives (White & Epston, 1990). Our interest is with NA as a diverse set of methods focusing on how something is said as well as what is said.

Rooted in literature, history, and sociolinguistics, narrative approaches assume that speaking and writing are forms of meaning-making. NA fall into two basic types: 1) *narrative analysis* of interviews designed to elicit storytelling; and 2) *conversation* and *discourse analyses* of naturally occurring speech. Narrative analysis, influenced by William Labov, Elliott Mishler, and Catherine Riessman, uses in-depth interviewing to encourage respondents to talk freely about their lives. Analyses involve repeatedly listening to a tape of the interview and scrutinizing the transcript to identify "stories" from which structural components are then delineated. In addition, the narrative analyst may examine how respondents "voice" themselves and others, thereby indicating social relationships and the meanings attached to them (Sands, 2004).

Naturally occurring conversations are ripe with meaning, whether between friends or virtual strangers. Conversation analysis (CA), with roots in sociology and ethnomethodology (Gubrium & Holstein, 2000; Sacks & Garfinkle, 1970), examines sequencing, turn taking, "holding the floor," interruption, and other aspects of conversation that reveal how social roles and identities are manifested during talk (Farnell & Graham, 2000). Audiotaped transcriptions of conversations between parents and children (or doctors and patients) can be analyzed with CA to offer clues to how interpersonal communication both shapes and reflects social interaction.

Discourse analysis (DA) emerged as a technique for identifying the social meanings reflected in talk and text (Gee, 2005). Meaning can be ascertained from a variety of indices, including choice of words and idioms, speaking rhythm and cadence, inflection, intonation, gestures, and nonverbal utterances (groans, sighs, laughter, etc.). Foucauldian discourse analysis, which draws on Foucault's critiques of hegemonic power and its influence on social meaning-making, tends to operate at a more abstract level than the everyday discourses of interest to most qualitative researchers. Standing in direct contrast to Foucauldian analyses are the best-selling popular books by sociolinguist Deborah Tannen in which she explores how men and women "just don't understand" one another (1990) and analyzes the volatile communications between mothers and daughters (2006).

Specific techniques for conducting the various narrative approaches differ, but all share a level of immersion and formality that places considerable demands on the researcher. Riessman and Quinney surveyed the social work literature and found many instances of narrative techniques in practice and teaching but few used in research, especially in the United States (2005). A requirement that the researcher become intensely involved in linguistic structures and meaning also raises concerns about losing the larger social context, although this need not be the case (Gubrium & Holstein, 2000; Riessman, 1993). When properly contextualized, studies of narrative can illuminate the foreground as well as the behind-the-scenes aspects of individual lives, programs, and practice.

Phenomenological Analysis

Phenomenological analysis (PA) explores the lived experience of a phenomenon. PA owes much to the early 20th-century writings of Edmund Husserl and to later developmental work by Giorgi (1985) and Moustakas (1994) in psychology and van Manen in education (2002). PA puts the focus on deeper meanings achieved by prolonged immersion. Their use has been heaviest in psychology and nursing.

In PA, the researcher must rely on "bracketing," or sidelining preconceptions about what is real (what Husserl terms "epoche"). Study participants are individuals who share a particular life experience (e.g., cancer survivors, crime victims, adoptive parents). Analyses of interview data are conducted to find the "essence" or common themes in their experiences. Phenomenological findings explore not only what participants experience but also the situations and conditions of those experiences.

PA interviews, conducted with around 6 to 10 participants, begin with broad, open-ended questioning to ensure the rapport and openness necessary to access the participant's lived experience. Multiple interviews with each participant are needed to achieve needed depth (Creswell, 2007). PA examines interview transcripts in search of quotes and statements that are emblematic in meaning. These are clustered into themes that form the architecture of the findings.

Guidelines for conducting PA are among the least explicit, a reflection of its philosophical origins in which exegesis takes diverse and complex directions. Nevertheless, PA is uniquely suited to leave readers feeling as if they have "walked a mile in the shoes" of participants.

Action Research and Community-Based Participatory Research

Action research (AR), traceable to the seminal work of Kurt Lewin (1946), has roots in pragmatism and Marxism (Tandon, 1996) as well as 1960s liberation movements. Closely linked to *participatory action research* (PAR) and *community-based participatory research* (CBPR), AR shares with PAR and CBPR fundamental commitments to community empowerment and egalitarian partnerships (Reason & Bradbury, 2001; Stringer, 2007). These may be applied to a de facto "community' of research participants. Wahab, for example, adopted a feminist participatory stance in collaborating with female sex workers in Seattle (2003), and Salmon deployed similar techniques (including shared data analysis) in interviews about alcohol abuse with aboriginal mothers in Western Canada (2007).

In the majority of instances, however, the partnership is with a geographically proximal "community," however defined by its members. The popularity of community-based participatory research (CBPR) can be traced to post-1960s movements advocating community empowerment in general (Fals-Borda, 1998; Freire, 1973) and power sharing in research in particular (Foster-Fishman, Berkowitz, Lounsbury, Jacobson, & Allen, 2001; Nelson, Ochocka, Griffin, & Lord, 1998). Impetus has also come from pragmatic concerns surrounding the necessary (but complicated) move away from academic-based, controlled trials to "real-world" interventions in communities (Hohmann & Shear, 2002). The problems attending such a change, often dismissed as "noise" by quantitative researchers, include low rates of recruitment and high rates of study attrition. Feasibility and relevance—clinical, cultural, and social—suffer when there is little or no buy-in from a community.

Closely linked to public health but also gaining ground in health services and primary care research (Jones & Wells, 2007), CPBR is a natural fit for qualitative researchers in social work and other practicing professions. Although not inherently qualitative òr quantitative in methodology, it is difficult to imagine CPBR operating without qualitative methods.

CBPR offers a paradigm for melding research and action (Israel, Eng, Schulz, & Parker, 2005). As such, it can be seen as embracing "three Ps." In other words, it is a perspective that ideally infuses a study from start to finish; it connotes a partnership of equals among researchers and community participants; it requires active participation by all parties. CBPR partnerships tend to work best when all parties are willing to commit time and resources. The potential for methodological tradeoffs and compromises is considered worth the benefits in the form of improvements in community health and well-being.

Although there are differences among action research, participatory research, and community-based participatory research (largely hinging on the extent to which research participants are full partners in the enterprise), they are united by a commitment to social change and community empowerment (Cornwall & Jewkes, 1995). AR uses both qualitative and quantitative methods but it is associated with the former given its ethos of community immersion which, in turn, favors minimally structured interviewing and rapport building. This degree of involvement is a good fit with activism and the "nothing about us, without us" ethos.

AR and CBPR have been increasingly popular in recent years in the fight against HIV/AIDS, cancer, violent crime, and environmental health hazards (Israel et al., 2005; Minkler & Wallerstein, 2003). Because time and resources are almost always limited, a premium is put on abbreviated and focused methods that can yield findings in a short turnaround time (sometimes within six months or less) and with wide impact on improving community health and mental health. As mentioned earlier in the section on ethnography, rapid-assessment techniques have become an essential part of the AR/CBPR toolkit. Projects may involve needs assessments, program planning and implementation, and program evaluation, their distinctive qualities ensuring a maximum of community involvement. Clearly, not all research topics point to AR or CBPR, nor are these approaches easy in any sense of the word. Yet their value in applied and practice-oriented research is unassailable.

Constructivist and Critical-Theory Influences

The aforementioned descriptions are of methods with distinct features and procedures, all deeply rooted in philosophy, linguistics, and the social sciences. As noted in Chapter 1, several have subsequently been affected by the rise of constructivism and the paradigm debates that ensued after the 1980s. Presented as a fully developed (and superior) replacement for positivism (Denzin & Lincoln, 2005; Lincoln & Guba, 1985), the constructivist movement introduced a degree of self-consciousness about epistemology not seen before (Morgan, 2007; Rodwell, 1998).

The embrace of constructivism and critical theories depended on the visibility and persuasiveness of their applications and by the degree of fit with each method. Narrative and phenomenological approaches had little distance to travel in this regard with their predisposition toward social construction and reflexivity. As noted earlier in this chapter, ethnography proved to be a ripe target for change as it shifted "from participant observation to the observation of participation" (Tedlock, 2000, p. 465). Multiple genres flowered, including critical ethnography (Kincheloe & McLaren, 2000), auto-ethnography (Ellis & Bochner, 2000), performance ethnography (McCall, 2000), feminist ethnography (Tedlock, 2000), and so on.

Annells (1996) and Mills, Bonner, and Francis (2006) find a strong constructivist thread running through grounded theory (even though it is usually the winner in the category of "qualitative method most likely to be post-positivist"). Critical theory is also compatible with GT. Cooney, for example, combined critical theory epistemology and grounded theory methods to analyze data from focus group interviews with Spanish- and English-speaking welfare recipients (2006).

A well-articulated version of constructivist grounded theory has been developed by Charmaz (2006). Charmaz distinguishes constructivist from objectivist grounded theory, noting that the former relies on interpretive frames and the latter focuses on explanation and prediction. Given the flexibility and neutrality of grounded theory—it predates and transcends the paradigm debates—such an adaptation extends rather than breaks with tradition. Charmaz' version is distinguished by its accessibility and comprehensiveness.

Action and participatory research have strong foundations in pragmatism and utility as they relate to solving real-life problems (Levin & Greenwood, 2001). Recently, however, constructivist iterations of CBPR have emerged. Eng and colleagues, for example, cite constructivism as their research paradigm in working with rural African American communities in North Carolina (Eng, Moore, Rhodes, Griffith, Allison, Shirah, & Mebane, 2005).

In summary, constructivism has found powerful allies among leading qualitative methodologists and has gained influence in many qualitative approaches. Even so, most qualitative studies pay relatively little attention to epistemology as a guiding principle. The various members of the qualitative methods family include those inclined to constructivist and paradigmatic allegiances and those who remain agnostic.

Mixing and Matching Qualitative Approaches

The risk of specifying six (or any number of) qualitative approaches lies in conveying a message of discreteness that belies the blurriness of definitions and applications in qualitative inquiry. It is not uncommon, for example, to see a qualitative study that is presented as phenomenological but uses grounded theory coding. Some case studies are hard to distinguish from ethnographies or biographies because they all adopt an in-depth holistic perspective. A lack of attention to precise terminology is not surprising given the diversity and lack of consensus in the field.

Meanwhile, qualitative researchers may deliberately mix and match qualitative approaches to find the right combination. This occurs within two plausible scenarios: 1) a fusion or hybrid approach; or 2) a juxtaposition of two approaches side-by-side or in sequence. Annells refers to this as "turning the prism" via theoretical and methodological triangulation (2006, p. 59).

Matters get complicated when considering: 1) the different points at which mixing may occur—from interpretive paradigm to overall approach to specific method of analysis; and 2) the extent to which one is concerned about paradigm and method congruence. Cross-paradigm mixing has been disparaged as incommensurable (Lincoln & Guba, 2000), although not everyone agrees with this contention.

A good example of this can be found in the groundbreaking work of Newman, Fox, Roth and Mehta (2004) in which they used a side-by-side paradigm approach to study school shootings in Kentucky and Arkansas (predating the Columbine and Virginia Tech tragedies). Newman and colleagues used both positivist and interpretivist lenses, drawing on "factual" data from forensic analyses and court records and also analyzing transcripts of interviews that provided conflicting (and conflicted) accounts by students, school staff, and parents of the shooters as well as the victims.

Mixing approaches and techniques can bring a new synergy. Although less common (and much more likely to be deployed at the analysis stage, hybrid mixing is described by Fereday and Muir-Cochrane (2006) in their blending of the inductive procedures of Boyatzis (1998) with "template style" coding (Crabtree & Miller, 1999) to study nursing performance. Similarly, Wilson & Hutchison (1991) propose the side-by-side use of phenomenology and grounded theory as complementary and mutually enriching perspectives.

Mancini sequentially mixed qualitative methods by carrying out a grounded theory study of persons suffering from severe mental illness (2005), then selecting two of the interviews for discourse analysis (2007). In another example of mixing in sequence, Teram, Schachter, and Stalker (2005) conducted grounded theory interviews with female survivors of childhood sexual abuse enrolled in physical therapy, then shifted to "pragmatic action research" to transform the analyses and findings via working groups of participants and physical therapists. The groups' joint production of a handbook for health professionals created a deeper, more sensitive set of guidelines for working with abuse survivors.

A few related caveats are pertinent here. First, incongruities can bring complications during the mixing of qualitative approaches. Phenomenological analyses of grounded theory interviews would be likely to suffer from the lack of deep attunement to meaning and lived experience (Wimpenny & Gass, 2000). Second, mixing carries the risk of "method slurring" (Baker, Wuest, & Stern, 1992) wherein one or both approaches loses its integrity and capacity to make a contribution. This is obviously a greater problem for hybrid than for juxtaposing formats. Finally, not all mixing is done for the purposes of *triangulation* (i.e., contrasting and/or corroboration). As will be discussed in Chapter 10, triangulation is not as straightforward as it sounds.

Qualitative Methods in Program Evaluation

The researcher's choice of qualitative method(s) may take place in the context of program evaluation. Qualitative evaluation has a long history, especially in the field of education (Bogdan & Taylor, 1975; Cook & Reichart, 1979; Fetterman, 1989; Guba & Lincoln, 1981, 1989; Patton, 2002; Scriven, 1967; Stake, 1995). Relying solely on quantitative methods risks losing an understanding of what is happening below the surface (where many an intervention succeeds or fails in ways unbeknownst to the investigator; Padgett, 2005). It also places enormous trust in quantitative measures of sensitive, fluctuating, and elusive phenomena.

Any number of hidden effects may occur. A program may be found successful, but not for the reasons assumed. It may appear to be a failure according to some outcome measures even though it might have been deemed a success by different methods. Narrow conceptualizations of "success" (e.g., symptom reduction) may overlook what clients value more (e.g., social services assistance). Positive outcomes may be an artifact of biased sampling or measurement error rather than "reality." A clinically tested treatment that succeeds under controlled conditions may fall apart when transplanted to a program beset by scarce resources, a demoralized staff, and unhappy clientele. These concerns point to the need for contextual methods sensitive enough to capture what is happening behind the scenes, not just on the stage. Box 2.1 describes the qualitative approaches used in the New York Services Study.

Summary and Concluding Thoughts

This chapter introduced six primary approaches in qualitative inquiry—ethnography, grounded theory, case studies, phenomenological analysis, narrative approaches and action or participatory research—as a menu of options for the would-be qualitative researcher. Not always willing to settle for just one, researchers often mix and match approaches to achieve the most suitable combination for their needs. The topic of interest and the goals of the study drive such choices. Constructivist iterations have also emerged to make matters more complicated and are especially well developed in grounded theory. Novice researchers are well-advised to read specialized texts and articles using these varied approaches to get a sense of how investigators make the most of what each has to offer. Qualitative inquiry is steeped in choices and decisions—a qualitative study can be seen as a series of critical junctures in which the decision trail is rarely, if ever, foreordained.

BOX 2.1   Qualitative Approaches in the New York Services Study

The central goal of the NYSS—to learn about the service system from the users' perspectives—pointed to an interview-dominant study, but this still left several options in choice of qualitative approaches. In Phase 1 of the study, we settled on grounded theory and case study analyses of life history interviews. Grounded theory was selected because we wanted to build an inductive theory or model explaining participants' experiences with homeless, mental health, and substance abuse services. This model, in turn, was meant to inform the study's Phase 2. Case study analysis was necessary in order to have a holistic view of each participant's life.

Both approaches were carried over into Phase 2 but with several modifications. In this second phase, participants consisted of 80 new enrollees in four homeless services programs for adults in New York City. Phase 2 interviews with clients consisted of three in-depth interviews over 12 months of follow-up. Baseline interviews were coded using GT. The two follow-up interviews used a template format in which open-ended questions were structured about domains. For these, we used Boyatzis' method of thematic development (1998) as more suitable for the data.

Phenomenological and narrative approaches were not used in the NYSS as they were not considered a good fit. We periodically regretted the absence of ethnography, however. Observation was considered to be too time-consuming given the study's priorities, but there were occasions when participants invited us to accompany them in daily activities or when we wished we could observe the agencies in their day-to-day operations. (We plan to use ethnography in future studies.) Action or community-based participatory approaches held great appeal but were well beyond the scope and feasibility of the study.

EXERCISES

1. Go to Google Scholar or use your college/university access to academic journals and locate examples of studies representing each of the six types of qualitative methods presented in this chapter. What types of journals carry these methods? Download and print an article and bring to class for discussion.

2. Choose a topic of interest and consult the listing of approaches and techniques at the beginning of this chapter. What combination of these is the best fit for your study?

3. How would you describe the strengths and limitations of each of the six approaches presented in this chapter?

4. Consider the many options possible in mixing among the six qualitative approaches. Discuss in class which appear most (and least) suitable for mixing.

ADDITIONAL READINGS

Ethnography

Agar, M. H. (1980). *The professional stranger: An informal introduction to ethnography.* New York: Academic Press.

DeWalt, K. M., & DeWalt, B. R. (2001). *Participant observation: A guide for fieldworkers.* Walnut Creek, CA: AltaMira Press.

Emerson, R. M. (2001). *Contemporary field research.* Prospect Heights, IL: Waveland Press.

Hammersley, M., & Atkinson, P. (1995). *Ethnography: Principles in practice* (2nd ed.), New York: Routledge.

LeCompte, M. D., & Schensul, J. J. (1999). *Designing and conducting ethnographic research* (Ethnographer's toolkit, Vol. 1). Walnut Creek, CA: AltaMira Press.

Lofland, J., & Lofland, L. (1995). *Analyzing social settings: A guide to qualitative observation and analysis.* Belmont, CA: Wadsworth.

Grounded Theory

Charmaz, C. (2006). *Constructing grounded theory: A practical guide through qualitative analysis.* Thousand Oaks, CA: Sage.

Dey, I. (1999). *Grounding grounded theory.* San Diego: Academic Press.

Glaser, B. G. (1992). *Basics of grounded theory.* Mill Valley, CA: The Sociology Press.

Glaser, B.G., & Strauss, A. L. (1967). *The discovery of grounded theory.* Chicago: Aldine.

Strauss, A. L., & Corbin, J. (1990). *Basics of qualitative research: Grounded theory procedures and techniques.* Newbury Park, CA: Sage.

Case Study Analysis

Stake, R. E. (1995). *The art of case study research.* Thousand Oaks, CA: Sage.

Stake, R. E. (2005). *Multiple case study analysis.* Thousand Oaks, CA: Sage.

Yin, R. K. (2003). *Case study research: Design and methods* (3rd ed.). Thousand Oaks, CA: Sage.

Yin, R. K. (Ed.). (2004). *The case study anthology.* Thousand Oaks, CA: Sage.

Phenomenology

Colaizzi, P. F. (1978). Psychological research as the phenomenologist views it. In R. Valle & M. King (Eds.), *Existential-phenomenological alternatives for psychology* (pp. 48–71). New York: Oxford University Press.

Giorgi, A. (1985). *Phenomenology and psychological research.* Pittsburgh, PA: Duquesne University Press.

Moustakas, C. (1994). *Phenomenological research methods.* Thousand Oaks, CA: Sage.

Polkinghorne, D. E. (1989). Phenomenological research methods. In R. S. Valle & S. Halling (Eds.), *Existential-phenomenological alternatives for psychology* (pp. 41–60). New York: Plenum.

Narrative Approaches

Clandinin, D. J. (Ed.). (2006). *Handbook of narrative inquiry: Mapping a methodology.* Thousand Oaks, CA: Sage.

Cortazzi, M. (1993). *Narrative analysis.* London: Falmer Press.

Gee, J. P. (2005). *An introduction to discourse analysis: Theory and method.* London: Routledge.

Josselson, R., & Lieblich, A. (Eds.). (1995). *Interpreting experience: The narrative study of lives* (Vol. 3). Thousand Oaks, CA: Sage.

Riessman, C. K. (1993). *Narrative analysis.* Newbury Park, CA: Sage.

ten Have, P. (1999). *Doing Conversation Analysis.* London: Sage.

Action and Community-Based Participatory Research

Cornwall, A., & Jewkes, R. (1995). What is participatory research? *Social Science & Medicine, 41*(12), 1667–1676.

Israel, B. A., Eng, E., Schulz, A. J., & Parker. E. A. (Eds.). (2005). *Methods in community-based participatory research for health.* San Francisco: Jossey-Bass.

Jones, L., & Wells, K. (2007). Strategies for academic and clinician engagement in community-based partnered research. *Journal of the American Medical Association, 297*(4), 407–410.

Minkler, M., & Wallerstein, N. (2003). *Community-based participatory research for health.* San Francisco: Jossey-Bass.

Reason, P., & Bradbury, H. (2001). *Handbook of action research.* Thousand Oaks, CA: Sage.

Stringer, E. T. (2007) *Action research: A handbook for practitioners* (3rd ed.). Thousand Oaks, CA: Sage.

3

Getting Started

Study Design and Sampling

D espite popular (mis)conceptions, qualitative research designs do exist (Miles & Huberman, 1994). They are flexible and iterative, but they also share with quantitative designs the need to be systematic, transparent, and as rigorous as possible. A qualitative design is systematic when it follows the methodological guidelines of a specific method or approach (i.e., a grounded theory study will unfold in distinctly different ways compared to a narrative analysis).

Quantitative designs are analogous to architecture or engineering; blueprints are carefully drawn in advance down to the smallest specification and then followed closely. Conducting these studies takes a lot of up-front planning. Qualitative studies are not intended to follow such a predictable step-by-step format and thus offer the opportunity for creativity as well as the challenge of decision making on an ongoing basis. Miles and Huberman refer to the "second chance" (1994, p. 38) afforded by the flexibility and groundedness of qualitative methods. Transparency entails keeping meticulous records of what is done and thus maintaining a degree of accountability for decisions made along the way. Standards for rigor in qualitative research are different from those in quantitative research. Although there is a lack of consensus on what constitutes rigor in qualitative methods, few would argue that adhering to some standards is not critical. (See Chapter 8 for further discussion.)

Some researchers begin with broad study questions that spring from intellectual curiosity, prior theoretical frameworks, personal experience and/or a commitment to social change, and human betterment. Study questions are distinct from research questions or hypotheses in being more broadly conceptualized and not directly researchable as stated. An example of a study question might be: How do refugee families adjust to postwar resettlement? Research questions might include: How are family relationships affected by displacement? How are decisions made about returning or staying in the new location? Are there signs of resilience and strength that distinguish some families from others?

Reviewing the Literature

Study questions and research questions do not get formulated in a vacuum. Although more often assumed than articulated, the fund of knowledge brought to bear by the researcher can make the difference between an innovative study and a ho-hum or wasted effort. One's fund of knowledge may include personal and professional experience, but its quality ultimately depends on an extensive and ongoing review of the research literature. Thus, a researcher may be interested in studying child sexual abuse because she is an abuse survivor and/or has worked extensively with other survivors, but her study would be impoverished both conceptually and empirically if developed from these sources of information alone.

Purist arguments that literature reviews taint the researcher's inductive capacities are attractive (phenomenological analyses come to mind). Such arguments, however, are rarely taken seriously these days. Reasons for this include the caution against re-inventing the wheel and ending a study with a resounding "what's new here?" from readers and audiences. Building upon previous work sets the stage for deeper description, conceptual development, and theoretical refinement. Not doing so runs a high risk of marginalization and irrelevance.

The length and organization of a literature review depend on the study's purpose. Dissertations have few if any restrictions on length and high expectations regarding comprehensiveness. In contrast, evaluation reports present background information in summary form. Similar to quantitative studies, qualitative literature reviews are extended arguments, critically evaluating previous research and situating the proposed study as occupying an important niche in knowledge development. The literature review is also an arena for conceptual thinking and for applying the theoretical lenses that will be brought to bear.

What distinguishes a qualitative literature review is its lack of conceptual finitude. Conceptual and theoretical doors are left open wide enough to permit new ideas and serendipitous findings to emerge. Whereas the natural closure of a quantitative review is the presentation of hypotheses and their component independent and dependent variables, a successful qualitative review relies upon questions posed in an open-minded, curious format.

Developing a Conceptual Framework

Literature reviews contain (and are often organized around) key concepts that are touchstones for the study and its research questions. A qualitative study's conceptual framework is not a contractual obligation. Rather, it is a guiding influence that ensures the study will transcend mere description (no matter how rich and compelling).

As discussed in Chapter 1, theories and concepts play an integral role in qualitative inquiry. This begs the question of how, when, and where this role gets played out. The various qualitative approaches answer this question somewhat differently, but all assume some reference to the world of ideas swirling around a particular topic. Conceptual frameworks are invoked in the literature review, lightly applied during analysis, and revisited during the interpretation of the findings. The key is to prevent them from becoming overseers of the study.

Formulating Research Questions

In quantitative studies, the research questions or hypotheses must pose testable propositions that encompass the key variables of interest. No such structural requirements are imposed on qualitative research questions. These research questions still must be intellectually interesting and point the reader in the direction the study will go. Of course, the phrasing and intent of research questions vary with the study's approach. Take, for example, an interest in studying young women who are HIV positive and engaged in prostitution or sex work. The following are some examples of research questions matched to the type of method.

> Ethnography: Are there tacit values, beliefs, and practices that characterize a local "culture" of prostitution? If so, how do these affect the women's decisions about personal health and HIV prevention? How do the women negotiate relationships with their clients and with fellow sex workers? What is daily life like for them?

Grounded Theory: How do women with HIV balance sex work with other life demands? Are there common elements to their experiences that can be identified as part of a grounded theory of AIDS prevention among sex workers?

Case Study/Life Course: What life events (childhood or recent) led the woman to sex work and to becoming HIV positive? How is her life story similar or different to that of other women like her? Does her life story reflect generational or cohort influences?

Phenomenology: What is the lived experience of being HIV positive? What is the lived experience of sex work? What are the essential elements of the life worlds of these women?

Narrative Analysis: What stories are embedded in their narratives? How do these women "voice" themselves and others in their social networks? What do these narratives reveal about exposure to HIV and AIDS prevention in sex work?

Action or Participatory Research: What are the needs of these women as they perceive them? How can researchers join with them in a partnership to conduct research that addresses these needs?

Any of these may incorporate theoretical and critical perspectives. For example, feminist researchers might include a focus on the constraints of gender roles in sex work and of sexism in AIDS treatment and prevention. What is least desirable are questions that resemble quantitative ones (e.g., "What are the barriers and incentives to seeking care for HIV?" or "Which services do women with HIV use?," etc.). Such questions yield thin responses.

The reader will notice here and elsewhere a strong emphasis on research questions as opposed to hypotheses (at least at the outset of the study). This is in keeping with the inductive approach of qualitative methods. However, some leading qualitative researchers (Miles & Huberman, 1994; Tashakkori & Teddlie, 2003) assert that hypotheses can be tested and confirmatory or explanatory analyses conducted using qualitative data. Indeed, grounded theory can be described as an inductive–deductive feedback loop in which hypotheses or hunches are tested as the conceptual model is built. While not ready to throw out hypothesis generation and testing entirely, I believe that expending too much effort in that direction betrays and undermines a unique strength of qualitative methods.

Designing the Study

The word "design" sounds almost too orderly for the iterative process that unfolds in most qualitative studies. Whereas quantitative researchers share a common language for designs (experimental, quasi-experimental, time-series, etc.), no such uniformity exists in qualitative inquiry (Tesch, 1990). Most qualitative researchers opt for a straightforward description of what they plan and how they plan to do it, using as many descriptors as are applicable (case study, ethnography, phenomenology, etc.). The latter is necessitated by the fact that many studies incorporate different qualitative methods and techniques rather than hew closely to a single approach (Bryman, 2006).

Qualitative designs are distinguished by their recursiveness and flexibility, often weaving back and forth between research questions, data collection, and data analysis. In this fashion, the researcher may reformulate his research questions based on new findings, may seek new samples of respondents, or may pose new questions to existing study participants. Similarly, data analyses can precipitate the collection of additional data.

In quantitative designs, a formulaic approach puts the emphasis on minimizing external "noise" and threats to validity (i.e., "What you see is what you get"). In contrast, qualitative researchers pride themselves on viewing such 'noise' as an inevitable and even welcome part of naturalistic studies. Yet they must also convince their audience that they can (and will) produce credible, trustworthy findings. This means offering an explicit message of "here is what I/we plan to do" tempered by the conditional message "these plans may be modified, but all analytic decisions will be justified and made transparent." Of course, like all complex endeavors, the "devil is in the details."

Questions Posed (and Needing Answers) by Qualitative Research Designs

Box 3.1 shows a series of questions typically posed by qualitative designs. Questions with relatively straightforward answers have them provided in parentheses. Questions without immediate answers are asterisked as "it depends." Perhaps not surprisingly, these questions cannot be answered without reference to the specific method being used as well as the scope of the study. Decisions about sampling, data collection, and data analyses are usually method specific, for example. Regardless, a qualitative research proposal should aim for as much specificity as possible. To be sure, over-attention to detail may drain away the creativity that lends qualitative findings their strength and longevity. But creativity need not preclude planning ahead.

BOX 3.1   Questions Posed by Qualitative Research Designs

"How many?" questions:

- How many study participants are needed?*
- How many interviews per participant? (Whenever possible, there should be at least two.)
- How many study sites are needed?*
- How many weeks, months, or years are needed to complete the study?*

"Should I?" questions:

- Pilot test the interview guide? (Yes!)
- Pay participant incentives? (Yes, if you can afford them.)
- Have comparison groups? (Only if your topic requires it.)
- Collect observational data if it is an interview-based study? (Yes!)
- Identify the strategies for rigor to be used? (Yes—see Chapter 8.)

"When?" questions:

- When should I start analyzing the data? (As early as possible.)
- When is there enough data to stop collection? (Usually at "saturation" point.)
- When should mentoring and supervision be sought? (Early and often.)

"How?" questions:

- How do I address ethical concerns? (More on this in Chapter 4.)
- How do I sample study participants? (Discussed later in this chapter.)
- How do I leave the field and end data collection? (See Chapter 7.)
- How do I analyze the data? (See Chapter 7.)
- How do I write and present the findings? (See Chapter 9.)

*It all depends.

The Element of Time

Flick (2004) notes the importance of time in design decisions. If concerned with temporal change, qualitative studies may be *retrospective* (e.g., life histories) or *prospective,* using longitudinal designs. When change is not the focus, qualitative studies may be "snapshots" (Flick, 2004, p. 148) or cross-sectional in design. Anthropologists, for example, talk about the "ethnographic present" as a compression of the lengthy period (usually a year or more) when they conducted their research in the field.

Prospective longitudinal designs are distinct from cross-sectional designs in which multiple interviews are conducted with study participants over several months (or even years). What makes a study "longitudinal" is: 1) its reliance on two or more waves of interviewing separated by a specified time interval; and 2) its ulterior motive of examining change over time. Iversen and Armstrong, for example, conducted ethnographic interviews with low-income families over a five-year period to portray their ongoing struggle with declining economic fortunes (2006).

Specific Aspects of Qualitative Designs

Notwithstanding the looping back and forth that characterizes most qualitative designs, the description itself is fairly linear. Building on the questions posed in Box 3.1, the primary items to consider are:

1. Which qualitative method(s) will be used? Include a rationale for this choice.
2. If the study is longitudinal, describe this, including procedures for retaining participants.
3. How many participants will there be, and how will they be sampled?
4. List the inclusion/exclusion criteria for eligibility.
5. How, where, and by whom will participants be recruited?
6. How will informed consent be obtained and human subjects protections maintained over the course of the study?
7. What types of data collection will be pursued?
8. How many interviews will be conducted per participant?
9. About how long will interviews last and where will they take place?
10. How (if at all) will incentives be paid and how much will they be?
11. How will data be managed and transformed, including transcription?
12. How will data be analyzed (including kind of software to be used)?
13. Which strategies for rigor will be used?
14. How will findings be presented and disseminated?
15. Give a timeline for completion of all study tasks.

Creating a timeline of tasks and/or a schema showing the study's stages is an excellent way of visually displaying what needs to be done and when, even if presented with a caveat regarding the flexibility that may accompany sampling or data collection. All descriptions should liberally cite the relevant experts in the literature and offer thorough descriptions and rationales.

One modest but essential way to enhance a qualitative study is to build in a pilot study. In quantitative research, pilot studies help smooth out wrinkles in the study's execution and refine its protocols. Little has been written about this in qualitative texts, in large part because of the unpredictable nature and absence of fixed protocols in qualitative studies. In the NYSS, we conducted two to three pilot interviews and sought feedback on their content, sensitivity, and length from the respondents. This in no way foretold all of the complications that lay ahead, but it did result in an improved set of questions for the interviews.

Using Multiple Qualitative Methods at Different Levels

As discussed in Chapter 2, the topic of interest and scope of the study may lead to using more than one qualitative method and technique. (Discussion of mixing qualitative and quantitative methods is reserved for Chapter 10.) It is helpful to distinguish between mixing at the method level (grounded theory, ethnography, etc.), at the level of data collection (focus groups, in-depth interviews, observation, etc.), and in use of analytic methods (coding, case study analysis, discourse analysis, etc.). Comingling at the approach level implies a study with sufficient expertise and coordination to manage the different tasks. A study of college drinking, for example, might pair ethnographic observation of campus social events with case studies of selected clubs and fraternities. (The amount of participation by the researcher, i.e., drinking beer with one's informants, should be monitored to ensure that field notes are accurate.)

Within a particular approach, it is not uncommon to use multiple types of data collection. Ethnography supplements its trademark participant observation with informant interviews. A grounded theory study might use interviews from focus groups as well as individuals. A life history study might go beyond first-person accounts to draw on participants' documents such as diaries, photographs, newspaper clippings, and so on. On the other hand, qualitative approaches such as narrative and phenomenological analyses do not lend themselves as easily to multiple data forms, given their almost exclusive reliance on interviews and narrative. A final note: Mixing may occur sequentially as well as concurrently, depending on the study design and scope.

Sampling Strategies

Qualitative researchers sample a number of things, including places (agencies, clinics, neighborhoods) and events (staff meetings, court sessions, religious services), as well as people. Sampling may begin with larger units such as schools or agencies and then proceed to selected individuals at these locations (e.g., teachers or staff).

By definition, qualitative studies rely heavily on people who are articulate and introspective enough to provide rich descriptions of their experiences. Observation-only studies are virtually unheard of nowadays. Interviews that produce sketchy answers from disinterested respondents are poor sustenance for a study. It is not easy to identify talkative individuals in advance; it is not unusual to discard an occasional interview as unusable. And yet, with the exception of children and severely demented elders, few if any individuals should be ruled out in advance as potential study participants. Stereotyped assumptions that persons with severe mental illness are incapable of participating in qualitative interviews have proven unfounded time and again. In the rare instance in which an individual in the NYSS was too symptomatic to be interviewed, we were usually able to reschedule the interview to a time when he or she felt better.

Of course, the ultimate decision about who to sample should be driven by the study's research questions and goals. As a general rule, qualitative researchers use *purposive sampling*—a deliberate process of selecting respondents based on their ability to provide the needed information. As Miles and Huberman note (1994), qualitative sampling is done for conceptual and theoretical reasons, not to represent a larger universe.

Purposive sampling implies that a researcher interested in how cancer patients cope with pain will seek out respondents who have pain rather than randomly sample from an oncologist's patient roster. As such, it should not be confused with convenience sampling, that is, selecting respondents based solely on their availability. Commonly used in clinical research (where ready access to specific types of patients overshadows concerns about non-representativeness), convenience sampling is generally antithetical to the aims of qualitative methods. Convenience may lead a researcher to a particular site (e.g., a domestic violence shelter where she has volunteered in the past), but this should be done only if that site is most appropriate for the study. Even when an appropriate site is available, the method for recruiting and selecting study participants should be purposive, not one of convenience.

Patton (2002, pp. 232–242) describes various types of purposive sampling. Some of these are suited to the outset of a study and others are for later use. Initial sampling techniques are described here:

- *Extreme or deviant case sampling* looks for cases that illuminate the "outer edges" of a phenomenon, for example, persons with major depression who have had multiple suicide attempts.
- *Intensity sampling* is similar to the above but the cases are not as unusual—persons with severe depression, for example.
- *Maximum variation sampling* captures heterogeneity across the sample population (e.g., recruiting breast cancer survivors who had all types of adjuvant therapy [chemotherapy, radiation, etc.] as well as those who rejected such treatments in favor of alternative remedies).
- *Homogeneous sampling* is the opposite of the previous point, for example, narrowing the sample to include only those cancer survivors who rejected adjuvant therapies.
- *Typical case sampling* recruits "average" members of the population (e.g., parents of autistic children who typify a profile of this population).
- *Critical case sampling* involves recruiting to illuminate the extremeness of a situation, for example, parents whose abuse resulted in the death of their child.
- *Criterion sampling* is selecting cases that exceed some criterion or norm (e.g., new mothers who score above a clinically significant level on a post-partum depression scale). A variant of this, nominations sampling, asks knowledgeable persons to name or select eligible persons based on the study criteria.
- *Snowball sampling* is used with isolated or hidden populations whose members are not likely to be found and cooperate without referral from others in their network. Examples include gang members, IV drug users, or members of a religious sect.

Analysis-driven sampling techniques occurring later on in a study may include any of the initial sampling techniques previously mentioned, along with:

- *Theoretical sampling,* which occurs when inductively derived analytic concepts are used to guide the choice of additional participants. For example, a grounded theory study of recovery from drug addiction finds that individuals with spiritual beliefs appear more likely to manifest a "natural recovery" without formal treatment. Further sampling of individuals who have experienced "natural recovery" would explore whether they had also used formal treatment and the extent of their spiritual beliefs

- *Confirming or disconfirming sampling,* which takes the logic of theoretical sampling a step further to seek out specific examples to test the validity of the grounded theory. An example could be looking for individuals who manifest natural recovery and spirituality without any formal treatment and (more importantly) those who do not. The latter, a variant of negative case analysis, ensures that qualitative findings are subjected to disconfirmation. Finding a "negative case" (e.g., a participant who naturally recovered but held no spiritual beliefs) may be the exception that either proves the rule or overturns it.

These categories offer the researcher much-needed terminology on specific sampling techniques. Not surprisingly, random sampling is a rarely used option in qualitative research. Aside from the fact that many study populations do not have a sampling frame from which to randomly select, the need for small but meaningful samples makes random selection techniques the least appropriate.

Sampling strategies should whenever possible identify inclusion and exclusion criteria to set boundaries on who is and is not eligible. Researchers must make special provisions if they seek to interview anyone who is under age 18 or a member of a vulnerable population (pregnant women, severely mentally disabled persons, and prisoners). Sharing the study's inclusion/exclusion criteria is essential for those helping to recruit for the study, for example, staff at an agency or clinic who are asked to pass out flyers or otherwise help to identify eligible participants.

Meeting the study's sampling goals requires tact, persistence, and foresight. Two related observations are pertinent here. First, sampling strategies may change in response to study needs. One might, for example, start out with maximum variation sampling and then turn to a more targeted technique such as deviant case sampling. Second, the researcher should take steps early on to ensure that flexibility in sampling can be pursued and sampling goals attained. For example, one might anticipate the need for snowball sampling when studying a relatively isolated population. If recruitment is being carried out among certain types of clients or patients, it is advisable to obtain assurances (and evidence) of sufficient accrual from their program gatekeepers or else expand recruitment to more sites. Experienced researchers often have agonizing accounts of how an intake coordinator promised a veritable flood of eligible study participants only to be confronted with a trickle when the study actually began.

Sample Size Considerations

In qualitative research, sample size considerations are directed to differing ends and proceed from different assumptions than in quantitative research. Here, the focus is on flexibility and depth rather than on mathematical probabilities and external validity. The phrase that quantitative research is "a mile wide and an inch deep," and qualitative research is "an inch wide and a mile deep" holds a grain of truth when it comes to sampling.

Different approaches have differing sample size considerations and there are no hard and fast rules. Case study analyses tend to have small samples even for multiple case studies—a single case may suffice in some instances. Similarly, phenomenological studies aim for depth—sample sizes of 6 to 10 participants are common but the numbers may be somewhat larger if resources permit. Grounded theory studies tend to have larger sample sizes, although still usually well short of a quantitative sample.

A few rules of thumb are helpful to remember: 1) the smaller the sample size, the more intense and deep are the data being collected; 2) larger sample sizes are needed for heterogeneity, smaller sizes for homogeneity; 3) avoid sacrificing depth (length of interviews or number of interviews) for breadth (number of participants). If, for some reason, you are unable to conduct more than one interview with each study participant, a larger sample may be desirable; 4) larger numbers need not be shunned as long as the study has sufficient resources and honors rule of thumb #3. Given the flexibility inherent in qualitative sampling, a study may end up with fewer participants than anticipated (because the data became saturated earlier on) or it may end up with a larger sample because of the need to pursue new leads from the analyses.

Qualitative sample sizes taken out of context can be deceiving to the uninitiated. Hirsch, Higgins, Bentley, and Nathanson (2002) conducted an ethnographic interview study of 26 Mexican women to examine male sexual fidelity and risk of HIV exposure. At first glance, such a sample size would make most quantitative researchers cringe. But further reading on the study's methods revealed that each woman was interviewed six times—a total of 156 interviews! Most qualitative studies are not as large-scale as this study, but the rules of thumb previously mentioned still hold (i.e., depth over breadth).

At the proposal stage, one needs to provide a projected sample size, but this should be accompanied by a caveat about the flexible nature of qualitative sampling to assure the reader that it is acceptable to end up with a sample size larger or smaller than anticipated. Because of a fundamental concern with quality over quantity, we sample not to maximize breadth or reach, but to become saturated with information about a specific topic.

Recruiting and Retaining Study Participants

Qualitative researchers go where respondents are rather than the other way around. These locations could be clinics, beauty salons, schools, churches, remote villages, homeless encampments, or any site where would-be study participants can be found. Gaining the cooperation of intermediaries such as gatekeepers is often critical.

Researchers in the helping professions are naturally drawn to studying the health or other problems of the populations they serve. However, this can be risky if they recruit study participants solely through treatment and service settings. Such a reliance excludes persons not in treatment and thus skews the sample toward the more severe or chronic cases and/or the highest service users. Of course, this may be the only way to access the population (or it may be the proper site given the study's goals), but intrepid researchers pursue alternative routes to recruitment such as advertising or snowball sampling.

Qualitative researchers use a variety of strategies for recruiting respondents. Human subjects committees are especially fond of advertising for volunteers because it is least likely to involve coercion. Cooperating sites and gatekeepers can help in distributing flyers or mailing introductory letters to potential participants. The researcher may make guest appearances at regular group meetings to describe the study and invite participation. At all times, he should have a script ready, either written or verbal, giving a brief description of what the study is about and what participation will entail. Attractive flyers with these points in bulleted form are the most efficient way to get the message out.

Obtaining the optimal sample takes careful planning and expenditures of effort. The wider one casts the net, the greater the need to screen in and screen out potential participants. This winnowing process involves rejecting some individuals who do not meet inclusion criteria and being rejected by some individuals who do not wish to participate.

Retaining study participants is a key element of study success. High attrition rates in studies owe much to the lack of attention to techniques designed to keep participants engaged voluntarily (which is the only kind of engagement permitted). While essential for longitudinal studies, study retention also pertains to qualitative research because multiple interviews with each participant are optimal.

The relational aspects of qualitative research generally confer an advantage in this regard, but there are specific techniques that a conscientious researcher should consider using. These include asking for contact information, paying incentives, and offering a telephone number and/or email address where participants may reach out with questions or concerns. Of course, qualitative studies can experience participant drop-outs, especially when participants are from vulnerable populations and have significant distractions in their lives.

Researcher–Participant Dynamics: Gender, Ethnicity, Age, and Social Class

The dynamic interplay between researchers and their respondents—each affecting one another in not easily predictable ways—is a defining (and exciting) feature of qualitative inquiry. Feminist researchers have led the way in discussing this as a methodological issue (Fonow & Cook, 1991; Reinharz, 1992). Accepting rather than condemning its existence, they have explored how subjectivity shapes the study findings.

Although the researcher–respondent relationship can be influenced by many attributes, the most tangible are the "fit" (or lack thereof) in gender, ethnicity, age, and other demographic characteristics. Sometimes the researcher has little in common with her respondents. Elliot Liebow (1993) acknowledged stark differences in sex, age, race, and social class when he began his study of African American homeless women in Washington, D.C. Yet he was able to forge enduring relationships with the homeless women and write a moving portrayal of their lives.

Rapport is hardly guaranteed by having a researcher–respondent match. Barbara Myerhoff was of the same sex and religion as her elderly Jewish respondents, but differences in age and lifestyle had to be overcome before she could be accepted by them. Feminist researchers have long noted that there are many occasions when shared gender is not enough to provide common ground (Hyde, 1994).

A practical discussion of these factors and how they may be dealt with will be offered in Chapter 5. Perhaps it is sufficient to say here that gender and other disparities in the researcher–researched dyad deserve attention in the design of qualitative research, whether that attention is concerned with training and supervision of the interviewers, with ethical issues, or with how the findings will be safeguarded from bias.

Introducing the Three Main Types of Data Collection

Three types of data collection are dominant in qualitative research: observation, interviewing, and review of documents. The latter is considered least intrusive or *reactive* (biased by the presence of the researcher). Secondary analysis of qualitative data is an option that is also low in reactivity, but can be problematic when earlier flaws are simply carried forward (Thorne, 1998). The variety of techniques nested within each of these broad formats will be the subject of Chapters 5 and 6. As shown in Box 3.2, the New York Services Study (NYSS) was large enough to encompass two types of research designs and purposive sampling techniques.

Summary and Concluding Thoughts

Qualitative studies require careful thought to settle on the optimal design. Their contours are visible in a thorough review of the literature—theoretical and empirical. The literature review sets the stage with over-arching study questions and specific research questions containing key ideas and concepts. The selection of qualitative approach(es), in turn, guides the design of the study and its implementation.

Like their quantitative counterparts, qualitative studies must address the element of time (longitudinal versus "snapshot" designs), choose a sampling strategy including the desired number, develop ethical protocols for recruiting and retaining participants, and specify the number of interviews per person and the types of data to be collected. In a qualitative study, it must be clear if and when incentives are paid, how data will be stored and managed, what data analyses will be performed, and what strategies for rigor will be employed. Unlike their quantitative counterparts, qualitative designs are not linear (even if their description appears as such). Instead, qualitative designs adopt an iterative back-and-forth rhythm between data collection and analysis.

This chapter has posed numerous questions whose answers form the backbone of a study's planning stage. Although each approach has its own procedures (e.g., ethnographic studies are different from narrative analyses), all share in common the need to transparently spell out what lies ahead.

BOX 3.2   Research Designs in the New York Services Study

The research designs for the NYSS indexed its specific aims. The study had two separate designs, the first based on life histories (collected in two interviews) and the second employing a prospective longitudinal mixed method (qualitative-dominant) design. Sampling in Phase 1 used something rare in qualitative methods—a sampling frame from an earlier experimental study comparing enrollees in a "housing first" (experimental) program to those in "treatment first" (control) programs in New York City. We chose a type of purposive sampling (*nominations sampling*) in which the roster of earlier participants was independently scrutinized by two experienced interviewers from the earlier study and categorized as either "successes" or "non-successes" from the experimental and control groups. "Success" was a judgment based on mental functioning, substance dependence, and overall life functioning. Once the roster was divided into the four groups (based on consensus discussion), recruitment was initiated to ensure adequate representation from each group.

The Phase 2 design required much more protocol development because it involved recruiting 80 clients from four city agencies, each of whom was interviewed three times over a 12-month period. In addition, each client's case manager was interviewed twice, once right after client entry and the second time after six months of program enrollment (or sooner if the client left the program). To enable tracking and retention, we planned monthly ten-minute check-in interviews with clients (for which they were paid $10).

Recruitment of client participants depended on ongoing relationships with the referring agencies because intake managers were asked to follow our inclusion criteria and inform eligible clients about the study. (The $30 incentive smoothed the way considerably.) Tracking clients who left the programs was a challenge, with many relapsing and returning to the streets. The turnover in case managers required vigilance as well.

Slippage in the best-intended protocols is not uncommon, especially with hard-to-reach populations. Compared to most qualitative studies (which are not longitudinal and multiphase), the NYSS was a large-scale effort.

EXERCISES

1. Chose a topic of interest and formulate one research question suitable for each of the types of qualitative methods: ethnographic, grounded theory study, case study, etc.

2. Using either the same topic you chose from #1 or a new one, plan and write out your research design for one particular type of qualitative method. Include answers to the "how many" questions as well as which type of sampling strategy you will use.

3. Think of a "hard-to-reach" population and identify one or more sampling strategy and recruitment technique that would be most effective.

4. Imagine that you are interviewing for an academic position and a member of the search committee says: "Your qualitative research looks interesting but I honestly don't see how much can be learned from such a small sample." How would you respond to that comment?

ADDITIONAL READINGS

Crabtree, B. F., & Miller, W. L. (1999). *Doing qualitative research* (2nd ed.). Thousand Oaks, CA: Sage.

Creswell, J. W. (2007). *Qualitative inquiry and research design* (2nd ed.). Thousand Oaks, CA: Sage.

LeCompte, M. D., & Schensul, J. J. (1999). *Designing and conducting ethnographic research* (Ethnographer's toolkit, Vol. 1). Walnut Creek, CA: AltaMira Press.

Marshall, C., & Rossman, G. B. (2006). *Designing qualitative research* (4th ed.). Thousand Oaks, CA: Sage.

Maxwell, J. A. (2004). *Qualitative research design: An interactive approach* (2nd ed.). Thousand Oaks, CA: Sage.

Patton, M. Q. (2002). *Qualitative research and evaluation methods* (3rd ed.). Thousand Oaks, CA: Sage.

4

Ethical Issues In Qualitative Research

The dynamic and ongoing nature of relationships in qualitative research raises a number of ethical questions (Christians, 2000; Punch, 1994). Although qualitative studies seldom entail a serious risk of harm for study participants, the sensitivity of their subject matter and closeness of relationships pose challenges that should not be taken lightly. Some ethical issues can be anticipated and dealt with in advance; however, the flexibility of qualitative inquiry means that unforeseen dilemmas can arise at any time. As will be discussed later on in this chapter, ethical guidelines designed for quantitative research do not easily fit the exigencies of qualitative studies.

Deception and Disclosure

Deception (concealing the nature of the study and the investigator's role) is prohibited in virtually all research these days. The history of research deception, from Holocaust medical experiments to the infamous Tuskegee study to Stanley Milgram's electric shock studies, makes its practice virtually indefensible. Of course, the harm incurred varies considerably—a high-risk medical experiment has far more potential for harm than an observational study of behavior in busy public spaces. Yet even the latter example is questionable given sensitivities about deception.

Three interrelated aspects of research deception are at issue in deciding whether it is defensible: 1) its necessity to carrying out the study; 2) its potential for harm; and 3) its intentionality. With regard to the first of these, human subjects committees have clear guidelines restricting use of deception to studies where the benefit outweighs the risk and the study could not be conducted otherwise. In these instances, researchers are required to put in place a number of safeguards such as debriefing subjects afterward.

The potential for harm is another variable. A number of landmark studies in the social sciences could not have been carried out without deception. LaPiere's (1934) study of racial and ethnic discrimination in the 1930s was based on his travels with a Chinese couple to various hotels and restaurants around the United States. The proprietors' discriminatory practices were, unbeknownst to them, contrasted with their previous survey responses stating they did not practice discrimination. If they had known the identity of LaPiere and his traveling companions, they likely would have behaved differently.

LaPiere's deception seems worth the risk, especially since harm was minimal or nonexistent given that no identities were revealed. Similarly, a researcher interested in unobtrusively observing panhandlers and pedestrians on a busy street can make a compelling argument for deception as having little potential for harm. To require informed consent would deny the naturalness on which the study depends because it would create serious distortion, or reactivity, in the behavior of those being observed.

Observational studies in public or semi-public places can be out of line if they involve reports of sensitive or stigmatized behavior. Laud Humphries' (1970) landmark study of gay men's behavior in public restrooms provoked cries of outrage when his deceptive tactics became known. Although Humphries countered that the study's findings justified the use of deception, few would defend his actions today.

If the reasons for intentional deception are few and must be carefully justified, what about unintentional deception? Human subjects committees would not countenance this on the face of things. However, in certain types of qualitative research (e.g., ethnography), it is virtually impossible to notify every individual who might cross the researcher's path. Consider a hypothetical study of staff–patient interactions in a hospital emergency department. A good faith effort requires that the gatekeepers (medical directors, administrators, and house staff) are notified in advance and that formal sit-down interviews occur only after gaining informed consent. Yet one cannot give advance notification to every individual passing through the ER—every ambulance driver, concerned family member, and janitor—by telling them that they will be observed! Nor can one be expected to obtain formal consent every time an impromptu question is asked.

Promoting candor and transparency does not mean that participants have to be told every detail of the study or that every person within eyesight of the researcher requires full notification—not even the most stringent ethical guidelines require this.

Informed Consent

Because the vast majority of qualitative research involves active, face-to-face engagement, informed consent is an "ongoing and negotiated" process (Waldrop, 2004, p. 238). The basic elements of informed consent are:

- A brief description of the study and its procedures as they involve participants (approximate number of interviews, duration of the study, etc.).
- Full identification of the researcher's identity and of the sponsoring organization (if any), including an address or telephone number for future contacts.
- An assurance that participation is voluntary and the respondent has the right to withdraw at any time without penalty or loss of services.
- An assurance of strict confidentiality (which may be accompanied by two caveats: one regarding mandated reporting by licensed professionals as required by state law and the other regarding the risk of a breach in confidentiality from other focus group members).
- Any risks or benefits associated with participation in the study. (Incentive payments are not considered benefits but, rather, reimbursement.)

It is also necessary to get explicit consent to audiotape interviews, along with assurances that participants may request that all or part of such recordings be withdrawn from the study. Most researchers bring two copies of the consent form (one for the researcher and one for the respondent to keep).

Special precautions are needed for studies involving members of vulnerable populations (e.g., pregnant women, prisoners, institutionalized mentally disabled, and children). For studies of children and adolescents under age 18, consent must be obtained from the parents and the child (children under age 12 may give verbal assent). For vulnerable populations such as the frail elderly, consent may need to be obtained from a guardian as well as from the respondent.

Signed consent may be waived under certain circumstances to protect the identities of vulnerable participants. A researcher studying gay and lesbian youth at a gay community center where they are considered emancipated would neither want nor need signed consent from their parents. The same would be true of undocumented immigrants who have reasonable fears that disclosing their identity would jeopardize their status.

The researcher should obtain the permission of gatekeepers whose approval is necessary to carry out the study, usually in the form of a signed letter. Such written permission is essential if their cooperation involves assistance in recruitment. *Gatekeepers* may include agency directors, clinic supervisors, hospital administrators, school principals, or the local health minister. To neglect this important task could cause delays and even imperil a study.

As discussed earlier, gaining informed consent for impromptu interviews during field observation is not plausible given their spontaneity and unplanned nature. In these instances, tacit consent is usually considered appropriate as long as the potential respondent is free to refuse cooperation by simply walking away.

Obtaining formal consent has its price. Many researchers have commented on the off-putting effects of asking participants to absorb two or more pages of information cast in bureaucratic language and then put their signature on it. This distancing and formality then has to be overcome to set the stage for the freer expression of an in-depth interview.

Coercion and "Deformed" Consent

The threat of coercion—whether heavy-handed or subtle—is a genuine concern in all research, especially in studies of vulnerable populations. Researchers tend to occupy higher-ranking social positions than their study participants and have institutional affiliations that can inspire feelings of coercion (not to mention real coercion). Thus, even carefully obtained consent can become "deformed" consent.

Human subjects committees have extensive guidelines to safeguard against coercion, including consent form language designed to assure prospective study participants that they are free to refuse participation and to withdraw from the study at any time without any loss of services to which they are otherwise entitled.

For clinical researchers, the potential for coercion becomes problematic when the study involves clients, students, or coworkers who are familiar to them. For example, an administrator may want to conduct a study in her agency or a teacher may ask his students to participate in his research project. Interrupting a professional relationship with one's client, student, or coworker to ask for consent can appear (and be) coercive even when handled sensitively. It is hard on the prospective respondents (who do not want to displease or who may fear retribution), and it can be hard on the researcher (trying to shift between research and work roles).

Qualitative research is incompatible with the practitioner's role when the two are carried out simultaneously. It is hard to see any satisfactory way to blend the two roles because the demands of being a practitioner preclude the free, open-ended flow of information that is the essence of qualitative research. Teachers and agency supervisors are similarly constrained when they consider studying their students or subordinates.

The payment of incentives for study participation is a common practice if the researcher's budget can accommodate them (more on this topic a bit later in this chapter). However, it may be construed as coercive if the amount is large enough to give the appearance of purchasing cooperation.

Confidentiality and Privacy

Qualitative researchers cannot offer the anonymity or safety in numbers that quantitative researchers can. They must, however, provide virtually ironclad guarantees of confidentiality. This means that every effort is made to ensure that the identities of participants are never revealed or linked to the information they provide without their permission. Breaches of confidentiality—one of the utmost violations of trust—are undertaken only in dire circumstances in which there are serious risks of harm to self or others, particularly children. For licensed clinicians who are also researchers, mandated reporting is a legal requirement and must be so stated on the consent form.

These precautionary measures represent a worst-case scenario that is extremely rare in qualitative research. Although they encourage candor and openness, qualitative researchers are not usually a sounding board for participants' thoughts of harming others (even when such thoughts exist). The same is not necessarily true of suicidal thoughts. In the NYSS, a few interviewees talked about suicidal ideation, usually as a thing of the past or in the context of help-seeking already undertaken. If a suicide attempt were probable and imminent, interviewers were trained to return to the topic after the recording had stopped, to ask if the participant felt he or she needed help and to offer to make a referral to a hotline or other source of help.

Less urgent but still concerning are respondents' accounts of activities that are nonviolent but nonetheless illegal, for example, shoplifting, prostitution, and drug dealing. Qualitative researchers cannot allow their personal or moral concerns about these behaviors to interfere with the promise of confidentiality. Intervening to prevent such activities would not likely be successful and in any case would end the research relationship (and possibly any chance of learning more about the respondents' risk-taking behavior).

Unlike quantitative research, a qualitative study runs a significant risk of breaching confidentiality in the reporting of results. Pseudonyms are typically used and inconsequential facts changed to help prevent this from happening; such breaches are less likely when the report relies on brief quotes or excerpts. More worrisome are vignettes or case studies in which individuals' life experiences are kept intact and their identities are traceable by others who know them. The more context and detail included in the report, the greater the risk. Moreover, gathering and storing visually recognizable images (photographs or video) of study participants runs a much higher risk of exposure of their identity (or at least a higher level of fear that this will happen). By comparison, audio taping does not pose the same threat, since utterances are less identifying than visual images.

This ethical bind emerges in sharp relief when the study's portrayal is perceived as sharply critical. Nancy Scheper-Hughes' study of mental illness in a remote Irish village was an award-winning ethnography that nonetheless drew widespread media criticism in Ireland for its portrayal of the Catholic Church and family life (1979). Given the extensive description in her narrative, fictitious names were quickly decoded and identities made public and widely discussed. In a dangerous coda to the controversy, the villagers expelled Scheper-Hughes during a return visit amidst threats of physical harm (2000). A possible preventative measure in such a situation—member-checking findings with participants—was not likely to be an option because the participants would have vetoed the author's interpretations.

There is one other (albeit remote) risk of breaching the promise of confidentiality in qualitative research. Unlike attorneys and physicians, researchers do not enjoy legal protection from demands that they disclose information on illegal activities committed by study participants. Thus, an ethnographic study of drug dealers could catch the attention of a local district attorney and inspire her to subpoena field notes and transcripts. If a study's participants are deemed vulnerable to such scrutiny, the researcher may wish to obtain a Federal Certificate of Confidentiality (CoC) from the National Institutes of Health (available to all researchers regardless of funding source). The CoC gives legal protection to participants for a specified period of time.

Thankfully, such dire outcomes are exceedingly rare. Prosecutors have better means (e.g., informants) to track down illegal activities and are usually reluctant to incur the wrath of local universities or research organizations. Of various threats to confidentiality, this is by far the least likely to occur.

Distress and Emotional Harm

Obtaining voluntary informed consent does not prevent one type of ethical problem from arising in qualitative research—the potential to cause emotional distress. Many qualitative interviews elicit intense discussions of painful life events such as divorce, death of a family member, and domestic abuse. Common sense dictates that such topics are not introduced gratuitously; they should be voluntarily brought up or, if necessary, inquired about carefully and empathically. Extremely sensitive topics (incest, child abuse, suicidality) must be handled with the greatest care.

When essential to the study, emotion-laden topics should be broached naturally and preferably not before the second interview. Although human subjects committees often assume that talking about sensitive topics is a recipe for psychological damage, emotional displays by respondents are not uncommon and are rarely cause for alarm (Seidman, 2006; Weiss, 1994). In the NYSS, interviewers were trained to anticipate this and have witnessed intense anger as well as mournful sobs. Such episodes turned out to be infrequent and transient. Rather than resent the qualitative researcher for eliciting such feelings, most participants remark that the interview is an emotional catharsis for them, a chance to express themselves before a nonjudgmental, sympathetic listener (Weiss, 1994).

The researcher should make advance arrangements for referrals to professional counseling if emotional responses are likely to occur. If a trained clinician, she should not provide this assistance directly (even if respondents request it). If offered, referrals should be made after the interview has ended. It is important to maintain this distinction between the data gathering part of an interview and the informal conversation and sharing that take place when the recorder is turned off. On one such occasion in the NYSS, a man with schizophrenia spoke of his deteriorating mental status and the likelihood that he would need to return to the hospital. The interviewer sympathetically asked him if he was in contact with his social worker and offered to help him make the contact, but also assured him that the ultimate choice was his to make. Despite hearing voices and knowing he was facing a psychotic crisis, the participant replied that he was ready to exercise that choice (and he did).

Incentives, Payback, and Maintaining Goodwill

Small monetary payments or other incentives encourage participation and partially compensate respondents for their time. As mentioned earlier, funded research projects routinely include incentive payments in their budget. The size of the payment depends on how much is being asked of the respondent in terms of time and inconvenience.

This decision regarding how much to pay respondents is ethical as well as financial. If paying too little, the incentive value is lost. But if paying too much (and especially if prospective respondents live in poverty), one risks taking advantage of their poverty by purchasing their cooperation. Novice researchers usually consult with more experienced colleagues to find out the current rates of compensation for study participation. Payment of cash incentives may not be feasible for researchers who lack funding, especially students who are themselves struggling financially. Doctoral students I have known have offered $10 gift certificates to a coffee shop or grocery or persuaded a local vendor to donate small items (tote bags, sundries, deli sandwiches, etc.).

Another form of compensation or payback takes place naturalistically during the study. For example, a researcher who is spending time at a hospice interviewing staff might be able to offer an on-the-spot tutorial on a computer software program to help them with an administrative task. In the NYSS, a study participant recently released from the hospital revealed that he was intimidated by the subway system but needed to leave soon for a doctor's appointment. In the best possible response, the interviewer offered to accompany him to the subway to show him how to buy and use a metrocard. Needless to say, payback has its limits—researchers should feel free to politely decline inappropriate requests such as going to a movie together, cashing or cosigning a check, hiding drug paraphernalia, and so on.

A final (and often overlooked) source of payback occurs after the study is completed—sharing the findings with the participants (Wolcott, 2001). Respondents often want (and deserve) to see the results of a study in which they played a key role, even if in the abbreviated form of an executive summary.

Institutional Review Boards and Qualitative Research

A discussion of ethics in research would be incomplete without referring to the federally mandated regulatory system promoting adherence to standards of ethical conduct in the United States. Begun for all of the right reasons—egregious abuses of human rights in biomedical experiments—the formal guidelines promulgated under federal ruling 45 CFR 46 (the "Common Rule") have since raised a number of vexing issues. These include the wide latitude given to institutional review boards (IRBs), shifting definitions of "research" and what thereby falls under their regulatory authority, and the methodological biases of these guidelines in terms of their "fit" with non-biomedical research. The distance between what is prescribed by the federal Office for Human Research Protections (OHRP; http://www.hhs.gov/ohrp/) and the actual rules and restrictions implemented locally is a reflection of the interpretive freedom accorded IRBs. Researchers in the social sciences have voiced concerns about IRBs since their inception in 1978. These complaints center in large part on the excessive attention given to procedural issues and the tendency to view all research as suspect (a "guilty until proven innocent" stance). In what has been an inevitable response to the expansion of their jurisdiction and the rapid growth in empirical research, IRBs have come to rely on administrative staff to handle applications, interpret Federal guidelines, craft replies to researchers/applicants, and monitor ongoing compliance. This bureaucratization has, in turn, produced a tendency to micromanage research practices. IRB members who are also researchers tend to bond with administrative support staff in a common "culture of oversight" that reinforces a sense of moral rectitude that places researchers in a defensive posture.

In October 2000, additional federal requirements were enacted such that all research "key personnel" were henceforth expected to pass a tutorial exam and become certified in human subjects protections. (This exam is usually offered by the home institution but is also available at the following Web site: http://bioethics.od.nih.gov.) One immediate problem emerged from confusion over who should be considered "key personnel." Such a determination becomes especially problematic in community-based research in which community partners have little access to federal human subjects certification materials and are unlikely to be familiar with the scientific language of regulatory authority.

For qualitative researchers, a major concern lies in the lack of fit between the biomedical model implicit in IRB activities and the flexibility inherent in qualitative studies. Ethnographers in particular have been repeat offenders or "IRB outlaws" (Katz, 2006). In a 2006 issue of the *American Ethnologist* devoted to this subject, the authors raised a few surprising points. First, a strict interpretation of federal guidelines under the Common Rule could be read as extending only to funded research, and federally funded research at that (Schweder, 2006). In this scenario, the vastly expanded reach of IRBs has been a local option designed to bring all research activities at an institution under a uniform set of standards. Second, IRBs are not required to review research protocols that fall under the exemption criteria, but most assume this authority anyway. Finally, federal guidelines urge timely reviews—expedited reviews to be done within five working days. Given the typical wait of weeks or months required for most IRB reviews and approval, such recommendations appear woefully out of touch with the bureaucratic realities they represent. These revelations are surprising not only for their content but also for their absence from public discourse on the regulatory oversight of human subjects protections.

The sometimes testy relationship between IRBs and researchers recalls that of an unhappy couple where one party to the relationship almost always has the upper hand. In 2003, scholars in oral history tried to exit this relationship by arguing that their work was not "research." Giving a nod to their counterparts in journalism as well as in the arts and humanities, this group of historians sought—and was granted—exemption by the federal OHRP. The wording of the decision regarding the federal definition of research was revealing. Thus, works that "do not reach for generalizable principles of social or historical development" and are not designed to have wider impact are not deemed to be "research." (Brainerd, 2003, p. A25). Museums and historical societies were exempt as long as they confined their work to collecting (not interpreting or generalizing) data from the past. This ruling brought the desired outcome but carried a price in potential loss of prestige for oral historians allied to the social sciences and other research-oriented disciplines.

Curiously, this federal decision causes the ultimate determination of what constitutes research to hinge on motivation or intent (i.e., whether one plans to reach for generalizability; Katz, 2006). This has serious ramifications for the vast arena of social and health care services in which management information systems and internal program evaluations can (and do) regularly verge into the terrain of "research." The primary deciding factors appear to be whether and when the program evaluator plans to draw broader conclusions. What if the program evaluator starts out with local (non-research) intentions but then changes her mind after pre-liminary analyses convince her that the findings should be used to generate broader knowledge? Here, one encounters the blurry line between primary and secondary analyses. Data collected without a priori informed consent is acceptable to an IRB only if it is fully disguised and part of an aggregate dataset. If so, it may be viewed as a secondary analysis worthy of exempt status. Qualitative program evaluation does not offer such anonymity, and so is rarely eligible for post-hoc transformation into IRB-approvable "research."

Common sense sometimes gets lost in bureaucratic inertia. In the NYSS, we had a study participant sent to prison soon after the baseline interview. As required, an amended consent form and protocol was submitted to our institutional IRB requesting permission to interview him at the prison. Although the protocols were approved, final IRB approval was contingent on obtaining a formal letter of cooperation from prison officials. The prison supervisor gave a verbal "yes" on the telephone but refused to provide a formal letter, stating that this would be against prison regulations. Getting back to the IRB, we argued that the interviewer had de facto permission to enter (we surely had no plans to break into the prison!) and perhaps an exit signature could be secured showing that we had been admitted to the facility. After a lengthy delay pending a hearing of this request, the IRB agreed and waived the requirement of a signed letter in advance. Meanwhile, we lost valuable time and prison officials became impatient (although we were ultimately able to conduct the interview).

The pervasive influence of the biomedical model shows up in other ways. At the outset of the NYSS, we were required by the IRB to ascertain participants' capacity to give informed consent because they had a diagnosis of serious mental illness. We counterargued (successfully) that an assumption of incapacitation, with the accompanying testing and implication of a guardian's consent, was itself a denial of study participants' free agency.

Many areas of IRB oversight remain open to varied interpretation regardless of the methodology being employed. For example, do student research projects fall under the "normal educational practices" exemption provided by federal guidelines? Is journalistic writing exempt from IRB review only when it is done by journalists? If a study's methods appear deeply flawed, should the IRB withhold approval given its apparent absence of scientific worth? How is enforcement of noncompliance with IRB rules carried out equitably? Do researchers who believe an IRB has overstepped its authority have avenues of appeal? Are there occasions when it is acceptable and even honorable to offer participants the option of revealing their identity? If so, how do IRBs view such voluntary breaches of confidentiality? Answers to these questions are largely at the discretion of a researcher's local IRB.

The explosive growth in qualitative research has led to wider understanding and acceptance of its flexible approaches. Medical schools IRBs, however, are often more concerned about qualitative studies than about venipuncture or other invasive medical procedures. For the time being, bureaucratic inertia and the continued dominance of the biomedical model will likely ensure that the authority and jurisdiction of IRBs are in no imminent danger of receding.

Dealing With Moral Ambiguity and Risk

The moral ambiguity that surrounds naturalistic inquiry ensures that ethical dilemmas can arise at any time. In-depth interviews can bring accounts of horrific or repulsive behaviors to the surface. Nora (not her real name), a participant in the NYSS, recounted being repeatedly raped by her biological father who also verbally abused her during the assaults. Carlos, another study participant, told of being held over a stove's flame by his mother as punishment for childhood misbehavior.

Respondents may reveal aspects of themselves that cause shock, anger, and feelings of exasperation. Nora ended her account to the NYSS interviewer by noting that she was planning to return to her childhood home to care for her elderly but still abusive father. Another NYSS participant boasted that he had fathered four children by two different women to "prove his manhood" despite having no income to support them.

The intensity and trust unique to qualitative research allows respondents to feel safe enough to utter despicable opinions or admit to illegal and morally reprehensible acts. The decision to intervene is rarely easy and frequently has unforeseen consequences. Steven J. Taylor (1987) wrote of an extremely difficult situation he encountered: physical and verbal abuse of mentally retarded adults by the attendants in a residential facility where he was conducting fieldwork. Although appalling, the attendants' behavior triggered a moral dilemma for Taylor when he reviewed his options for responding.

Intervening with the attendants might have inhibited their abusive behavior (at least in Taylor's presence), but at a cost of breaching confidentiality and losing rapport (thereby ending his inhibiting presence and the study). Blowing the whistle and notifying the authorities (facility administrators, the police, or the media) was made complicated by the fact that facility administrators knew about the abuse, tolerated it, and even covered it up when confronted by family members. Taylor noted that pointing the finger at a few attendants was not likely to prevent future abuse because it was so prevalent and tolerated. Blowing the whistle also comes at a cost—breaching confidentiality and effectively ending the study.

Although acknowledging that there are occasions when intervening is worth it, Taylor ultimately decided to take no immediate action against specific individuals (thereby protecting confidentiality). Instead, he carefully documented his observations. After completing the study and writing about the prevalence of institutionalized abuse in treatment of the mentally retarded he led a media campaign to expose the abuse and worked with legal advocacy groups to draw attention to its prevalence. What at first seemed morally unacceptable—continuing the study—gave him the commitment and knowledge to pursue these activities after the conclusion of the study (Taylor, 1987).

The primary issue for conscientious qualitative researchers caught up in such situations is not whether to do something, but what, how, and when to do it. The lesson of Taylor's experience is that initial impulses to take action should be weighed against foreseeable consequences. Put another way, the timing of taking action should be calibrated to fit the immediacy of the threat and the likelihood that such action will produce the desired result.

Moral ambiguity can happen in any study. Consider a few examples. A young woman with an ovarian tumor says that she will not seek treatment because she fears it will make her infertile. A gang member describes an upcoming initiation rite involving gang rape. An immigrant mother insists on finding a doctor to perform female circumcision on her infant daughter. The options for the researcher are the same as Taylor's: do nothing, end the study relationship, intervene with the respondent, or blow the whistle to the authorities. Unfortunately, there are no clear-cut rules for which course of action to take and when to take it.

Clearly, all of these strong emotions and raw experiences can take their toll on the researcher. In these instances, it is wise to practice bracketing (Ely et al., 1991). Bracketing refers to a conscientious effort to suspend assumptions, beliefs, and feelings in order to better understand the experience of respondents. Debriefing is also important. In the NYSS, we scheduled weekly meetings to talk about the interviews, including their emotional impact. Interviewers and transcribers were also urged to voice any concerns individually.

Emotional stress is not the only risk a qualitative researcher may encounter. Although extremely rare, threats to physical safety may come from respondents, especially those with violent histories. Sexual come-ons and innuendo can also occur. Riessman (1990) found herself deflecting sexual advances by male respondents. Weiss (1994) reported sexual overtures from his female interviewees. Such events can be discomfiting, especially when the interview takes place in the respondent's home or a private location where the researcher feels vulnerable. A rule of thumb in these situations is to plan ahead whenever possible (i.e., by not sending a female to interview a male alone in his apartment) and to maintain professional poise (and leave the premises) whenever the discomfort level becomes intolerable.

Socially Responsible Research as Ethical Research

Social responsibility as an ethical stance includes being sensitive to diversity—gender, social class, age, ethnicity, and sexual orientation—but it also encompasses much more. Professional organizations, as evidenced in the National Association of Social Workers (NASW) Code of Ethics (http://www.naswdc.org/pubs/code) urge their members to pursue research while being mindful of the potential for harm. The NASW Code of Ethics also promotes social justice as fundamental to research as well as practice and policy.

When it comes to social responsibility toward research participants, qualitative researchers have a distinct advantage because they are obliged to "go where the respondents are." Beyond concern for individuals, however, socially responsible research implies taking the larger structural context into consideration when interpreting and understanding the data. A study of persons with schizophrenia might, for example, conclude that they prefer to be isolated if the focus is narrowly on what they say. Considerations of stigma and social exclusion bring an enlarged and more realistic perspective on their social isolation.

The incorporation of broader socioeconomic and cultural perspectives may seem to conflict with a focus on the intricate textures of people's lives seen from the inside (the emic perspective) rather than from the outside (the etic perspective). In fact, some qualitative approaches are less open to addressing structural issues—narrative and phenomenological analyses come to mind—whereas others such as critical theory and feminism are avowedly structural in focusing on inequality and its consequences. The majority of qualitative studies, however, occupy a middle ground in which the researcher may choose to incorporate structural concerns at some (or all) stages of the study.

Socially responsible research does not mean presenting a one-sided portrait that leaves out the less savory aspects of respondents' lives. Qualitative researchers are not investigative reporters digging for dirt, but they are also not obliged to produce an uplifting portrayal devoid of nitty-gritty reality. This delicate balance between accuracy and sensitivity to respondents' needs affects studies of the despicable, the heroic, and the everyday people in between.

Summary and Concluding Thoughts

Ethical issues are omnipresent in qualitative inquiry. As with all research, qualitative studies must adhere to federal guidelines ensuring voluntary informed consent; freedom from deception, coercion, or emotional harm; and protection of confidentiality and privacy. However, many gray areas remain when it comes to interpreting these guidelines and addressing ethical issues lying outside of IRB jurisdiction.

The intensity and duration of the qualitative research relationship, in combination with its lack of strict neutrality, ensure that boundary maintenance requires constant vigilance. Notwithstanding good intentions, researchers who encounter morally ambiguous situations risk inappropriate responses such as giving into the temptation to get too involved, showing disapproval of unsavory behavior, or letting their enthusiasm verge into coercion. The vast majority of qualitative studies poses a risk for harm no more severe than those encountered in everyday life. If properly observant of ethical guidelines, qualitative researchers can take comfort in the fact that their studies are likely to provide a satisfying and memorable experience for respondents.

EXERCISES

1. Go to the National Institutes of Health Web site (http://grants.nih.gov/grants/policy/hs_educ_faq.htm) or to your own institutional review board Web site and take the tutorial on human subjects protections. What are the basic elements of ethical research conduct?

2. Draft a sample consent form that includes the essential protections of human subjects for studying each of the following groups: 1) hospice patients dying of cancer; 2) parents of children with autism; 3) adolescents aged 12–16 who smoke cigarettes.

3. Consider the possibility of conducting ethnographic research in a busy pediatric asthma clinic serving a poor inner-city population. How would you approach informed consent since you will be visiting for prolonged periods and at different times but cannot possibly request informed consent from everyone who will be visiting the clinic?

4. Go to the NIH Web site explaining the federal Certificate of Confidentiality (http://grants.nih.gov/grants/policy/coc). Discuss what types of study populations are most likely to need this extra protection.

ADDITIONAL READINGS

Christians, C. G. (2003). Ethics and politics in qualitative research. In N. K. Denzin & Y. S. Lincoln (Eds.), *The landscape of qualitative research: Theories and issues* (2nd ed., pp. 208–244). Thousand Oaks, CA: Sage.

Guillemin, M., & Gillam, L. (2004). Ethics, reflexivity, and "ethically important moments" in research. *Qualitative Inquiry, 10*, 261–280.

Katz, J. (2006). Ethical escape routes for underground anthropologists. *American Ethnologist, 33*(4), 499–506.

Malone, R. E., Yerger, V. E., McGruder, C., & Froelicher, E. (2006). "It's like Tuskegee in reverse": A case study of ethical tensions in institutional review board review of community-based participatory research. *American Journal of Public Health, 96*, 1914–1919.

Mauthner, M., Birch, M., Jessop J., & Miller, T. (Eds.). (2005). *Ethics in qualitative research*. London: Sage.

Morse, J. M. (2007). Ethics in action: ethical principles for doing qualitative research. *Qualitative Health Research, 17*(8), 1003–1005.

Thorne, S. (1998). Ethical and representational issues in qualitative secondary analysis. *Qualitative Health Research, 8*(4), 547–555.

5

Entering the Field and Conducting Observation

I n early ethnographies, the "field" was a faraway place where anthropologists went to spend a year or longer learning about the local culture. Nowadays, it can be a variety of places and situations, ranging from a finite location such as a clinic, school, or prison to a dispersed population such as transgender youths, persons living with AIDS or methamphetamine abusers. What distinguishes being in or out of the "field" is the stage of the research vis-à-vis data collection.

Based on the premise that all qualitative research takes place within a "field" of action, this chapter will focus on observation as a form of data collection. Because gaining rapport is an essential ingredient for success, the early phases of reaching out to prospective study participants and sites are crucial. Success also depends on getting appropriate permission from gatekeepers and ongoing attention to the researcher's role as engagement with study participants intensifies.

On the Importance of Observation

Naturalistic observation, the hallmark of qualitative methods, has been relegated to a distant second place, with interviewing becoming the most prevalent qualitative method. This turn of events has its origins in the confluence of several interrelated trends. The first trend has been the enthusiastic embrace of qualitative methods by talk-based professions such as teaching, nursing, and social work. Second, talking and dialogue have intrinsic appeal due to their familiarity in everyday lives (Atkinson & Silverman, 1997)—the same cannot be said of participant observation. Finally, research interviewing has flourished as part of a larger phenomenon—the rise of an "interview society" in which television and radio talk shows (not to mention psychotherapy) feature "narratives of suffering" (Atkinson, 1997, p. 325) as the most authentic means of communicating the human experience.

This trend is not without consequences. Bemoaned as the "precariousness of a one-legged stool" (Hall & Rist, 1999, p. 291), interview-only qualitative research conveys the erroneous impression that anyone living in the "interview society" can do it—only good intentions are needed (Sandelowski, 2002). Beyond this naïve take on methodology are deeper concerns about the assumptive world in which interview-only studies take place. Thus, free-flowing narratives are considered to be superior because they give voice to study participants and provide a window into their "real" world. Such a realist assumption, more commonly associated with quantitative interviews, treats what participants say as having an inherent authenticity (Atkinson & Silverman, 1997; Sandelowski, 2002).

Taking everything said at face value is an error of commission as well as omission. Committing what Silverman calls an "Oprah Winfrey cop-out" (quoted in Gergen & Gergen, 2000, p. 1031), researchers dare not interpret what they are hearing as this would dishonor participants. The pendulum appears to have swung from one extreme (the all-knowing researcher) to a romanticized other extreme (the all-knowing study participant). The error of omission comes from not considering the larger context of what is being said. In writing about his study of homeless booksellers in New York City, Duneier notes, "if I had simply taken the men's accounts at face value, I would have concluded that their lives and problems were wholly of their own making" (1999, p. 343). Homeless men are hardly the sole architects of their fate, nor are they helpless victims of larger political and economic forces. Either of these two assumptions, taken alone, is obviously incomplete.

It is often tempting to stay at the concrete level. In the NYSS, participants offer deeply moving accounts of life on the streets, in and out of hospitals and jails, and caught in the throes of drug addiction, all of which make for captivating reading. And, like the men studied by Duneier, their reflections often produce self-recrimination.

Is there a happy medium? To paraphrase a noted social scientist, "you can't generalize from the local, but you can't generalize without it" (Kotkin, 2002, p. B11). Readers of qualitative research are asked to trust the authors as guides leading them into new understanding, but researchers must earn this trust. To do so, we provide sufficient detail to assure them of our immersion in the setting and data, but we are also obliged to make connections "up and out" to the larger context of opportunities and constraints. The reader may be asked to take a "leap of faith" (Duneier, 1999, p. 343) in this regard but the leap should have a credible landing.

Here is where interview-only (as opposed to interview-intensive) research is problematic. Confining a study to one source of data deprives it of the broader interpretive power that comes from observation (Agar & McDonald, 1995). An interview-intensive qualitative study can benefit from systematic and recorded observations of the interview context (the setting, nonverbal communication, etc.). Beyond the immediate surroundings of the interview lie opportunities to shadow participants and enter their worlds naturalistically—admittedly not always possible but at least worth considering (McDonald, 2005).

Without a doubt, interviews will continue to be the staple of qualitative research—talking and listening are deeply woven into the fabric of our being. This chapter represents an attempt to swing the pendulum back a bit by emphasizing observation. We begin with preparations for entering the field.

Getting Permission(s) and Announcing the Study

After spending a considerable amount of time conceptualizing and designing the qualitative study, the cerebral gives way to the social. For most researchers, this is energizing, the time when all of the planning finally gets put to the test. What is meant by "gaining entry"? Qualitative studies may be site-specific, person-centered, or both. Either way, it is common for a study to have some sort of institution and other authority involved. Here are a few examples from doctoral advisees with whom I have worked.

- Patricia's study of Orthodox Jewish runaways involved contacts with youth-oriented rabbis and a small community drop-in center.
- Susan sought to interview young women who self-mutilated by advertising at college student health centers.
- Reji advertised her study of arranged marriage on Web sites serving South Asian immigrants in the United States and Canada.

In Phase 2 of the NYSS, we recruited all new enrollees from four agencies and needed formal permission letters from their executive directors. The clients we recruited were themselves "gatekeepers" whose consent was required in order to interview their case managers at the agencies.

Gaining entry requires differing degrees of outreach and engagement ranging from placing an Internet notice or posting flyers to protracted negotiations including additional reviews by institutional review boards (IRBs) at various study sites. It is best not to take anything for granted. An administrator, agency, or community may have been friendly in the past and then bristle at the prospect of being put under scrutiny in the name of research. Similarly, study participants and communities often have legitimate concerns about the potential for human subjects abuse or negative portrayals (Malone, Yerger, McGruder, & Froelicher, 2006). Qualitative researchers have to accept the fact that the word "research" may conjure images of "human guinea-pig experiments" and exploitation. (The use of the label "subjects" reinforces this image.) Substitution of terms such as "research project" or "study participant" is less distancing and more consonant with the realities of a qualitative study.

It is entirely the responsibility of the researcher to demonstrate that the study is valuable and feasible. Although students are often granted more latitude and acceptance than professional researchers, no one can assume cooperation to be forthcoming.

Finding the gatekeeper(s) and getting permission is an essential first step. The gatekeeper could be an agency administrator, prison superintendent, school principal, or any other authority figure whose support is needed to gain access to a community. In approaching such individuals, the researcher should be direct and forthright about the study's overall goals and the human subjects protections being offered. The study's benefits (as well as its risks) should not be overstated; it is also important to inform gatekeepers and others about the time-consuming and involved nature of qualitative research. If an incentive or other reimbursement is being offered, it should be identified as such and not used as leverage or coercion.

It helps to anticipate gatekeepers' concerns or questions. In the NYSS, program directors expressed doubts about paying cash incentives, worried that study participants would spend the money on drugs and alcohol. Although we were prepared to substitute movie tickets or subway metrocards as a last resort, our counterargument that study participants deserved the same choices as other adults was eventually accepted.

Getting a gatekeeper's attention can itself be a challenge. Agencies, schools, and correctional facilities are busy places. Such facilities are increasingly savvy in the ways of research and skeptical of any added value coming from a proposed study. Medical settings are a veritable beehive of clinical research. Academic teaching hospitals are usually juggling several different study protocols at the same time. One advantage of qualitative research in these situations is its user-friendly, low-tech approach. Still, it is advisable to get a head start in learning about the settings and their gatekeepers, even those whose cooperation involves little more than posting a recruitment flyer on a bulletin board.

Announcing the study refers to laying the groundwork for observation and/or interviewing that is specific to a site. As with the usual procedures of informed consent, this involves full disclosure of one's identity, the purpose(s) of the study, its voluntary nature, and the protection afforded by strict confidentiality. If field notes will be taken, this must also be noted so that everyone knows that they might be observed. Other expectations of cooperation, such as help in recruiting, participation by staff in focus groups, and so on, must be clearly specified. For a clinic or agency, this can usually be handled by attending staff meetings to explain the study and answer questions. For larger entities such as multisite programs or school districts, letters of approval by gatekeepers can be sent to local authorities to smooth the way. Studies of neighborhoods often depend on cultivating the goodwill of civic leaders, clergy, and similar authority figures.

Observational studies bring special considerations. With the exception of busy and open public spaces, the researcher needs to broadcast information about the study as widely as possible. During intensive participant observation, the researcher's prolonged presence gives ample opportunities for such self-identification. For sporadic or less intense involvement, having flyers and gatekeeper permissions handy and being available for questions goes a long way toward allaying suspicions. Of course, any contacts that lead to formal interviewing will trigger the need for informed consent.

If a site is being asked to provide assistance with multiple tasks over a period of time, a *memorandum of understanding* (MOU) is helpful at the outset to specify responsibilities of the respective parties. Although not as necessary in qualitative research as in clinical trials (where randomization, wait list controls, and fidelity measures often intrude on program operations), a MOU can be a reference point for everyone to clarify roles and reduce misunderstandings. A simple one-page, bulleted list of responsibilities for the site and the researcher is a good start. Of course, a MOU should not lock the research in too stringently because protocols need to remain flexible.

All of this interaction can produce a difficult situation if researchers find themselves too closely identified with gatekeepers who participants view with suspicion or distrust. Potential participants can also be confused when well-meaning but overly enthusiastic gatekeepers assist in study recruitment. In the NYSS, for example, we asked intake coordinators to avoid pressuring their clients to participate and to make it clear that we were not affiliated with their program. Of course, not all qualitative studies have to seek permission from formal gatekeepers (e.g., those soliciting volunteers through advertising or informal networks).

Obtaining and Maintaining Rapport

Once all formal permissions have been obtained, what James Spradley refers to as the "rapport process" (1979, p. 78) takes center stage and continues until the study is over. Rapport can begin on a number of levels, depending on the complexity and length of the study. At a minimum, rapport refers to the sense of respect, trust, and positive regard between researcher and study participants that enhances openness in information sharing. Rapport also refers to maintaining good relations with study sites and their representatives. Paying participant incentives facilitates the development of rapport but can never substitute for interpersonal skills.

Spradley (1979) cautions that the mutual enjoyment typical of study participation does not necessarily translate into deep friendship or affection. A researcher and study participant do not have to like one another to have rapport. The first encounter, often awkward, should set the stage for future exchanges. Once a participant is engaged in the study, rapport is maintained or deepened by careful attention to changes that might signal distraction or fatigue. It is also enhanced by engaging in small talk before and after the interview (with the tape recorder turned off) as well as by the psychological benefits of the interview itself. Ultimately, the recipe for maintaining rapport includes equal amounts of respect and attentiveness leavened by ongoing self-reflection on the part of the researcher.

Presentation of Self in the Field

Qualitative researchers vary in how they present themselves depending on their personal preferences as well as the particular setting being entered. Erving Goffman (1961), for example, adopted a marginal stance, detaching himself as he observed asylums and other institutions. At the other end of the continuum, feminist researchers advocate a research partnership in which roles are blurred and researchers are actively engaged in coproducing findings with respondents (Reinharz, 1992). Most qualitative researchers present a "self" somewhere in between that of a marginal outsider and an intimate insider.

The researcher is obliged to enter the field "with an open mind, not an empty head" (Fetterman, 1989, p. 11). In other words, the researcher should be knowledgeable enough about the topic to prevent unnecessary interruptions that disrupt the flow of the interview. In the NYSS, interviewers were trained to be familiar with the slang words for drugs (e.g., crack cocaine is "rock," marijuana is smoked in "blunts," and "benzos" are anxiety medications abused on the streets). Similarly, the terms "SSI" and "rep payee" were common parlance in interviews. These short-hand references to federal disability income and representative payee status can be mentioned by the study participant without having to explain to the interviewer what they mean. This leaves time for explorations with more depth and nuance, for example, questions about what it means to have SSI as a steady source of income or to have someone else in control of one's finances.

The interviewer's mode of dress and demeanor also deserve attention. Because dressing up can appear elitist or patronizing and dressing down can come off as disrespectful, dressing in a casual and neat manner usually works the best. Demeanor is a bit trickier because it involves one's personal style of communication and engagement with others. The researcher's creativity and intellectual curiosity should not be squelched; qualitative interviews usually rise above the mundane when the researcher is enthusiastic. However, when a researcher expresses too much individuality it can detract from the real experts (the study participants). Optimally, the researcher is empathic and understanding without sacrificing professionalism. Maintaining a sense of humor, a willingness to be wrong (a lot), and an eagerness to learn is a winning combination.

Issues of Identity: Gender, Age, Race/Ethnicity, and Social Class

Whereas mutable characteristics such as dress and demeanor can be adjusted, relatively fixed traits such as sex, age, race/ethnicity, and social class must also be considered. Socially constructed meanings associated with gender, race, and class identity often come into sharp focus in qualitative research relationships. There are potential advantages as well as disadvantages to this situation. In her study of psychiatric outpatients living in the community, Sue Estroff made these observations:

> Being female helped and hurt. Over half of the subjects were men. My gender served as an entree to contacting them and eliciting some interest, but it created tensions as well. Many had never had a female friend, that is, a symmetrical, platonic, heterosexual relationship. This led to some confusion on their part when their sexual advances offended me, and to reluctance on my part in entering situations . . . which might be misconstrued. (1981, p. xvii)

The consequences of sex, race, social class, and other differences can be either disastrous or negligible. In most instances, a relationship of mutual respect need not be based on sameness; the ultimate success of the study depends primarily on the skills of the researcher (Manderson, Bennett, & Andajani-Sutjaho, 2006). In addition to their demographic traits, researchers carry a number of identities into the field that they have acquired over time. These identities can be professional (student, professor, practitioner), personal (partner, parent, sibling), political (feminist, antiwar activist, animal rights advocate), and recreational (soccer fan, pianist, marathon runner). How, if at all, these identities influence the study is largely a matter of context and appropriateness.

Researcher Self-Disclosure: How Much Is Enough? How Much Is Too Much?

There are no prohibitions on personal disclosure in qualitative inquiry; some is to be expected as part of the give-and-take required to maintain rapport and trust. The overriding questions are: Which "selves" should the researcher reveal? When is it appropriate to do this? Are there dangers to such revelations?

Qualitative researchers generally adhere to the advice to be "truthful but vague" (Taylor & Bogdan, 1984). One should never lie if asked a question, but should use considerable discretion in how much to reveal. Weiss suggests providing the basic "business card" information (1994), but others assert that sharing personal information encourages fuller disclosure by respondents and promotes greater equality (Gair, 2002; Reinharz, 1992).

Personal disclosure is usually easier for researchers who are studying what is familiar. Catherine Riessman (1990) reported that sharing her divorced single-parent status with her respondents enhanced their willingness to talk about their own experiences with divorce. When studying the unfamiliar, personal information may humanize the researcher and make her appear to be less of an outsider.

Interviewees often parry with questions that come out of the blue and require on-the-spot decisions on whether and how to respond. Take the hypothetical example of a doctoral student–researcher who is a licensed social worker, a parent, an Army veteran, and an avid fan of heavy metal music. She is obliged to reveal her status as a doctoral student right away because this is the requisite "self" conducting the study. If the study involves potentially harmful subject matter, she will also have a caveat in the consent form regarding her legal status as a mandated reporter of child or elder abuse. Whether she has the occasion to reveal her musical tastes or status as a veteran and parent depends on the context.

Disclosure can have unintended consequences. Ben Henwood, an interviewer for the NYSS, noted that the case managers he interviewed sometimes mentioned his student status (one paternally urging him to "stay in school") yet he was unsure whether to mention that he was also a licensed social worker like them. The rapport-enhancing advantage of doing this could be outweighed by the risks of: 1) unintentionally stirring up social class resentment (he is able to afford a doctoral education); 2) finding out that they know some of the same people professionally (raising respondents' fears of exposure); and, 3) changing the tenor of the interviews to "insider" exchanges between two professionals. Ben decided to err on the side of caution, resolving to disclose his profession only if asked. As it happened, none of the case managers asked.

A researcher's disclosure of his various selves and life experiences cannot follow a strict protocol but is usually better confined to the before-and-after chat that accompanies each interview. During the interview, such decisions should take into account a risk-benefit equation balancing rapport with the potential for bias or intrusiveness. It can be entirely appropriate for the researcher to identify himself as being a military veteran or a recovering addict, but this should not be done gratuitously or appear as attention-seeking behavior.

Observation in Qualitative Studies

As discussed earlier, many researchers consider interviewing preferable to the less familiar terrain of observation. But imagine trying to fully understand how a hospice, methadone clinic, or soup kitchen operates by relying solely on verbal description. First of all, those who have more to hide usually hide it more. Second, many individuals are either unaware of goings-on in their midst or have spotty recall. As discussed in the previous chapter, the days of deception in observation are largely over. With rare exceptions, qualitative researchers develop and follow observational protocols that involve full disclosure.

It is helpful to distinguish between observation as a mode of qualitative data collection and *participant observation,* the centerpiece of ethnographic fieldwork (Emerson, 2001). While the latter assumes the primacy of immersion and interaction within a specific environment, the former is less site specific and often used in conjunction with interviewing (thus being less intense and time consuming). Although the dividing line between these is often blurry, I will focus more on the former (ethnographic fieldwork)—with varying amounts of participation accompanying the observation.

Even minimal amounts of participation require careful consideration given the potential for *reactivity* (changes due to the researcher's presence). Think of a continuum ranging from full participation (living with the study population for a prolonged period and carrying out daily activities much as they do) to unobtrusive observation with little or no interaction. The risks at the high-involvement end of the continuum include researcher fatigue and some version of "going native" (losing sight of the researcher role). At the low level of involvement, avoiding interaction means foregoing a valuable means of learning in situ.

Both extremes are more difficult to accomplish compared to mid-level participation that is selective and contextual. If the study is site centered, attendance at carefully sampled events—staff meetings, street festivals, political protests, support group meetings, and so on—can be extremely useful in documenting the range of activities. If the study is largely person centered, getting permission to shadow study participants on their daily rounds of activities or on selected outings gives added value to what is otherwise entirely dependent on the participants' verbal accounts. Sampling of events may be representative (e.g., varying by time of day, types of participants) or purposive (e.g., attending case conferences reserved for the most troubled clients or shadowing a study participant on the first of the month after the disability check has arrived).

Ultimately, the degree of involvement and participation depends on the study goals. Eliot Liebow (1993) spent many hours at a homeless women's shelter in Washington, DC, where he shared in the daily activities of women residents. He did not become homeless himself, but he was far from a detached observer. Similarly, Sue Estroff (1981) carried out ethnographic research among persons with schizophrenia by sharing in virtually all aspects of their daily lives. She even took Prolixin to experience firsthand the powerful antipsychotic drug's side effects (a degree of immersion few would be willing to undertake today).

Some qualitative methods do not draw on observational data, for example, those relying on historical documents or narrative and other textual analyses. Some behaviors are too intensely private or risky to observe, for example, unsafe sex, self-mutilation, and IV drug use come to mind. Leaving aside these exceptions, it is safe to say that most qualitative studies benefit from collecting observational data, even those that are interview intensive.

"Doing" Observation: The Best (and Only True) Way to Learn

Despite volumes of "field wisdom" passed on by ethnographers (Sanjek, 1990), the demands of qualitative observation can only be appreciated with hands-on experience. Students in my qualitative methods doctoral course react similarly during their first participant-observation assignment—an initial response of "how easy" and "what a refreshing break from the usual class assignments" gives way to reality after an hour spent observing in the field. Post-hoc comments run along these lines: "I couldn't decide what to write down," "There was so much going on, I didn't know where to start," and "I've never had to do anything like this before."

We are all participant observers in a way—nothing less is required when entering an unfamiliar situation, whether it is the latest nightclub or a coveted job interview. Yet qualitative research demands a more systematic, thorough, and nonjudgmental form of observation than the necessarily self-interested and selective observations one makes in daily life.

According to experts in ethnographic techniques (Agar, 1980; LeCompte & Schensul, 1999; Spradley, 1979), the best approach is to begin by casting a wide net and then move to more focused observation as the study's aims and major themes begin to crystallize. All of the senses are involved—sounds and smells can convey important meaning and context. Ethnographers usually seek out one or more *key informants* (knowledgeable individuals who can supply valuable information). Although the term "informant" is a regrettable holdover from earlier days, it connotes what is being sought because the individual is not asked to talk about personal experiences.

To illustrate the unique powers of observation with all of the senses, consider a typical homeless men's shelter. In photographs, it can appear relatively benign, for example, rows of beds with men sitting or lying on them. But a few visits for field observation will bring the sensory experience of the shelter to full life. Pervasive theft, drug use, and physical intimidation are the norms of life in the public shelter system, as recounted by residents and often barely concealed from visitors. The sensory stimuli add an extra dimension or two. The smells—body odor (few working showers), poor sanitation (nonfunctioning toilets), greasy cooking, and powerful chemical disinfectants—can be overpowering. However, the noise and lack of privacy are often the most disturbing aspects of shelter life—the cacophony of sounds from dozens (or hundreds) of men crowded into close quarters, cursing and shouting (including guards and staff), some in the throes of drug-induced or mental psychoses. Usually required to leave the premises for the day, weary occupants return at night for rest, but get little. Residents' accounts of municipal shelter life are often dismissed as exaggerated or flimsy excuses for preferring the freedom of the streets. But researchers' firsthand observation more often than not validates these portrayals of homeless shelters as multisensory hazards to health and well-being.

Recording Observational Data

"Observation protocols ... cannot be treated as faithful reproductions or unproblematic summaries of what is experienced, but should be seen, rather, for what they are: texts written by authors, using their available linguistic resources, to give a meaningful summary of their observations and recollections after the event ..." (Luders, 2004, p. 228)

Field notes are the necessary if imperfect representation of what is experienced during observation (Emerson, Fretz, & Shaw, 1995). Their quality is improved significantly by adhering to two practices. First, field notes should be taken either in real time or very soon thereafter because memory erodes dramatically within the first 24 hours after an event. Second, it is important to avoid the clouding or distorting effects of "filters," whether personal predilections or theoretical allegiances. This can happen by referring to a man and a woman arguing on the sidewalk as a "couple" without knowing what their relationship actually is. It can also occur when using psychological terms such as "denial" when referring to a respondent's reluctance to address a sensitive issue. No observer is a bias-free instrument, but attending to this fact is the requisite first step.

Much has been written addressing the "why, what, and how" questions of field note-taking. Answering "why" is the easiest to do: Logging one's observations produces valuable raw data that can lead to more focused follow-up via interviewing or additional observation. The "what" of field note-taking depends on the topic of interest as no one can presume to record everything. General suggestions regarding what to look for in the initial phase include physical space, actors, behaviors, inter-actions, relationships, and affect (expressions of feelings or emotions; Lofland & Lofland, 1995). If one is observing a bounded physical space, it is useful to draw a map or floor plan to add a spatial dimension to understanding what is happening. An agency where staff share cramped cubicles will have a different feel from one where private work space is the norm.

The "how" of field note-taking requires a good deal of flexibility, sensi-tivity to the situation, and practice. It is easier to take notes (or speak into a recorder) in busy public spaces where one can remain relatively incon-spicuous. But there are many occasions when writing notes would intrude on the natural course of events and even provide cause for offense. For these occasions, Lofland and Lofland (1995) describe a sequence of taking mental notes—committing to memory as much as possible—followed by brief jottings or speaking into a tape recorder. (Retreating to the bathroom is a favorite technique for accomplishing this.) At the end of the day, one can write in greater detail. Box 5.1 offers an example of notes from the NYSS.

BOX 5.1   Field Notes From a Visit to the Homeless Outreach
Center (HOC)

October 2, 2005, 2–3 pm. Recorded by Courtney Abrams, NYSS Interviewer

From the outside, the HOC (all names are pseudonyms) is unassuming—a plain building nestled between similar structures. It was a temperate autumn day and there was a casual mix of local street traffic on the block, hip-dressed employees of local businesses and a few hardscrabble-looking individuals milling about. We were buzzed inside and met by a receptionist behind thick glass. The entranceway was a small space for the three of us plus the other employee, so along with the glass, it was somewhat uninviting. But the employees were pleasant and cheerfully asked the purpose of our visit. Deborah asked whether we might wait inside for our scheduled meeting with George [HOC Director] since we had been advised upon arrival that he was handling an emergency and would be late for our meeting.

(Continued)

(Continued)

We sat in a small waiting area which offered a row of three metal-and-plastic chairs. This area was a hub of activity; we later learned that half the residents live on this floor. To our left was a staircase that led to the rest of the facility. Directly in front of us, but up high, hung a brightly colored, neatly arranged collage made with feathers and paint. It looked as if a resident had made it, but it wasn't signed. On either side of the collage, we faced two wide doorways: One led to the kitchen, and the other led to the nurse's station. We could hear casual conversations emanating from each room and it probably would have been awkward had we just wandered in. The aroma of hot institutional food filled the waiting area.

While we waited, men and women came and went. It seemed to be a mix of employees (food service and custodial workers, perhaps) as well as some possible residents (although we later learned all but the newest residents should have been away at their day programs). After about 10–15 minutes, an African American female employee came to tell us we could wait on the second floor. At this point, we weren't told that George was, in fact, out for the day. The building is not very old, and the stairway was wide and typically institutional. It was all concrete, with grey floor and walls that were half orange, half white, with a bright yellow line separating the orange and white. There was some signage in the stairs but we were talking so I didn't make note of it. We walked up to the second floor.

The door opened into a small, brightly lit corridor with offices in many directions. We could see into a cheerfully decorated large room. Pretty soon a young white woman (early 30s) walked out of a nearby doorway and introduced herself. She was Sarah [Assistant Director]. She informed us in a very friendly and apologetic manner that George was not in that day but perhaps she could help us. Did we want a tour, did we need information, or did we need to wait and reschedule? We opted to talk, and she led us into a relatively cramped and disarrayed meeting room.

The décor consisted of more collages and art. Sarah had a notepad and took notes while we talked. We were all impressed with her manner. She was confident, direct, engaging, professional, and focused. She was clearly proud of the HOC's role in helping the homeless in New York City. She was generous, offering us access to anything she could think of and volunteering information that might help us. She never

> once said she would have to check with someone and I found myself
> wondering whether she might later rescind any of her offers.
>
> After the meeting, we adjourned to Sarah's office so she could print
> out the intake and other forms we needed. She had a lot of personal
> items and it was a small space. She cheerfully handed us what she had
> printed, we said our goodbyes, and we were free to show ourselves
> out. We retraced our steps down the stairs, which were being mopped.
> There was a lot of traffic and the mopping seemed to actually make the
> stairs dirtier, now full of wet black footprints. We said "hello" to every-
> one we passed, and they returned the greeting. As we left, there were
> loiterers hanging around outside, in small groups or alone, leaning
> against the building.

Lofland and Lofland (1995, pp. 89–90) provide a number of helpful hints for field note-taking:

1. Aim for the concrete and specific in describing behaviors and events. At the beginning, try to avoid any inferences, whether your own or volunteered by others.

2. Try to distinguish between the different types or levels of observational data based on their proximity to the event being observed. First-order data such as verbatim accounts are recorded either during, or immediately after, the period of observation. The second level of data involves paraphrasing conversations and less certain recall after observation has taken place. Ideas regarding new directions and inferences are further along the continuum of removal from the event and are periodically recorded in analytic memos. The final level of abstraction, concept development and theory generation, involves generating a meaningful explanatory framework that has been developed from the ground level up.

3. Record observations of yourself—your impressions, feelings, and concerns. You can bracket this information in your field notes or log it separately in a diary. Keeping a running commentary of personal reactions and feelings serves two related purposes. First, it is an outlet—a place to unload the inevitably human reactions to prolonged contact with others. Second, it provides a means of identifying personal biases and devising ways to manage them.

4. Strive for balance—don't let yourself become lost in a forest of minutiae, yet don't lose the tendency for compulsiveness that motivates the best field observers. Even small amounts of time spent in the field translate into lengthy notes. The ratio is around 6 to 1—6 hours of recording for every hour of observation.

The average field notebook is not scintillating reading—it will appear long and tedious to an outside reader. At times, the burden to record as much as possible can be onerous; most ethnographers have at least one story of hiding from an informant to avoid yet another encounter. After all, a 15-minute conversation might turn into an hour or more of write-up!

Uses of Video and Photography

Field note-taking in real time can divert attention away from observation (Agar, 1980). A question often arises at this point: What about video and photography as ancillary means of observation or as stand-alone methods of data collection? Film and video have long been used in ethnography, pioneered by Margaret Mead and Gregory Bateson during their fieldwork in New Guinea in the 1930s. As presentational forms, ethnographic films such as the 1920s classic *Nanook of the North* and Frederick Wiseman's *Titicut Follies* in 1967 chronicled the decline of traditional culture on the one hand and the horrors of insane asylums on the other. "Visual anthropology" and "visual sociology" are fast-growing subfields devoted to the still image in photography as well as the moving image of film and video.

The ubiquity of digital video capacity makes videotaping a readily available companion to field notes for anyone with a cellular phone or camera. However, use of videotaping and photography presents special legal and ethical issues. Compared to audiotaping, it is much easier to violate a person's privacy because visual images are more identifying and exposing than voice recordings.

The combination of privacy laws and human subjects protections requires that signed releases and informed consent be obtained from all persons in advance of photographing or videotaping them. Some study participants may want to be identified and credited and this should be an option if anticipated. In oral history research, for example, participants may want their names and faces to be known because their identity is an important aspect of the historical record. Indeed, all forms of media—audio, video, photography—are an invaluable means to preserving historic and rare phenomena. Barnes, Taylor-Brown, and Weiner (1997) combined a social work videotape intervention with research on HIV-infected mothers. The twelve women who volunteered for the project gave deeply moving accounts and advice to their children that were videotaped and then analyzed using grounded theory methods.

Photovoice techniques, which originated in public health research, offer an appealing option that enables study participants to control the camera and tell the story themselves (Carlson, Engebretson, & Chamberlain, 2006; Wang & Redwood-Jones, 2001). Influenced by the emancipatory writings of Paolo Freire in combination with feminist theory, photovoice adroitly merges research with community empowerment. Its implementation, which usually involves collaboration between researchers, community representatives, and photography instructors, is a means for individuals and communities to document their strengths as well as their concerns in order to effect positive change (Wang, Morrel-Samuels, Hutchinson, Bell, & Pestronk, 2004). Although still needing to adhere to human subjects protections and obtain signed releases, photovoice projects in health promotion and community empowerment have provided valuable opportunities to democratize research practices and achieve collective action. (Carlson, et al., 2006).

In addition to ethical and legal concerns, visual media are difficult to incorporate into written reports except as stills or photographic prints. With photovoice and other visually oriented research, the end product may be part of a public forum and eventually posted on an Internet Web site for easier access.

Rapid Ethnographic Assessment (REA) and Time-Sensitive Qualitative Methods

Despite increasing demands for time-sensitive methods, the burgeoning literature on qualitative inquiry has been relatively silent on ways to conduct research "on the run." Perhaps not surprisingly, most of the pioneering work in this area has been done by international health organizations allied with anthropologists working in developing countries. Anthropologists led the way in developing *rapid ethnographic assessment* (REA) as a means of conducting research in nutrition, sanitation, family planning, and HIV/AIDS (Beebe, 2002; Manderson & Aaby, 1992; Scrimshaw, Carballo, Ramos, & Blair, 1991). Like its parent method of ethnography, REA is used in culturally specific situations and is not exclusively qualitative. Key informant interviews, for example, could be combined with a brief survey measuring nutritional intake. It is no surprise that the success of REA is enhanced considerably when one or more of the investigators has prior knowledge of the local culture as well as the requisite methodological skills. It would be difficult to imagine, for example, trying to start a family planning program in eastern Kenya (or East Los Angeles) without knowing a great deal about the governmental agencies and health officers involved as well as local religious beliefs, marital practices, and views on women's roles and rights.

Of course, time is not always of the essence. This adherence to a naturally evolving, often unpredictable timeline is a defining characteristic of qualitative inquiry. Although REA and other time-sensitive techniques are needed for public health research and program evaluation, their salience rests on the sturdy foundation of qualitative methods that are developed and carried out in the pursuit of meaning, not deadlines.

Summary and Concluding Thoughts

In qualitative studies, the "field" can be a particular site (or sites), the nexus of experiences shared by a group of individuals, or both. Regardless of the form it takes, entering the field requires careful planning amidst near-certainty that things will not work out as planned. Earning the trust of study participants and establishing rapport are necessary preconditions to navigating through such uncertainty, but flexibility in design and implementation are also vital. Working without the protective layers of distance and presumed neutrality, the qualitative researcher-as-instrument must maintain a level of vigilance toward others as well as toward the self. One enters the field mindful not only of the physical presentation of self (e.g., dress and demeanor), but also of the many identities that may come into play. Personal disclosure by the researcher is a natural consequence of the give-and-take that often occurs before and after an interview (preferably not during).

The immersion and intensity of qualitative inquiry make observation a natural and necessary part of data collection despite its low visibility in the ever-growing corpus of interview-based qualitative studies. At a minimum, such studies are enhanced by recording observational data surrounding the interview, including the interviewee's nonverbal behavior and the interview setting. Adding a request to "shadow" interviewees can enrich understanding by extending beyond verbal renditions of events.

When the study is focused on a specific place, observation becomes crucial. Whether the researcher acts fully or partially as a participant, the concern is with being as unobtrusive as possible and taking deeply descriptive field notes. Observing the myriad goings-on in a clinic, an agency, or a public meeting is not easy; it can cause understandable trepidation among novice and experienced researchers alike. Practicing the art and science of field note-taking is the only way to learn this important skill.

Can an observer fully achieve an insider perspective on what is happening in the field? There is bound to be an impact on what is being observed and what gets recorded, and the researcher must enact a particular role even as rapport and familiarity build. Observation in general and field notes in particular have been criticized as biased and incomplete (Tjora, 2006). Such questions about the nature of ethnographic representation are understandable, but it is the best approximation we have.

EXERCISES

Entering the Field

1. Choose a setting familiar to you such as an agency, clinic, day care center, or similar setting. Think of how you might study it from an ethnographic perspective. Start by drawing a map or floor plan and ponder how this might reflect a "social order" and affect behavior. Who are the actors in this setting? Who is the likely gatekeeper? Is there an individual who might become a key informant? Is there a social hierarchy among the actors?

2. In the classroom, have a role-play exercise in which one student acts as an agency administrator and another poses as a researcher seeking permission to conduct a study.

3. Design and print a flyer that you would like to post at this agency (from Question 2) seeking clients for interviews.

Observation in Context

1. An Hour in the Life . . .

Spend an hour or more in the "field" as an ethnographer. This may be in a park, playground, cafe, subway station, or sports arena—any public space where behavior can be unobtrusively observed. As you carry out your observations, take in-depth field notes. Report on the physical space, actors, behaviors, emotions expressed, and ambience of the setting (time of day, unusual events, etc.). After your field notes are written, bring them to class and share with a fellow student. Working together, place brackets around portions that appear more interpretive than descriptive. In other words, try to separate straightforward reporting from assumptions or biases.

2. Memory Fails . . . Field Note-Taking

Show 10–15 minutes of a movie or video to students and ask them to write a description of what they have seen 24 hours later. Meeting in groups at the next class, students should compare their "field notes" and talk about the selectiveness of memory. Show the movie excerpt again, and then discuss the importance of taking field notes as soon as possible after the observation.

ADDITIONAL READINGS

Agar, M. H. (1980). *The professional stranger: An informal introduction to ethnography.* New York: Academic Press.

Emerson, R. (2001). *Contemporary field research: Perspectives and formulations.* Long Grove, IL: Waveland Press.

Emerson, R. M., Fretz, R. I., & Shaw, L. L. (1995). *Writing ethnographic field notes.* Chicago: University of Chicago Press.

Gilbert, K. R. (Ed.). (2001). *The emotional nature of qualitative research.* Boca Raton, FL: CRC Press.

Lee, R. M. (2000). *Unobtrusive measures in social research.* Philadelphia: Open University Press.

Lofland, J., & Lofland, L. (1995). *Analyzing social settings: A guide to qualitative observation and analysis* (3rd ed.). Belmont, CA: Wadsworth.

Madison, D.S. (2005). *Critical ethnography: Method, ethics, and performance.* Thousand Oaks, CA: Sage.

Manderson, L., & Aaby, P. (1992). An epidemic in the field? Rapid assessment procedures and health research. *Social Science & Medicine, 35,* 839–850.

Prosser, J. (1998). *Image-based research: A sourcebook for qualitative researchers.* London: Falmer.

Scrimshaw, S. C., Carballo, M., Ramos, L., & Blair, B. A. (1991). The AIDS Rapid Anthropological Assessment Procedures: A tool for health education planning and evaluation. *Health Education Quarterly, 18*(1), 111–123.

Smith, C. D., & Kornblum, W. (Eds.). (1996). *In the field: Readings on the field research experience.* Westport, CT: Praeger.

Spradley, J. (1979). *The ethnographic interview.* New York: Holt, Rinehart, & Winston.

Wang, C., & Burris, M. A. (1997). Photovoice: Concept, methodology and use for participatory needs assessment. *Health Education & Behavior, 24*(3), 369–387.

Wolf, M. (1992). *A thrice-told tale: Feminism, postmodernism, and ethnographic responsibility.* Stanford, CA.: Stanford University Press.

6

Interviewing and Use of Documents

N otwithstanding the importance of observation, this chapter starts from the realistic premise that high-quality interviews are the linchpin of success for the vast majority of qualitative studies. We begin with informal field interviews then proceed to in-depth interviewing—both individual and via focus groups. The chapter ends with the third and last type of data—documents, archives, and printed materials—then segues to secondary analysis of qualitative data (a relatively new development in qualitative research).

Informal Field Interviews

It is fitting to begin this discussion with the type of interview that the previous chapter introduced—the informal give-and-take that is so much a part of observation and interaction in the field (Dick, 2006; Spradley, 1979). Such interviews are context driven and rarely amenable to advance preparation. In his book on homeless women, Eliot Liebow (1993) explained his approach:

I was under no pressure to bring ready-made questions into the study situation. I did ask questions, of course, but these were not questions I brought with me from the outside. They are "natural" questions that arose spontaneously and directly out of social situations. . . . They were situation-specific questions, not research questions. (p. 321)

Liebow had many years of experience to anchor such a relaxed approach. Most researchers go into the field with ready-made questions but expect and seek out the impromptu. On-the-spot queries can be straightforward ("Is attendance at group meetings required?") or may entail a brief sit-down ("Can you tell me how patients are educated about diabetes self-care at this clinic?"). Such exchanges with informants allow researchers to gather valuable information and affirm their role as learner. They also serve as the interstitial "glue" that binds long hours of observation with more formal in-depth interviews. Without these ad hoc questions, the informational gaps would make in-depth interviews much longer and more tedious. Informal field interviews may be audio recorded but they usually end up in field notes. Box 6.1 offers some general tips for interviewing in qualitative studies.

Focus Group Interviews

Group interviews are useful because they draw on the synergy between members. Focus group methods originated in sociology (Merton, Fiske, & Kendall, 1956) and were developed especially for use in marketing and polling so that small groups of unrelated individuals could be brought together to discuss a new product or political candidate (Krueger, 1994). The size of a focus group should be large enough to generate diversity of opinions but small enough to permit everyone to share in the discussion—about 7 to 10 participants is optimal, but size can range anywhere from 3 to 15 (Morgan, 1997).

As originally conceived, the focus group comprised persons from similar backgrounds who did not know each other very well—because familiarity can lead to more habitual ways of interacting and inhibit fresh opinions from emerging. Focus groups that include persons from different levels of a status hierarchy are considered problematic because the subordinates have understandable concerns about the repercussions of being candid. In practice, both of these assumptions are violated (Morgan, 1997). In a typical social service agency, for example, it would be near-impossible to convene focus groups of staff who do not know one another. Less common but also possible are focus groups in which some supervisory staff are included and the topic seems benign enough to allow this to take place.

BOX 6.1   Tips for Qualitative Interviewing

---

1. Familiarize yourself with your questions as much as possible in advance.

2. Ask follow-up questions based on what you are hearing; use the participants' words when possible.

3. Avoid leading questions.

4. Explore issues but don't interrogate the participant.

5. Feel free to *not* understand (but don't come across as patronizingly unintelligent).

6. Try not to lead with questions about feelings—let feelings emerge naturally and then ask about them.

7. Encourage participants to share anecdotes and specific experiences—avoid generalities.

8. Monitor personal disclosure; emphasize rapport-building over drawing attention to yourself (e.g., "I'm a Virgo too!" is better than "I have the same back pain problems that you have").

9. Don't interrupt or try to control the conversation.

10. Accept pauses as natural; break the silence only if the participant seems stuck.

11. Feel free to laugh and appreciate humor.

12. Avoid becoming informal and "knowing" in follow-up interviews.

13. Take notes for follow-up questions but don't let them become distracting.

14. Remember that everyone has a "bad interview day"!

Focus-group interviewing typically involves a moderator who asks open-ended questions, but the degree of direction and structure can vary depending on how narrow or broad the topic of inquiry is. In addition to the need to be sensitive, flexible, and empathic, the moderator must avoid certain pitfalls common to group situations (Fontana & Frey, 1994). These include domination by one person or a clique and lack of participation by some group members. Poor group leaders—those who dominate the discussion or are too passive—can make focus groups a lost cause. Even skilled moderators, however, can find it difficult to channel members away from internal dissension or divisive tactics such as intimidation and ridicule.

The logistics of focus groups require special considerations, both methodological and ethical. These days, scheduling a time and place for several individuals to meet can be a real challenge—early evenings often work best but not always. Inducements such as refreshments usually help with attendance and comfort level. Payment of incentives is also desirable if the budget allows.

The optimal structure of the focus group format is where turn-taking is frequent and the moderator exerts control only to ensure a smooth and informative discussion. If at all possible, group moderators should not be tasked with taking notes because their attention needs to be on the group members and what they are saying. For example, MacGregor, Rodger, Cummings, and Leschied (2006) conducted focus groups with foster parents that were cofacilitated by a parent coordinator and university professor, with a graduate research assistant in charge of recording and taking notes.

With respect to data collection, audio taping is increasingly used but some researchers and/or group participants prefer to have either a scribe or note-taker only. Either way, complications may arise when trying to distinguish speakers without revealing their identity—some moderators ask members to adopt a pseudonym or ID number at the outset and use it each time they speak.

As with any method of data collection, focus groups have limitations. An ethical problem can occur when a group member breaches confidentiality. The researcher has no control over this rare but unhappy event, and can only warn prospective group members of this possibility in the consent form. If a group member decides to withdraw from the study, the researcher may be obliged to expunge his or her statements from the transcript.

Focus groups developed and matured outside of the evolving traditions of qualitative methodologies, and their economy and convenience sometimes lead to less-than-rigorous methods (Kidd & Parshall, 2000). Agar and McDonald raise concerns that "a few hours with a few groups guarantees only that the 'quality' in qualitative will go the way of fast food" (1995, p. 78). No matter how successful, the format of a focus group entails artificial conditions that may discourage going into deeper or sensitive areas—hence their popular use in marketing (Morgan, 1997).

Despite these potential drawbacks, focus-group interviewing can bring clear advantages to a qualitative study, including savings in time and resources and the elicitation of insights from individuals stimulated by the group dynamic. It is particularly well-suited to studies in organizations or communities where there is a web of social networks already in place. Group interviews are useful in conducting needs assessments, in studies of organizational change, and in community-based studies. Quantitative research offers no equivalent to what focus groups can accomplish.

In-Depth Interviews

Unlike brief field interviews, intensive interviewing is scheduled in advance, takes place in a private setting conducive to trust and candor, and requires careful preparation. That said, there is immense variation in how an intensive interview is planned and how it unfolds (Fontana & Frey, 1994; McCracken, 1988; Weiss, 1994).

In-depth interviews follow different "rhythms of directivity" based on the type of method being employed. Some studies derive their interpretative power from unbroken narratives in which the way a person tells the story is of interest as well as the content of what is being said. Examples include phenomenological, life history, and narrative interviews. In these instances, probes or follow-up questions are minimized to avoid unnecessary interruptions. Other interview methods (e.g., grounded theory) are more dialogic. At the most structured end of this continuum—but still far from the rapid back-and-forth of a quantitative survey—are semi-structured interviews in which the same set of open-ended questions is asked in sequence.

Interviews in the NYSS differed significantly across its two phases, the first phase eliciting free-flowing life histories and the second a somewhat more structured inquiry into participants' experiences with drugs and other substances, their social networks, and their utilization of mental health and other services. Both phases placed a premium on open-ended questions, but Phase 2 included "must-ask" questions to ensure that certain domains were addressed uniformly with respondents.

Qualitative interviews are minimally structured but they are not complete improvisation. Typically, the interview guide reveals the study's key domains (i.e., classes of information from which a variety of questions could be asked, some prepared in advance and others elicited through probes). Deciding on what constitutes must-have information is important because anything not routinely elicited will emerge only if volunteered or resulting from an ad hoc probe. In the NYSS, we chose not to directly ask about traumatic experiences because such information was not essential to the study's goals. We also wanted to respect participants' privacy and their sometimes precarious emotional state. Although previous research indicated the strong likelihood of traumatic events such as physical assault and rape, we decided to allow these accounts to emerge naturally rather than risk appearing voyeuristic. Such information did come up, mostly from women in the study, in startlingly graphic detail (Padgett, Hawkins, Abrams, & Davis, 2006). At the same time, we cannot report traumatic events in terms of prevalence because reports of such events were not routinely elicited.

Interviewing Children and Other Vulnerable Populations

As mentioned in Chapter 4, human subjects committees have federally mandated protections for vulnerable populations (e.g., pregnant women, prisoners, children under age 18, and persons with severe mental impairment) that require specialized consent (or verbal assent) procedures as well as additional protection against coercion. Because qualitative interviews with prisoners and pregnant women are more a matter of avoiding coercion than using specialized interview techniques, I will focus here on the latter groups beginning with minor children.

Qualitative interviews with young children are a distinct challenge because young children lack the verbal abilities, life experiences, and insights that adults bring to study participation. Older children and adolescents have more verbal capabilities but may be uncooperative or resistant to questioning. Highly appropriate for younger age groups is the use of observation (e.g., a study of children's social skills in classroom and playground settings). Irwin and Johnson (2005) offer specific guidelines for researchers whose studies depend on such interviews.

Persons with mental disability may have organic impairment due to brain injury, or they may have a serious mental illness such as schizophrenia. For those on the severe end of the disablement continuum, qualitative interviewing is not feasible. However, the decision to exclude participants with mental impairment should be made carefully because stereotypical assumptions can interfere with their right to be heard (not to mention the researcher's need to learn from them). A few years ago, I met with a doctoral student interested in homeless mentally ill women. This student planned to interview these women's case managers. When asked why she did not talk to the women directly, she insisted that they did not have the verbal or cognitive abilities to engage in qualitative interviews. This decision denied her access to the true experts.

Elite and Expert Interviews

Elite or expert interviews may target highly regarded practitioners (e.g., a famous heart surgeon), policymakers (e.g., a state legislator in charge of mental health appropriations), or other public figures (e.g., a leading advocate for persons with AIDS). These individuals add a top-down perspective to a study that would otherwise be missed without their participation. For a qualitative study of foster care in which I was involved, the design called for purposive sampling from key stakeholder groups including youths but also family court judges and attorneys (Freundlich, Avery, & Padgett, 2007).

In what anthropologists fondly refer to as "studying up" (Nader, 1969), interviews with elites require special planning and foresight. Busy professionals and civic leaders have little to gain from talking to a researcher, and some may fear they have plenty to lose despite assurances of confidentiality. Questions usually need to be tailored individually to ensure maximum use of time and draw on the unique perspective of the interviewee.

The NYSS study design called for interviews with 10 New York City area leaders in the provision of mental health and substance abuse services. These interviews turned out to be the most difficult to conduct in the entire study. The hassles began with scheduling and repeated postponements or refusals (handled indirectly through a staff subordinate) and continued with the interview itself. With a few exceptions, the NYSS interviewer was questioned about her background and qualifications for 30 or so minutes before the questioning could begin. Although all expert interviewees eventually spoke freely and informatively, several started out defensively and took time to warm up to the interview process.

Once engaged, experts and those in power often enjoy having the opportunity to speak confidentially to a neutral party. Despite the headaches, the expert interviewees in the NYSS provided a fascinating glimpse into the hurly-burly world of New York City and state policies affecting the homeless mentally ill. In a state that expends upwards of five billion dollars per year on mental health alone, policy decisions and competition for contracts are hotly contested arenas—the politicization of mental health care and homeless services was never more apparent than in these interviews.

A few words on ethical issues with this special population: It is harder to disguise the identities of experts—the more well-known and opinionated, the more difficult this task can be. Quotes from a well-known judge, an outspoken defender of prisoners' rights, or the leader of a religious sect may be revealing for their content alone. Because experts deserve the same protections as other study participants, the use of direct quotes might need to be curtailed in the report. On a lighter note, should one pay incentives to experts? No expert interviewee in the NYSS chose to accept our $30 incentive, but we thought it prudent to at least offer. We also did not distinguish this group of "subjects" in our application for approval from a scrutinizing human subjects committee.

A Few Guidelines for Starting Out

A qualitative interview is goal-directed. It is conversational without being a conversation, a distinction that is not always easy to recognize or put into practice. A few helpful hints come in handy when contemplating qualitative interviewing. These are drawn from the works of seasoned qualitative researchers such as Weiss (1994), Lofland and Lofland (1995), and Seidman (2006).

First, *clarify your stance* as much as possible, situating it along a continuum of structure and directedness—the phrase "minimally structured" is a good descriptor in most cases. Although study participants are encouraged to see the interviewer as a curious, uninformed learner, the interviewer provides gentle guidance and directs the flow of the interview. It may be a partnership, but the roles remain different and complementary.

Second, *develop an interview guide* well in advance and pilot test it on a few individuals (preferably drawn from the population of interest). As mentioned earlier in this chapter, interview guides consist of open-ended questions structured around the study's domains or categories of informational needs. Keep in mind that vague and ambiguous questions can lead to vague or testy answers (Levy & Hollan, 2000). Thus, asking "tell me about your family" might get the reply "what (or why) do you want to know?"

The spontaneity and flexibility that make qualitative interviews special tend to come from *probes*, some of which can be anticipated and others emerge on an ad hoc basis. Interview guides may be standard for all participants, tailored uniquely to each person, or a combination of both standard and person-specific questions. Questions should allow for contingencies such that the interviewer may skip a question that is not relevant or already discussed (e.g., leaving out questions about substance abuse if the interviewee says she has never used drugs or alcohol). Giving the interview guide a trial run almost always leads to changes, whether major cutbacks in the number of questions or minor tweaking of wording or sequencing.

Sequencing of questions is very important. Avoid starting out with demographic and other factual questions that give the wrong impression of the purpose of a qualitative interview. Also avoid starting out with highly sensitive questions—save these for later, when rapport is established. The best opening gambit is to ask an open-ended but non-threatening question, one that engages the study participant without putting him on the spot.

Third, if the study is a team effort, *build in plenty of time for training interviewers,* mixing didactic instruction with role-playing exercises. If time permits, transcribe the training interviews and use the transcripts as teaching devices to point out strengths and weaknesses in technique. If time is short, use the early interviews for the same purpose.

Fourth, *plan for the location of the interviews,* attempting when possible to leave this up to the participant. This can present a number of dilemmas because privacy, comfort, and safety are paramount—locales providing all three can be few and far between. Interview sites may include the participant's home, a private office set aside for the purpose, or a quiet public space. In the NYSS, we were fortunate to have ample office space for interviewing, although study participants often preferred to stay at home (if they had one). With regard to safety—always a concern but rarely as much as some think—we had an informal policy that no female interviewers would be expected to interview a male in his apartment.

Last but not least, it is always a good idea to *start and end the interview with small talk* when the recorder is not running. This helps produce a smoother beginning, particularly after the dry (but necessary) exercise of going over the informed consent form. At the end of the interview, casual repartee leaves participants with a sense of being appreciated, a chance to pose questions or make comments (including asking for referrals for additional help), and to lay the groundwork for future interviews and contacts.

Conducting the Interview

In-depth interviews have a performative quality in which the players enact their roles while a recorder captures the drama. The interviewer is a low-key presence on the stage, more an enabler than a co-star. The "script" is not written in stone; a free-flowing narrative depends on creating space and comfort for the interviewee to speak. Techniques vary, ranging from a quasi-formal back-and-forth to the emotional closeness and mutuality of a feminist or participatory approach (Oakley, 1981; Salmon, 2007).

Some of the most valuable information in qualitative interviews comes from probes, of which some are planned but many are spontaneous. The interviewer must remain alert to subtle cues. Probes are critical for getting beyond rehearsed accounts and prefabricated renditions. Box 6.2 gives an example of the importance of probes from a previous study in which I was involved.

BOX 6.2   The Importance of Probes Both Planned and
Spontaneous: "Air Theory" and Breast Cancer

In an earlier study in which I was involved (The Harlem Mammogram Study), we were interested in why some African American women neglected to follow up with diagnostic testing after receiving notice of an abnormal mammogram. In the interviews, we asked about their beliefs regarding what caused breast cancer and its spread throughout the body. Almost in passing, a few women mentioned a firm conviction that "air" is partly or fully responsible. An alert interviewer felt comfortable enough to probe further. Respondents obliged by explaining that opening up the body during surgery exposed dormant cancer cells to the air and precipitated their growth and spread to other areas of the body. During our regular interviewer debriefings, we agreed that this unforeseen information should be gently probed for because it could shed new light on why women do not follow up on recommendations for surgical biopsies and other diagnostic services. We preferred contextual probes rather than direct questioning; the latter might be perceived as too leading or presumptive.

Subsequent interviews and probes revealed varied forms of "air theory" attributions among several of the women, all sharing a general concern with the dangers of ambient air during surgical procedures. A couple of years later, in a surprising twist of fate, this potentially harmful "folk belief" turned out to have more credence than previously thought. In short, it received the biomedical seal of approval when surgical researchers at Columbia University reported that airborne pathogens may explain the greater recurrence of cancer after open-incision surgery compared to closed-incision (laparoscopic) surgery!

Lofland and Lofland (1995) recommend appending facesheets and interviewer reaction sheets to the interview guide. The *facesheet* is a standardized document for recording the date, time, and location of the interview as well as the demographic characteristics (age, sex, race, ethnicity, etc.) of the informant. The *interviewer reaction sheet* is a place to log observations about the interviewee (the informant seemed hostile, distracted, overly eager to please, etc.) and about the setting (the informant's home was immaculately kept; the clinic waiting room was chaotic; etc.). It is also valuable to jot down any concerns about the participant and ideas to follow up. Box 6.3 provides an example of an Interview Feedback Form (IFF) from the NYSS (with some facts changed to shield the participant's identity).

As shown in Box 6.3, interviewer observations capture many things unsaid. Tone of voice (sarcasm, sadness, light-heartedness), speech impediments, facial expressions (grimaces, winks, smiles), body language, and the ambience of the setting (noise, filth, interruptions) provide a feeling for the context that is missing from the transcript if not otherwise noted.

Here are a few additional examples of nonverbal information coming from NYSS interviewers:

- A male participant re-enacted a botched robbery attempt in which he had stuck his finger under his jacket to mimic a gun (both in the original incident and during the interview).
- A male participant acted out his newfound pleasure at having his own apartment by gesturing (e.g., unlocking his apartment door, opening his refrigerator).
- A male participant insisted that he was socially isolated even as friends and neighbors stopped by repeatedly during the interview in his apartment.
- A female participant's words were slurred, but it was due to missing teeth and over-medication, not inebriation.
- A male participant kept nodding off during the interview because he had just received his methadone dose.
- A male participant was often sarcastic in tone (e.g., "I'm really popular with women" meaning quite the opposite).

Whether it is the kinetic joy of having one's own apartment or the tone of voice that belies what the speaker is saying, nonverbal communication is an essential part of qualitative research. Box 6.4 offers a psychological rationale for face-to-face interviewing being essential to observing as well as to listening.

What if the respondents' words contradict their actions and circumstances? Take, for example, the respondent described in Box 6.3, who denied ever having a problem with alcohol. In trying to recontact him, we

BOX 6.3   An Example of Interviewer Feedback From the NYSS

NYSS Interview Feedback Form
(Note: This form should be filled out soon after the interview and brought to the weekly debriefing meeting. If possible, a typed transcript should be included.)

Participant ID #___000_____ M/F_ M_____ Age___47_____

Race/ethnicity ___white (Eastern European)_ Date of Interview_ 03/09/06_____
Site of Interview ___NYSS office___ Interviewer_ CA
Time begun_4:00_ Time ended___5:30_____

1. Note study participant (SP)'s demeanor and mood during the interview (anxious, impatient, relaxed, angry, etc.).

Emotional, but within reason. SP is an expressive, animated individual. At times he spoke quickly, passionately, and loudly (e.g., about the war in Iraq, other political causes, & his many conspiracy theories). He seemed quite sad when discussing his diabetes and physical pain. He expressed no emotion when discussing other people (family, girlfriend, therapist, etc.). All did not seem important to him. Overall he had an air of fatalism or bleakness—he lacked hope that anything can change (e.g., "I'm going to die here," "No one cares about a crazy old man," etc.). SP was always very warm towards me and at the end, he said "I love you," thanked me profusely for the chance to "tell these things to someone," and asked for another interview.

2. Note observations of SP's posture or nonverbal behavior. (Remember to include gestures, expressions, and utterances such as laughter or crying in transcript!)

Constant gesturing throughout the interview. Mostly hand gestures to emphasize points. In addition, I recall SP showing the size of his room to be about 12' × 12.' He showed the pain in his body as beginning in his right foot and going all the way up his right side to his head, and then back down again.

3. If the interview took place at SP's home: note physical setting, orderliness, personal artifacts such as photos, and so on.

Not applicable, but he did have a "Power Puff Girls" (child's) backpack although he does not have children. Also, at one point we were discussing what he likes to do and he pulled an art museum brochure from his backpack. It was addressed to him at the SRO where he is staying.

4. Summarize briefly SP's history of drug/alcohol use and current status.

SP claimed to have no problems with alcohol or drugs. Said he will smoke an occasional joint if he encounters someone with one, but that he doesn't have a problem. Doubt if he is being truthful about ending his long-term alcohol use but did not press him on this.

5. What (if any) service contacts appeared to be more successful in terms of engagement and retention in care for mental health or substance abuse treatment?

None. SP claimed never to have had a problem with substances. He saw a private therapist for a long time but he is not currently attending treatment.

found out from a neighbor that he died suddenly from an alcohol-related illness. In these instances, it is best not to point out the discrepancy or force a confrontation over what version of events is the "truth." Prolonged engagement with respondents will likely bring this out in time (although a briefer relationship might leave the researcher guessing). In any event, such observations of participant discrepancy need to be noted—a narrow reliance on verbatim transcription would lose this valuable information.

Probes: An Essential Part of the Qualitative Interview

For some interviewees, one question will release the floodgates, but most qualitative interviews rely on probes to obtain the depth and richness desired. As follow-up questions predicated on earlier answers, probes can be used to:

- *Go deeper* ("Can you tell me more about . . . ?").
- *Go back* ("Earlier you mentioned_____ , please tell me. . . .").
- *Clarify* ("And were you homeless when you were arrested?").
- *Steer* ("That's very interesting, but can we return to . . . ?").
- *Contrast* ("How would you compare your experiences in foster care with living with your adoptive family?").

BOX 6.4   The Importance of Face-to-Face Interviewing

In this era of the electronic commons and highly mobile lifestyles, it is tempting to conduct interviews over the telephone, by email, via Internet chat rooms, and so on. Distance interviewing is appropriate for some studies, but it comes with a significant price: the loss of information that comes from an in-person encounter. Psychologists have noted that the brain's orbitofrontal cortex (the center for empathy) modulates the amygdala (center for impulsivity) during social interactions. Such neurological processing depends on a cascade of socially coded cues including tone of voice, facial expressions, and body posture (Goleman, 2007). There are numerous ways that individuals convey meaning during face-to-face contacts—a raised eyebrow, sarcastic tone, a smile, and a wink all have connotations and these may be further differentiated by culture. Whereas telephone conversation captures some of the aural cues, online communication offers none (hence the use of emoticons such as ☹). For the qualitative researcher, authenticity and candor are the *sine qua non* of in-depth interviewing. A study participant is less likely to shade the truth or hold back when sitting across from the interviewer.

Each of these types of probes has a role depending on what is being said and what is being sought. The "go deeper" probe usually opens the door wider than the others. Here, the interviewer must avoid gratuitous questions that can appear voyeuristic if not part of the study's goals and the interview's flow. Probes about sexual functioning can be appropriate if part of a discussion about the side effects of antipsychotic medications but inappropriate if brought up with young adults talking about their dating experiences.

The "steering" probe is used judiciously so as not to interrupt the flow. Respondents are known to go off on tangents, some of which might later yield nuggets of insight while others are yawn inducing. It is not unusual for an interviewer to listen attentively through lengthy harangues about the police, boasts of sexual conquests, and arguments in favor of the legalization of drugs. Steering probes come into play when time grows short and content becomes thin.

Less commonly used are *prompts* (i.e., suggested options offered when a question is vague but a "checklist" approach is not appropriate). In the NYSS, we asked participants if they had used health services and then prompted them by mentioning "clinic visits, emergency rooms, and the like" to illustrate what we were after. Obviously, care needs to be taken in using prompts because they may put words in a respondent's mouth.

Should probes be built into the interview guide or emerge spontaneously during the interview? Renowned interviewers such as Elliott Liebow and Studs Terkel assert that they used the latter approach, but few researchers can attain success this way. Most studies balance both approaches, planning for some probes in advance but giving the interviewer the latitude to improvise on the spot. A qualitative study that relies on multiple interviewers must ensure that such improvisation does not introduce "solo performances" by interviewers keen on making their stylistic mark.

Developing the Interview Guide

Most qualitative studies implicitly or explicitly rely on domains or topical areas organized around the study's conceptual framework. The following are two examples of domains from the NYSS and sample questions and probes associated with each. In the interview guide, we put the probes in italics to remind the interviewer that they were to be asked only if the interviewee did not cover that information spontaneously. Note that one of the probes also comes with a prompt and that "SP" means "study participant.")

Domain: Entering the Program

Sample Question #1: How did you get to this program?

Probe for:
- *Source of referral*
- *Degree of choice in entering the program*
- *If SP was homeless prior to coming to program*

(Continued)

(Continued)

Domain: Social Networks

Sample Question #1: Who if anybody can you count on the most to help when you need it?

Probe for:
- *Relationship to SP*
- *What type of help → Prompt: financial help, child care, food, cash, other*
- *How they respond when asked for help by SP*

Sample Question #2: Is there anyone who counts on you for help?

Probe for:
- *Relationship to participant*
- *Type of help given*

Sample Question #2 ("Is there anyone who counts on you for help?") almost got left out given the prevailing mindset regarding persons with serious mental illness as "burdens." It was at first considered a probe under Sample Question #1 but subsequently earned its way to full question status. The usual rule is to upgrade a probe to a question if it is "must-have" information that cannot be left to discretion. As it happened, this question not only revealed neglected facets of participants' lives but also helped enhance rapport by signaling that the interviewers were not focused one-sidedly on problems and woes.

When developing an interview guide, pay close attention to the wording of questions to avoid confusion or leading respondents toward certain answers. In-depth interview questions need to encourage lengthy replies and engage respondents. To be avoided at all costs are questions that sound quantitative or are off-putting in any way.

Consider a scenario in which you are interested in whether and how participants plan for the future. As with any domain, there are many ways to ask about this. The worst from a qualitative point of view would be a question along the lines of "What are your goals for the next five years?" Not much better would be "What are your goals for the future?" (although this might well be effective as a probe). The tacit message here is one that many individuals cannot relate to, especially if they are having personal problems and find goal-setting language to be judgmental and too direct. In the NYSS, we settled on easing into the subject by asking "What is the next step for you?" A good follow-up to this would be "Where do you see yourself in the near future?" The "next step" question turned out to be a winner for us, giving participants a chance to reflect on the near or far term as they saw fit and to talk about their hopes as well as concrete plans. In the final NYSS interview, we inserted a probe after the "next step" question, asking "And how about the longer-term future— where do you see yourself?"

How Many Interviews? Issues of Quantity and Quality

There are qualitative studies in which one interview per participant is the only option and even a few where this is preferable. As a general rule, however, it is optimal to conduct at least two interviews per person and allow for more than two when possible (Seidman, 2006). A single interview starts the process and builds rapport and forward momentum for the next interview(s). Multiple interviews provide greater evidentiary adequacy (Morrow & Smith, 1995).

Follow-up interviews fill in missing information, but they are also important as a venue for pursuing leads from earlier interviews. In grounded theory studies, this may occur under the rubric of theoretical sampling where reinterviewing or sampling new participants is an anticipated stage in theory development. Repeated interviewing brings engagement and sets qualitative methods apart from their quantitative one-shot counterparts. When using single interviews, the onus is on the researcher to make the most of these encounters.

Matching Interviewers to Respondents: The Effects of Age, Gender, Race, and Other Characteristics

Given their intrinsic nature as interactive and ongoing social relationships, it is no surprise that "discrepancies and proximities" between interviewers and interviewees deserve serious attention (Manderson, Bennett, & Andajani-Sutjaho, 2006, p. 1333). Some researchers advocate matching interviewers with respondents by sex, age, race, and so on. Defenders of matching tend to cite greater acceptability and understandability as advantages because certain topics can be more easily addressed. In the Harlem Mammogram Study (of which I was a co-investigator), we wanted African American women as interviewers to maximize participants' comfort level when discussing sensitive issues surrounding bodily functions, sexuality, and concerns about racism in health care.

Yet it is not easy to anticipate which interviewer characteristics will help or hinder a study. Robert Weiss (1994) noted:

> When I interviewed men who were IV drug users, I was an outsider to the drug culture but an insider to the world of men. When I interviewed a woman who was an IV drug user living in a shelter and also the mother of two children, I was an outsider to the world of women, drug users, and women's shelters, but an insider to the concerns of parents. (p. 137)

Using members of the study population and community as interviewers is laudable (and an essential ingredient of participatory research) but it carries some risks as well. Respondents may fear a loss of privacy by speaking to "one of their own" or they may slant their responses to avoid loss of face with a compatriot. For some studies, the effectiveness of the interview may depend on matching, but for most, being a skilled interviewer is sufficient.

Common Problems and Errors in Qualitative Interviewing

Ideally, the qualitative interviewer has: 1) a broad fund of knowledge that makes the inevitable departures from the interview questions productive; and 2) the maturity to be patient, to know when to make these departures, and to know when to remain silent. Even veteran interviewers have had that sinking experience of losing control, what can feel like "taking a puppy for a walk" (Steinmetz, 1991, p. 64). Trying to rein in unruly focus groups can be like trying to herd cats.

It helps to anticipate some of the common pitfalls of qualitative interviewing. One occurs when the desire to control or lead compels the interviewer to interrupt the narrative flow. Few things are more disappointing than reading a transcript (or listening to a recording) in which the interviewer dominates the proceedings and cuts off the interviewee. Then there are occasions when the interviewee is uncooperative. A suspicious administrator, a sullen adolescent, or a harried parent may be evasive or hostile. It is frustrating to sit across from someone who answers questions in monosyllables, then sits impassively waiting for the next question. The interview stops and starts, frustrations rise, and the interviewer feels at her wit's end. In the NYSS, we are mindful of the fact that the $30 incentive can be a serious attraction, but try to ensure that the relationship transcends its pecuniary beginning.

Respondents who resist cooperating can be exasperating, but the best tactic is to remain calm, be diplomatic, and stop if necessary. No amount of information is worth risking coercion (or a migraine headache). If the resistance appears transitory, another interview can always be scheduled.

Finally, inadequate training and supervision of interviewers in team projects can lead to slippage and unproductive improvisation. Either through carelessness or well-intentioned ad-libbing, poorly supervised interviewers can reproduce all of the pitfalls previously mentioned. Interviewers sometimes get a little too zealous in probing, especially when skeptical about a participant's claim. They could also become too familiar and the interview becomes conversational and veers off the topic. Once, when perusing transcripts, I came across an interviewer who prefaced a question about drug use with "Sorry, but I have to ask this next question." This seemingly minor act of distancing himself from the study sent a message of not taking the question seriously, thereby practically inviting participants to fudge the truth.

During a successful interview, qualitative researchers strike a balance between the general and the particular, the need to stay focused versus the need to probe deeper. Simultaneously, the interviewer is expected to listen empathically, monitor body language, anticipate the next question, and mentally or literally take note of red flags (e.g., discrepancies, statements signaling deeper meaning). When everything is clicking, both interviewer and interviewee part company feeling they have had a mutually beneficial encounter. Even a less-than-perfect qualitative interview leaves most interviewees gratified by the experience of being respected and listened to.

Emotional Issues in Interviewing

The sensitive nature of qualitative research almost guarantees that emotionally laden information will surface. Study participants may laugh, cry, or grow angry during an interview. Levy and Hollan (2000) write about exaggerating the fragility of the interviewee as a recurring problem for novice researchers (and as well for those in the practicing professions accustomed to being in a helping mode). Sensitive topics and traumatic stories can and do bring painful emotions to the surface; interviewers should never gratuitously probe or show insensitivity in other ways. Yet to avoid addressing this information simply because it is emotion-laden deprives the study and assumes that participants are incapable of handling themselves and their emotions. Indeed, the vast majority welcome the opportunity to tell their story to an empathic, nonjudg-mental listener. It is rare that emotions cause more than momentary interruptions.

Human subjects committees often object that studies of sensitive topics will set off a chain reaction of emotional turmoil that harms research participants. Weiss (1994) argues forcefully that the nature of qualitative interviewing mitigates against this. Even when interviews prompt strong reactions, a skilled interviewer can show concern and then gently steer respondents to a calmer state of mind. In any event, the qualitative inter-viewer does not try to elicit strong emotions, only to create a safe space for their expression if they need to occur.

What about the effects on the interviewer—the backwash of emotions that follows an intensely personal and painful encounter? In their grounded theory study of qualitative researchers' experiences, Dickson Swift, James, Kippen, and Liamputtong (2007) found that maintaining rapport, monitoring self-disclosure, and dealing with guilt can take their toll. Satisfaction with a job well done may be tempered by exhaus-tion and numbness. Gair (2002) provides a moving account of her dissertation research on adoptive mothering, her feminist approach affording a degree of self-disclosure and closeness that required con-stant monitoring on her part. Participants' teary-eyed stories about their adoptive children, their anger at social workers (the author's profes-sion), and their gratitude at being able to tell their story brought feelings out that sometimes threatened to tilt the relationship to friend or confi-dant. That Gair's journey to becoming a "qualitative research disciple" (2002, p. 138) was successful is testimony to her ability to maintain her equilibrium.

Unlike the relationship between practitioner and client, the qualita-tive interviewer does not have the protection of clinical distance, set-tling instead for an "emotional middle distance" (Weiss, 1994, p. 123). One important way to maintain this is through debriefing (more about this in Chapter 8). In the NYSS, the team met weekly to debrief about each interview that occurred in the previous week. Although most interviews take place without incident, the infrequent exception is worth discussing further, whether it is a study participant or interviewer who needs help.

Interviewing in a Non-English Language

It is an understatement to note that many individuals of interest to qualitative researchers do not speak English. Yet the vast literature on qualitative methods since the 1970s has been virtually silent on this issue, leading one to erroneously conclude that qualitative research is an English-only enterprise (Esposito, 2001; Shibusawa & Lukens, 2004; Twinn, 1997). Anthropologists, long accustomed to cross-language research, have traditionally relied on translators when they were unable to master the language themselves. However, ethnographers over the decades have often treated language barriers as a technical hurdle unworthy of lengthy consideration.

The neglect of language differences can be seen as a consequence of the explosive growth in qualitative methods with a heavy concentration in the United States and other English-speaking countries (Canada, Great Britain, Australia, and New Zealand). Working in education, nursing, and social work, qualitative researchers naturally gravitated toward studies closer to home, both geographically and topically. The move toward interview-intensive studies also tipped the balance toward monolingual studies. Methods of qualitative analysis became more dependent on deriving meaning from texts (verbatim transcripts in particular), so venturing beyond the English language risked distortion and complicated research designs and sampling.

Qualitative interviewers who do not speak the language of their study participants must rely on translation (an awkward undertaking) or include bilingual interviewers as members of the research team. Although some qualitative methods do not work well with linguistic distance (e.g., phenomenological interviewing), most can be used with intervening translation. Care must be taken, however, to reduce distortions and misunderstandings as much as possible.

Noting the overwhelming influence of the English language on qualitative methods and studies should not lead one to overlook one important fact: Non-English-speaking qualitative researchers have pursued studies with noteworthy success (Flick, 2004). One need only peruse the *International Journal of Qualitative Methods* (http://www.ualberta.ca/~ijqm) to see excellent works published in Spanish, Portuguese, French, Russian, Afrikaans, and Tagalog.

Interviewing at a Distance: Telephone and Computer-Mediated Interviews

Notwithstanding the cherished status of in-person encounters in qualitative research, there are occasions when these are either not feasible or not the point. Email and other forms of computer-mediated interactions—not to mention the old-fashioned telephone—have risen in popularity in qualitative research (Illingworth, 2001; McCoyd & Kerson, 2006). There are, of course, differences between these two modes of communication. Telephone interviews share with in-person interviews the need to schedule the encounter (not so easy these days), but they have the advantage of the possibility of being audiotaped, thus retaining access to voice and intonation. Although there are always exceptions to prove the rule, telephone interviewing should be seen as a stopgap or fall-back measure. Ideally, it is reserved for second (or later follow-up) interviews and when respondents live far away or are not available for other reasons.

Though heavily dominated by surveys (where the efficiency is hard to beat), the Internet has also become the province of qualitative research. Internet interviewing has taken on a life of its own, opening new ways to reach and communicate with isolated, stigmatized populations as well as with technologically savvy respondents who prefer the relative anonymity of the Internet (Illingworth, 2001; Markham, 2005). Unlike telephone or in-person interviews, Internet communications do not need to be scheduled (although this is an option) and are far more convenient to respondents sitting in the comfort of their home, office, or Internet cafe (Miller & Slater, 2000). Internet communications can also be accessed in an archival sense and treated as documents and other data.

McCoyd and Kerson took advantage of an opportunity to compare in-person, telephone, and email formats for intensive interviews with women who had terminated a pregnancy because of fetal anomalies (2006). They found several advantages to email interviewing, including: 1) obtaining a credible sample (referrals through physicians being less effective); 2) receiving the data in typed form (saving on the costs of transcription); and 3) affording opportunities for the spontaneous outpouring of thoughts and feelings at any hour of the night or day. The same advantages of face-to-face interviewing outlined in Box 6.4 can put respondents on the spot or cause them to feel less safe. In a sense, email interviews give respondents more control (McCoyd & Kerson, 2006). This can increase rapport as long as the researchers can balance free-wheeling communication with the need to obtain needed information.

Internet communications can be the best or only way to tap into a network of individuals assuming that they share a propensity to use online support groups, chat rooms, and the like. Of course, online interviews still leave out individuals without access to a computer or the wherewithal to use one. This bias obviously tilts against the economically disadvantaged (in the NYSS, computer-mediated interviewing would not have been feasible even if desired). As with so many options in qualitative research, the decision should be driven by appropriateness rather than convenience.

Use of Audio Recorders and Other Logistical Considerations

Technological advances in audio recorders and computer software have greatly enhanced data collection and management. Audio recording of interviews is the norm these days, and the superior technology and lower costs of digital voice recorders have made them accessible for most budgets. The newer recorders usually come with the software to enable one to download the interview onto a computer and transcribe it directly using controls displayed on the screen (with headphones plugged into the computer). Although longed for by weary transcriptionists and resource-tight qualitative researchers, voice recognition software (allowing one to sidestep listening and typing interviews verbatim) is not up to the task of replacing the human ear (as of this writing).

Audio recording allows the interviewer to concentrate on what is being said. It also has an advantage over note-taking in capturing laughter, sighs, and sarcasm—aural aspects of the interview that are vivid and revealing.

Logistical concerns relate to the timing, length, and location of the interview. Given the balance of power in the researcher–respondent relationship, qualitative researchers must maintain flexible schedules, operating at the interviewee's convenience, not their own. The interviewer must also remain alert when respondents feel like talking beyond the time allotted and be prepared to conduct interviews in unusual places. Some settings tax the patience of even the most dedicated researcher—crying children, complaining spouses, ringing cell phones, and other ambient noise can be annoying and distracting. Fire trucks and car alarms were the background "music" for many NYSS interviews, but one of our most memorable was conducted in the apartment of a participant who had turned his bedroom into an aviary—the sound of birds nearly drowned out his soft voice in the tape.

Incorporating Standardized Measures Into Qualitative Interviews

A qualitative researcher not averse to mixed methods might reasonably wonder if a standardized measure could be used for one or more of the study's domains. There are a plethora of measures available for all manner of cognitive, emotional, and behavioral phenomena. The inclusion of such measures and indexes usually implies that they are nested within what is otherwise a predominantly qualitative study (more about mixed methods in Chapter 10).

Miles and Huberman (1994) suggest that checklists or measures be used when the domain:

- Is conceptually important.
- Can be unbundled easily into distinct indicators or components.
- Is part of a study that needs comparability across cases.
- Has the potential for comparison to other studies measuring it in a similar way.

As shown in Box 6.5, we used some checklists and indexes in the NYSS. Yet the decision to do so is not without consequences. First, standardized measures detract from what is otherwise a more free-flowing experience. When used, they should be reserved for the interview's end or a follow-up interview. Second, their quantitative properties introduce numbers into the analyses, even though sample sizes are rarely large enough to sustain statistics beyond the descriptive level of frequencies, ranges, and averages (more on this subject in Chapter 7).

With or without the inclusion of measures, qualitative interviewing is defined by its intensity and by a researcher–participant relationship without parallels in quantitative interviewing. Box 6.6 addresses the effects of qualitative interviews as "unintentional interventions." As with all research interviews—such effects can be negative (although rarely harmful). But the empathy and trust in which qualitative interviews are steeped more often bring therapeutic effects that leave participants gratified at being able to speak their minds and use their own words. Under these circumstances, negative outcomes are more likely to come from ending the relationship than from its continuation.

Using Documents, Archives, and Existing Data

A variety of documents and materials is of interest to qualitative researchers. These include printed matter such as court records, case

---

BOX 6.5   Checklists and Standardized Measures in the NYSS

Checklists turned out to be useful in Phase 2 of the NYSS for two domains—service needs and markers of recovery. We used a Services Needs Checklist (SNC) to capture participants' perceived needs in a range of areas (housing, substance abuse treatment, food stamps, etc.). The Mental Health Recovery Index (MHRI) was more complicated to operationalize. We consulted the expanding but still relatively sparse literature on serious mental illness and recovery and found a few measures in which the emphasis was on programs rather than clients (Onken, Craig, Ridgway, Ralph, & Cook, 2004). We revisited the recovery literature (Ridgway, 2001) and the writings of Patricia Deegan, a leading advocate for mental health consumers who recovered from schizophrenia (www.patdeegan.com). From this, we derived several key indicators of recovery, including:

- *Having a partner or close friend who you trust*
- *Having a job or way of making a living*
- *Using psychiatric medications as needed*
- *Going to self-help groups as needed*
- *Belonging to a social group*
- *Being active in society as a citizen*

To these six items we added: "Having a safe, affordable place to live," because we were studying homeless adults. What is missing from this checklist is something that virtually all recovery advocates agree is crucial—hope (Ridgway, 2001). Although we may live to regret it, we chose not to ask directly about respondents' sense of hope, reasoning that this would elicit socially desirable or inauthentic responses. Instead, we plan to rely on qualitative observations from interview transcripts and interviewer feedback during case study analyses to detect signs of hope from how participants talk about the future.

---

reports, minutes of meetings, brochures, diaries, photographs, letters, and so forth. Archived videos, films, and photographs are also useful. Documents and existing data have advantages over interviewing and observation, including their lack of reactivity. In contrast, the presence of an observer or interviewer has an impact on the natural course of events

---

BOX 6.6   Interviews as Unintentional Interventions

A study of vulnerable or disadvantaged persons casts most interviewers (wittingly or unwittingly) as members of a privileged class. In the NYSS, this relative affluence did not go unnoticed by study participants (SPs). Comments such as "I want to dress in a clean shirt and pants like you" or "You're lucky you have nice teeth" are reminders that interviewers' appearance and behavior are an integral part of the exchange.

In-depth interviews afford unique opportunities for participants to self-reflect. Sitting across from an empathic interviewer who asks about life experiences and personal relationships can prompt SPs to think about their lives and what might need changing. Sometimes SPs seek to transform the interview into an intervention (e.g., asking for advice on handling a child custody battle or getting into a job training program).

While overt helping is generally avoided in qualitative interviewing, the very existence of the interviews and the relationships they entail constitute a form of intervention for good or ill. Higher levels of involvement bring more intense relationships. In the NYSS, for example, we interviewed SPs three times over 12 months and conducted monthly check-in interviews via telephone or in-person. These encounters are accompanied by cash incentives, and the meetings are respectful and empathic, leaving time for small talk and inquiries about how things are going. SPs often note to NYSS staff that their study participation constituted a significant event in their lives. It would be naïve to think otherwise—although no such assumption should be made automatically. Still, it is a good idea to address the possibility of "unintentional intervention" and ensure that the relationship continues in and ends on a positive note. SPs should be fully cognizant that an end to the study will surely come and promises of confidentiality will not be broken. Likewise, interviewers often need debriefing themselves to deal with the separation.

---

no matter how unobtrusive one tries to be. Use of documents is also less time consuming and emotionally taxing compared to observation and interviewing.

However, documents have some disadvantages, mostly because they were not produced for research purposes. They may be inaccurate, uneven, or incomplete. Some of this is due to hurried record keeping but it can also be deliberate. For example, minutes of staff meetings may be doctored to cover up embarrassing revelations, or a physician may omit mention of a psychiatric history in a medical file to protect her patient from stigma. Clearly, a study dependent on documents and existing research data is constrained by what is available and its quality.

In addition, access to such data varies. Individuals may freely share personal documents with a researcher (e.g., diaries, photographs, letters). Less available are documents covered by privacy protections, copyright laws, and the like. The advent of federally mandated HIPPA regulations in the United States has made one source of data—medical records—retrievable only with special consent from the patient. Internet-based information may be subject to copyright protection or its use may constitute an invasion of privacy (e.g., online support groups). As with all forms of data, appropriate permissions must be sought.

Cultural anthropologists have long been interested in "material culture" as a way of understanding social structure, religious practices, and the like. Archeologists and historians are accustomed to relying on archives, artifacts, and other physical traces of human activity. Many behaviors leave behind detectable traces—broken windows in a parked car, crack vials in a schoolyard, cast-off fast food wrappers—that are revealing in themselves. These usually exist as objects of recording (presence or absence, location, frequency, larger context) that stand in contrast to "deeper" documentary data such as court documents, diaries, or family photographs. What all of these sources of data share in common is their existence as independent of the researcher's actions.

Internet communications are a growing source of existing data. Blog, listserv, and chat room conversations can be analyzed in the same way as hard copy documents, although ethical considerations and proper approvals must be given top priority because such information can be poorly protected and secured (Hessler, Downing, Beltz, Pellicio, Powell, & Vale, 2003). The threshold between interviewing via email and "existing data" can get blurry. In their study of diaries kept by adolescents and sent via email, Hessler and colleagues avoided elicitation and attempted to be as unobtrusive as possible, so the diary entries were aggregated and treated as archival materials (2003).

Given the overwhelming emphasis on interviewing in qualitative research, documents as a source of data have fallen out of favor in much the same way as observation. They should not be considered an afterthought, however. Although not created for research purposes, their advantages in low reactivity and availability offset many such limitations.

Secondary Analysis in Qualitative Research

The explosive growth in the popularity of qualitative research has under-standably led to the stockpiling of large stores of data in electronic files as well as in hard copy format. These may include audiotapes, interview transcripts, field notes, and documents. Secondary analysis of qualitative data, traditionally the province of quantitative research, is increasingly an option in qualitative research (Thorne, 1998). Although analyzing existing data does not provide the warmth and good cheer that follow a successful interview or day in the field, their ready availability is a viable tradeoff (Williams & Collins, 2002). The next chapter will provide more details on this subject.

Ending Data Collection and Leaving the Field

The decision to end data collection depends on a number of factors, both methodological and practical. With regard to the former, closure usually comes when *saturation* has been achieved (i.e. when additional analyses of the data bring redundancy and reveal no new information; Morse, 1995). This somewhat vague prescription is often juxtaposed against practicalities such as deadlines imposed by the study's sponsors or by resource constraints. A general rule of thumb on saturation: Studies with relatively homogeneous domains and/or sampling strategies are likely to reach this endpoint faster than those with broader reach and ambition. Discussion of saturation related to data analysis will follow in Chapter 7.

Two aspects of data collection are peculiar to the timeline of qualitative research—the flexibility of the design and the likelihood of return visits to the field (Iversen, 2008). Just as a baseball game is played until finished, qualitative studies resist arbitrary endpoints. There are the usual exigencies (e.g., transcription delays, participants become elusive, or the researcher gets distracted by other responsibilities). Data analyses are rarely amenable to precise time estimations because they can lead to further data collection in an iterative manner.

Some qualitative methods, most notably ethnography and community-based participatory research, need longer periods of time to come to fruition. In this context, the relationship between researchers and partici-pants continues, but it may ebb and flow depending on the stage of the study and the availability of resources to carry it out.

As discussed in Box 6.6, stopping qualitative data collection can have an emotional component missing from quantitative studies. Study participants may regret losing the respectful camaraderie, and many a qualitative researcher has felt deeply bereft by study's end (although we should not assume that participants need or want us to stick around!).

Ely, Anzul, Friedman, Garner, and Steinmetz (1991) recommend keeping the door open in the final interview with an understanding that follow-up contacts may be needed. Modest payback in the form of mailings containing summaries of the findings constitutes a way to demonstrate respect in the study's aftermath. Study participants sometimes ask if they can call to say hello or to check on the progress of the study—this is a reasonable request that should be honored even if they choose not to follow through on it.

Summary and Concluding Thoughts

This chapter complemented the previous chapter in discussing the two additional sources of data in qualitative research: interviews and existing documents and other materials. Interviews may be an informal part of ethnographic fieldwork or a sit-down affair lasting several hours. Although typically done via face-to-face meetings, qualitative interviews may also be conducted via telephone or email. This convenience comes at a significant price, however, in the loss of visual and other sensory cues that give meaning to interpersonal communication.

Among types of interviewees, children as well as persons with severely limited mental capacity are less likely to provide the depth and insight that qualitative studies require. Persons in power and experts are harder to engage and often reluctant to speak candidly in an unrehearsed manner. Language differences are surprisingly neglected in the literature on qualitative methods, but they merit serious consideration given the potential for distortions and cultural misunderstanding.

Qualitative interviewing occurs in different ways and contexts, but its signature format is in-person, individually or in small groups. Advance preparation involves developing and pilot testing an interview guide, familiarizing one's self with its contents, and practicing the gentle art of probes, both planned and spontaneous. Conducting the interview is an exercise in multitasking (i.e., asking questions, observing nonverbal behavior, and unobtrusively taking notes on follow-up questions). Audio taping relieves the interviewer of the onerous (and error-ridden) task of verbatim note-taking. When at all possible (and most of the time it is), each participant is interviewed more than once to ensure depth and completeness.

The third type of qualitative data—documents and other materials—are the tangible and nonreactive byproducts of human activity. Documents originate from a number of places, both personal and organizational. Because they were not produced for research purposes, archival materials raise understandable concerns about their accuracy and completeness. Their strengths—availability and naturalness—are balanced by these potential flaws.

Data collection ideally comes to an end when saturation or redundancy has been achieved, but external factors such as deadlines and diminishing resources can also impinge on this. The emotional sequelae of qualitative data collection reverberate throughout the study, often coming into sharp relief as it draws to an end. Safeguards such as periodic debriefings help deal with intense feelings—both positive and negative. Simply paying attention to the possibility (or inevitability) of such feelings and addressing them with sensitivity can make closure much easier for all concerned.

EXERCISES

Exercise #1: Conducting an Interview

This exercise exposes the student to the intensity and flexibility of a qualitative interview. It also vividly illustrates how time-consuming interviewing and transcribing are.

1. Choose a topic of interest and seek out a knowledgeable respondent for an open-ended interview. Develop an interview guide of four to five questions.

2. Conduct the interview using an audio recorder. Make sure it lasts at least 30 minutes.

3. Transcribe the interview verbatim.

4. Share the transcript with others and look for areas of improvement. For example, did you interrupt the flow? Ask leading questions? Become too conversational?

Exercise #2: Using Available Documents: What Can Be Learned?

Think about your workplace or another familiar work setting as the object of an ethnographic study. This would ideally be an agency, clinic, or other type of human services program. Now consider that you have been asked to study this program only using documents, archival materials, and so on—no observation or interviewing allowed. Address the following:

1. Develop a list of the types of documents available.

2. How would you evaluate the relative quality and quantity of these materials?

3. Do you have any concerns about their accuracy and completeness? If so, what are they?

ADDITIONAL READINGS

Atkinson, R. (1998). *The life story interview.* Thousand Oaks, CA: Sage.

Best, S. J., & Krueger, B. S. (2004). *Internet data collection.* Thousand Oaks, CA: Sage.

Fontana, A., & Frey, J. H. (1994). Interviewing: The art of science. In N. K. Denzin & Y. S. Lincoln (Eds.), *Handbook of qualitative research* (pp. 361–376). Thousand Oaks, CA: Sage.

Gubrium, J. F., & Holstein, J. A. (Eds.) (2002). *Handbook of interview research.* Thousand Oaks, CA: Sage.

Hewson, C., Yule, P., Laurent, D., & Vogel, C. (2003). *Internet research methods: A practical guide for the social and behavioral sciences.* Thousand Oaks, CA: Sage.

Irwin, L.G., & Johnson, J. (2005). Interviewing young children: Explicating our practices and dilemmas. *Qualitative Health Research, 15*(6), 821–831.

Krueger, R. A., & Casey, M. A. (2000). *Focus groups: A practical guide for applied research* (3rd ed.). Thousand Oaks, CA: Sage.

Kvale, S. (1996). *InterViews: An introduction to qualitative research interviewing.* Thousand Oaks, CA: Sage.

Manderson, L., Bennett, E., & Andajani-Sutjaho, S. (2006). The social dynamics of the interview: Age, class and gender. *Qualitative Health Research, 16*(10), 1317–1334.

Markham, A. N. (2005). The methods, politics, and ethics of representation in online ethnography. In N. K. Denzin & Y. S. Lincoln (Eds.), *Handbook of qualitative research* (3rd ed., pp. 793–820). Thousand Oaks, CA: Sage.

McCracken, G. (1988). *The long interview.* Newbury Park, CA: Sage.

Miller, D., & Slater, D. (2000). *The Internet: An ethnographic approach.* New York: Berg.

Mishler, E. G. (1986). *Research interviewing: Context and narrative.* Cambridge, MA: Harvard University Press.

Morgan, D. L. (1997). *Focus groups as qualitative research.* Thousand Oaks, CA: Sage.

Oakley, A. (1981). Interviewing women: A contradiction in terms. In H. Roberts (Ed.), *Doing feminist research* (pp. 30–61). London: Routledge & Kegan Paul.

Rubin, H. J., & Rubin, I. S. (2005). *Qualitative interviewing: The art of hearing data* (2nd ed.). Thousand Oaks, CA: Sage.

Seidman, J. (2006). *Interviewing as qualitative research.* New York: Teachers' College Press.

Spradley, J. P. (1979). *The ethnographic interview.* New York: Holt, Rinehart & Winston.

Stewart, D. W., & Shamdasani, P. N. (1990). *Focus groups: Theory and practice.* Newbury Park, CA: Sage.

Thorne, S. (1998). Ethical and representational issues in qualitative secondary analysis. *Qualitative Health Research, 8*(4), 547–555.

Weiss, R. (1994). *Learning from strangers: the art and method of qualitative interview studies.* New York: Free Press.

Wilson, J. C., & Powell, M. (2001). *A guide to interviewing children: Essential skills for counselors, police, lawyers and social workers.* New York: Routledge.

7

Data Analysis and Interpretation

A nalysis of qualitative data begins soon after data collection begins. Here, the differences from quantitative research are striking. Given preformatting and standardization, a research assistant may assume most of the tasks of collecting and entering quantitative data for statistical analysis. This formulaic approach reduces the amount of discretion open to the investigator. Decisions usually come down to which statistical tests to deploy.

Qualitative data analyses are steeped in choices and decisions. They may emerge from an explicit epistemological framework. They may hew closely to specific procedures or venture into realms of imaginative artistry. Yet all must contend with masses of raw data that need to be reduced and transformed through an iterative process of reading, describing, and interpreting. Pre-existing theories and concepts may be invited into the proceedings but are asked to stay only if they fit (Charmaz, 2006). The balance between staying close to the data and thinking abstractly and conceptually is a defining feature of qualitative analysis.

Given their origins in naturalistic settings, qualitative methods have an "arts and crafts" approach to analysis—as far from the controlled conditions of the laboratory as one can imagine. Their localized adaptability has, however, come with a price—a historic tendency to mystify and obscure methods of data analysis. While ethnography has retained much of this mystique, grounded theory opened the door to greater transparency in methods, particularly in data analysis. Indeed, the plethora of qualitative methods texts published since the 1970s represent a concerted effort to satisfy the growing demand for how-to instruction. Legitimate concerns can be raised that such a trend will lead to predictability and staid formulism. However, creativity and interpretive latitude are still what make qualitative inquiry the "art" as well as the "craft" that it is.

Specific forms of analysis cover a wide range of possibilities, from the particularistic (narrative and discourse analyses) to the holistic (case study and ethnography) to approaches falling somewhere in between (phenomenological analysis and grounded theory). All require prior management of the raw data to enable the researcher to interact with it systematically. This chapter will begin with the logistics of management and preparation of data, and then provide an overview of the separate analytic approaches. Greatest emphasis will be placed on the form of analysis most common in qualitative methods—coding and thematic development.

Data Management:
Dealing With Volume Early On

Proper management is essential given the massive amount of raw data needing storage and accessibility for retrieval. The tasks begin with fully disguising participants (usually with ID numbers) in all transcripts, audio files, field notes, and other documents. When case study analyses are used, an ID number helps to keep the various data sources linked together for each particular case. Inexperienced qualitative researchers are often surprised by the sheer quantity of raw data generated by studying relatively few people. Manwar, Johnson and Dunlap (1994) studied 80 crack dealers in New York City and generated more than 25,000 pages of text! Sue Estroff (1981) described a typical approach to data management that she used in her ethnographic work:

> When I refer to data, I mean primarily volumes of field notes filled with verbatim and reconstructed conversations, my own thoughts and feelings, descriptions of events and individual behaviors, synopses of discussions, and miscellaneous information collected from a variety of sources. The other materials I used were notes made by clients (some solicited and some unsolicited) and staff; Community Adaptation Schedule (CAS) responses that were computed, coded, and scored; some transcribed tapes of in-depth interviews with staff members; and veritable mountains of newspaper

clippings, books, and scholarly articles. I created a file for each client that contained essential information such as demographic, admission, and discharge facts. In addition, these files contained medication, employment, and personal histories as well as current status—all as reported to me by the clients. (p. 33)

Using Qualitative Data Analysis (QDA)
Software Part I: Storing and Managing Data

Not surprisingly, computerized versions of the manual filing system described by Estroff have become a staple of qualitative data analysis (QDA). QDA software has acquired a 'must-have' status for many researchers, lending technological cachet to a methodology known for being low-tech.

Initially, computerized word processing programs were used to perform the cut-and-paste tasks of coding and analysis, but the popularity of dedicated QDA software such as ATLAS/ti, NVivo, NUD*IST, HyperRESEARCH, and The Ethnograph has spread rapidly. The Centers for Disease Control and Prevention offer a free downloadable version of QDA software known as "CDC EZText" that performs the same functions.

The regularity of QDA software upgrades and the learning curve required to use them make it advisable here to stick with a general overview and suggest additional readings and resources including free trial downloads. (See the end of this chapter.) In general, QDA programs work on PCs rather than Macintosh operating systems. (HyperRESEARCH being the exception.) Most have a smooth interface with word processing programs, allowing input of documents as well as selected file downloads for printing hard copies. Memos are stored separately but can also be coded as text. Innovative features include the incorporation of graphic, audio, and video files and exporting of files to SPSS or EXCEL. The central functions of QDA software—to store data and facilitate coding and analysis—make it possible to search for connections or hierarchies among codes, to produce graphical displays of codes, and to easily retrieve information in an organized fashion. (More about this later in the chapter.)

The decision about whether to use QDA software usually rests on the scope of the project (including its budget) and the researcher's comfort level with learning the ins and outs of the software. A study with substantial amounts of data and multiple users will probably make the cost of the software worthwhile. Yet most basic QDA functions such as cutting, pasting, and retrieving text can be done manually or on regular word processing programs without this added expense.

Multiple Users and Cross-Site Databases

Large databases with multiple users have long been the province of quantitative research. The standardization of quantitative studies facilitates tasks such as entering data from different sites, managing and cleaning the data, merging files, and making subsets of data available to multiple users. Recently, the rise of large-scale qualitative (and mixed methods) studies has opened the door to similar multiuse scenarios, albeit with some daunting challenges (Manderson, Kelaher, & Woelz-Stirling, 2001). The Three Cities Study, a massive undertaking involving over 2,000 low-income families in Chicago, Boston, and San Antonio, was funded by no less than seven federal agencies and 14 private foundations (http://web.jhu.edu/threecitystudy). The study's design, which included three waves of data collection and four years of ethnography (1999–2003), required the cooperation of multiple investigators and institutions.

The site-specificity and flexible designs of qualitative research mitigate against such large-scale collaboration, although it is possible with proper planning and sufficient resources. At a minimum, advance thought needs to be given to coordination across sites to ensure that datasets can be integrated. QDA software can be invaluable for these long-distance transactions (Drisko, 2004). The timing and scope of the cross-site collaboration are key questions that lead to still more questions: Will all data be sent to a central repository or remain local? If the former, when will the data be sent and in what form? If the latter, how will cross-site quality control be monitored? Will full collaboration be activated from the earliest stage of the study or after the data have been collected? How will the collaborative team divvy up tasks? Whereas data collection is inherently site-specific, data analyses and writing may be integrated across sites and/or take place at a single "headquarters" site. Finally, how will the allocation of responsibilities be reflected in authorship of reports and publications?

Aside from concurrent data collection, multiple uses may occur sequentially as new investigators seek access to archives of qualitative data. As will be discussed later in this chapter, secondary analyses are becoming increasingly common—and they present their own challenges.

Transcribing Interviews

Transcription of audiotapes receives relatively little attention, perhaps because it is mistakenly assumed to be a mechanical task amidst the many cerebral activities associated with data analysis. However, transcription is a form of data transformation that can either enrich or deprive a study depending on how carefully it is done (MacClean, Meyer, & Estable, 2004). The best approach is to transcribe one's own interviews as much as possible and to train and supervise all other transcribers, including making them aware of the need for full confidentiality. Interviewer self-transcription has several advantages, including the ability to: 1) fill in unclear passages; 2) insert explanations or clarifications; and, 3) obtain timely feedback on one's interviewing technique.

There is no substitute for hearing one's own voice and reliving the interview. For example, an interviewee might use gestures for emphasis or to replace words altogether (e.g., a wink or a smile to mean "I was only joking," a shrug instead of "I don't know," or eye-rolling to signal impatience). Participants often tell animated stories in which they act out scenes for the interviewer's benefit. "Outside" transcribers are left scratching their heads in such instances.

Be sure to develop basic rules for transcription and ensure that they are followed consistently. These include transcribing nonverbal utterances such as sighs, sobs, and laughter (setting these off with parentheses is helpful). Pauses by the respondent lasting more than a few seconds are worth noting parenthetically. Sometimes the interviewer needs to add a clarifying phrase so that future readers of the transcript will not be confused or misled. In the NYSS, for example, one study participant (SP) spoke repeatedly of "Susie" which led me to think he had a girlfriend, until the interviewer correctly identified "Susie" as SP's dog in the transcript. Sometimes an interviewee slurs incomprehensibly or talks very softly—this can be noted in brackets as [unclear]. Another use of bracketing is to provide translation of foreign-language words or idioms.

The transcriber should studiously avoid editing and cleaning up grammar or off-color language. Respondents have a right to have their stories transcribed without cosmetic (and potentially distorting) revisions. This concern with fidelity is not the same as "triaging" transcription (i.e., selectively transcribing to omit tangential portions of the interview). Given time and labor costs, researchers may instruct transcribers to overlook small talk at the beginning and end of the interview or long-winded repetitions of the same story. In these instances, careful supervision is needed to ensure that useful information is not lost.

Here are a few logistical suggestions for transcription:

1. Leave ample margins (for memos and coding) and number the lines sequentially from start to finish.

2. Use a header on every page noting the interviewer's initials, date of the interview, and date(s) of the transcription.

3. Put interviewer questions in bold font to make it easier to scrutinize the content of questions as well as their length (going on too long is a problem).

4. Start every answer with the participant's identification number so that any chunks of narrative moved to new files will be identifiable; including the line numbers for the moved narrative makes its provenance even clearer.

5. It is usually okay to skip over the many "uh-uhs" and "umms." (The exception being conversation analyses where such utterances are important.)

6. Back up all work early and often and keep back-up files in different places. Although some variant of this story has become the stuff of urban legend, a doctoral student I knew experienced the ultimate nightmare—while in the midst of moving apartments she had all of her data—original and back-up—stolen from the trunk of her car!

Using "Outside" Transcribers

Given its intense labor, qualitative researchers frequently opt to pay others to do the transcription. This is expensive but it also saves a lot of time. (Transcribing a 90- minute interview can take 8 to 10 hours and produce more than 30 pages). If the option to use an outside transcriber is pursued, it should be done with the knowledge that it forecloses the possibility of a close relationship between the researcher and his data. One compromise is for interviewers to transcribe their own interviews in the early phases and sporadically thereafter but hand most of them over to others for transcription.

With regard to remuneration, it can be made per tape, page, or hour. Local norms on this vary. MacClean and colleagues (2004) recommend paying by the hour (rather than by the tape) to ensure full attention to detail. Whatever payment system is devised should be flexible enough to reward accurate and efficient transcription.

Transcribers should be treated as members of the research team rather than as technicians (Gregory, Russell, & Phillips, 1997). Often drawn from the ranks of graduate students and the underemployed, transcriptionists play key roles in protecting confidentiality and in making decisions about what gets transcribed and how. Interviews are entertaining and informative but they can also be intensely personal—listening to teary accounts or hate-filled harangues can take its toll. Although the vast majority of qualitative interviews resolve such emotions by the end, transcribers may feel genuine concern toward a participant. Assurances that the study has procedures for making referrals for counseling and that most interviews are quasi-therapeutic (or at least do no harm) are essential. Like other members of the team, transcribers can benefit from periodic debriefing to express their concerns and suggestions.

Protecting Confidentiality During Transcription

Whether given verbally or via a signed form, transcriptionists must promise to maintain strict confidentiality. This still leaves open the question of how much identifying detail should be left in the transcript. Using identification numbers for study participants does not eliminate the overall risk of breaching privacy because interviewees often refer to others by name during an interview or talk explicitly about programs and places they have experienced. At the same time, instructing transcribers to disguise all names (e.g., by typing only the first letter), removes valuable information from later analysis. In New York City, for example, Lincoln Hospital in the Bronx is a very different place from Lenox Hill Hospital on Manhattan's East Side. Similarly, a SP may mention a particular provider whose name comes up in other interviews as an unusually caring individual. Transcribing verbatim the names of jails and prisons where SPs served time also conveys important information. Although it is clearly essential to fully disguise all names in public presentations of the data and findings, it is better to retain such details in the transcripts.

Human error is a constant factor in transcription. In addition to encountering unfamiliar terminology, transcriptionists may fill in the blanks when the speech is muffled or background noise intrudes. They may decide to edit out foul language or "mispronunciations." Sometimes it is difficult to know who is correct—the transcriber or the interviewee. (See Box 7.1.)

Translating From a Non-English Language

As discussed in the previous chapter, the post-1970s literature on qualitative methods has been virtually silent on the issue of non-English translation (Esposito, 2001). The newly developing interest in what is said as well as how it is said raised the bar considerably when it came to cross-language interactions. In ethnography, prolonged immersion leaves time to correct misunderstandings or inaccuracies, and the risks of distortion by the translation are lower. In contrast, grounded theory and other language-based methods rely heavily on transcripts of interviews that have been filtered twice—once by translation and again by transcription. In this context, use of qualitative data in a non-English language raises a

---

BOX 7.1   A Brief Quiz on Transcription "Errors"

Interviewees may use colorful phrasing and transcribers may err in capturing them or (worse) deliberately change the language. The following quotes contain some examples of transcriber error interspersed with actual statements made by study participants in the NYSS. Can you detect which is which? (The Answer Key follows.)

1. "I was diagnosed as schizo-defective."

2. "The doctor kept saying 'take a seat,' 'take a seat' and I didn't want to hear 'take a seat.'"

3. "I want to stay at the Plasma Hotel."

4. "I am very bi-popular."

5. "My boyfriend was built like a brick tree-house."

Answer Key: #1, #3, and #5 were actual statements made by participants; #2 and #4 were transcriber errors. #2 should read "Hep C" (hepatitis C) instead of "take a seat," and #4 should read "bipolar" instead of "bi-popular."

---

host of new questions not only about the accuracy of translation but also about its timing relative to transcription and textual analysis (Shibusawa & Lukens, 2004).

Errors in translation can result from a lack of familiarity with local dialects and meanings as well as deliberate (if well-intentioned) bias. Translators may feel that they need to safeguard their community values (e.g., a Spanish-speaking translator decides to leave out embarrassing details about sexual activities recounted by a Mexican woman). Even conscientious and thorough translation cannot capture the nuanced meanings embedded in language. In addition to culture-bound idiomatic phrases, meaning arises from the texture of speech—the words, cadences, and inflections that non-native speakers often fail to understand. For example, the Japanese term *amae* has no English counterpart in its connotation of interdependency and indulgence on the part of siblings caring for an ailing brother or sister (Shibusawa & Lukens, 2004). Concerns about literal translation are further compounded by the inevitable nonverbal cues sent by facial expressions, body language, and so on. As noted by anthropologist Clifford Geertz, a wink may have many cultural and situational meanings or it may just be an involuntary twitch (1973).

Identical to earlier recommendations regarding transcribers, translators should be included in the research team as full members. They too are privy to the intense human emotions evoked by qualitative interviewing and may benefit from debriefing. In addition, sharing a deeper understanding of what the study is about helps transcribers to reduce errors and makes them feel valued as having a substantive contribution to make.

Analyzing Qualitative Data: The Search for Meaning

Some qualitative researchers assert that findings are discovered (as if they are lying in wait) and others say that findings are social constructions. Beneath this semantic and epistemological divide is a common substrate of activities that involve pattern recognition and thematic development (Boyatzis, 1998; Patton, 2002; Ryan & Bernard, 2003). Such activities are influenced by whether the study is concerned with change over time and whether its "cases" (individuals or other units of analysis) are treated holistically or as part of an aggregate whose words or utterances constitute the raw material of analysis.

Although all data are filtered in some way, qualitative data can be viewed as existing on a continuum based on the degree of abstraction and processing involved. Raw data include audiotapes and visual media such as photographs and documents; partially processed data refer to field notes, transcripts, translations, and interviewer observations. For many qualitative studies, the next level of processing involves codes—concepts or meaning units drawn from raw and partially processed data— followed by themes or categories. Parallel to data analysis and transformation are auditing and operational tasks including memo-writing of analytic decisions and journal-keeping to record the researcher's personal reactions, biases, and concerns.

Boyatzis (1998) distinguishes between manifest and latent analysis, the former referring to surface description and the latter to an interpretation of underlying or hidden meaning(s) that goes beyond description. One does not usually plunge into analyzing the latent before gaining a comprehensive understanding of the manifest. Ethnographers, for example, stay at the descriptive level for a long time in order to make their interpretations "deep" and "thick" enough to uncover the tacit meanings of cultural beliefs and practices.

Whereas some methods offer specific (albeit flexible) guidelines for data analysis, others are less explicit in the how-to aspects. Still other qualitative approaches, such as case studies and ethnography, exist as "meta-methods" (i.e., broad enough to incorporate differing modes of data collection and analysis). Regardless of approach, qualitative analyses depend on close and careful readings of texts, multitasking to attend to what and how something is said or done, and using filters and analytic axes to organize the process as it unfolds. Qualitative data analysis rarely follows a predictable course, so keeping track of its progress via memo-writing is critical.

Use of Case Summaries and Data Displays

Most researchers are familiar with coding as the gateway to data analysis, but there are additional ways to get a handle on one's data. Miles and Huberman (1994) discuss two basic types of data display techniques—matrices and networks. The former consist of rows and columns and the latter a series of nodes with links in between. Although superficially similar to quantitative approaches such as cross-tabulations and path analyses, qualitative data displays use narrative or text rather than numbers. Both are used to facilitate visual inspection in the search for patterns and connections, not as the basis for statistical predictions.

Case summaries, another heuristic device, involve assembling and summarizing all available data about each particular case so that they may be viewed holistically. Case summaries can take the form of stories or vignettes, but they may also be structured around the study's topical domains. Study participants volunteer a lot of information—some important and some not; the case summary organizes this for greater retrievability. In the NYSS, for example, case summaries could be readily consulted to find out how many children a participant had, current substances being abused (if any), and so forth.

When constructing matrices there is the risk of losing important information—even a densely packed matrix locks the data into a small number of dimensions. Qualitative studies that focus on group comparisons or discrete events have an analytic axis built into their design, but others might be more fully inductive. Problems arise when researchers try to shoehorn data into matrices that do not fit the format, thereby sacrificing nuance and deeper meanings. As noted by Walker and Myrick (2006), the conditional matrices used by Glaser and Strauss can also be used later on in grounded theory analysis.

As with other types of qualitative data analyses, the utility of matrix and network displays depends on their "fit" for the particular study. Case summaries, on the other hand, are useful in virtually all qualitative approaches.

Theories and Concepts in Qualitative Data Analysis: A Continuum of Involvement

As discussed in Chapter 1, theories and concepts play an important but often contested role in qualitative research. During data analysis, their role is that of informing without determining, lending concepts and ideas without imposing them. Charmaz aptly refers to "theorizing" as the optimal description of what goes on during qualitative data analysis (2006). Theorizing allows for conceptualizing without necessarily producing a theory—the reality for the vast majority of qualitative studies including those using grounded theory. It also implies a dynamic process with varying inputs and outputs depending on the study's aims, research design, and stage of analysis.

The most prepackaged stance toward concepts and theories conforms to what Crabtree and Miller (1999) call a *template approach*. Using this approach, a researcher relies on a codebook largely or entirely developed in advance. Content analysis is closely associated with this option, but any qualitative study that needs to follow a prescribed conceptual grounding may go this route. At the other end of the continuum are studies that reject the use of preexisting concepts in favor of naive immersion in the data. A phenomenological approach, for example, places high priority on exploring the lived experience de novo to reduce filtering and distortion that can undermine authenticity.

Along the continuum's middle ground lie most qualitative studies, especially those using grounded theory. In these instances, the researcher may use sensitizing concepts from existing theories, but their place in the findings is by no means guaranteed. In this way, the sine qua non of qualitative research—its capacity for surprise and new insights—remains intact. For the most dedicated grounded theorists, the development of a theory or model (whether having low, medium, or high explanatory power) is the desirable end result.

Data Analysis in Diverse Qualitative Approaches

The following are general descriptions of data analysis used in the qualitative approaches that do not depend on coding as their initial means of interacting with the data. This does not preclude their use of coding (although narrative approaches are not likely to do so), but each has its own historic development that is independent of grounded theory and other methods reliant on coding as the first step.

Content Analysis in Qualitative Research

Content analysis has a separate and largely quantitative history of use in the field of communications (Berelson, 1952). It was originally developed to quantify the number of incidents of some phenomenon. Content analyses of newspapers, magazines, television, and (more recently) Internet communications could be used to reveal, for example, the frequency of pharmaceutical advertisements, the number of violent incidents involving children, or the prevalence of ethnic and racial slurs in Internet blogs.

Qualitative researchers sometimes use content analysis when examining documents and other textual materials. Although the boundaries between thematic coding and content analysis are not always clear, content analysis deals with the manifest rather than the latent. If forced to choose, most qualitative researchers would opt for an interpretive method that takes full advantage of the depth of qualitative data.

Ethnography and Data Analysis

Ethnographic methods have the exotic image of involving far-away places. Regardless of whether they are conducted in Samoa or Springfield, these methods produce a wealth of data that can quickly overwhelm the researcher unaccustomed to multitasking with minimal guidance. The following quote (Estroff, 1981) describes this laborious tradition:

> Working with these materials was a messy, exasperating, and complicated procedure. I began by reading all the field notes and raw materials repeatedly until I knew what was in each volume and where it was, creating a sort of mental map and table of contents. Then, as the structure and order of presentation of topics became clearer, I literally surrounded myself with data. I made concentric circles of important pages of field notes, articles, books, and drafts, and I perched in the middle of these to think, sort, and combine. Each of these circles became a chapter, but only after it had become a shambles. Days were spent shuffling and grabbing, realizing a whole section needed rewriting and so beginning again, or rescuing all from numerous disasters with the paws of muddy dogs who assaulted me for attention. (pp. 33–34)

Estroff's analyses relied on manual sorting, visual examination, and intense contemplation about what was being observed and interpreted. In addition to field notes, ethnographic data include interviews supplemented with documents and records. They may also include quantitative measures and analyses.

As a meta-method, ethnography encompasses diverse forms of data. Learning how to "sweep back and forth" and "swoop in and out" of the data is one of the most challenging aspects of analysis. A number of ethnographic experts have stepped forward over the years to demystify and instruct, including Agar (1980), Bernard (1994), Lofland and Lofland (1995, and LeCompte and Schensul (1999). In the end, the best way to demystify ethnographic data analysis is hands-on experience.

Case Study Analysis

Like ethnography, case study analysis is a meta-method embracing multiple forms of data and analytic techniques (including quantitative) and lacking detailed procedures for its performance. Stake (1995) distinguishes between *instrumental, intrinsic,* and *multiple* case studies. Whereas instrumental case studies are illustrative devices used to highlight discussion of a larger issue or concern, intrinsic case studies focus on the entity itself as worthy of intensive scrutiny. Multiple case study analysis follows the same principles of a single case study but, for reasons of replication or expansion, depends on more than one case.

A primary feature of case study analysis is going "deep" before going "out" (to larger issues and theories) or, for some studies, going "across" (to other cases). Doing within-case analysis means delving into historical background and/or exploring the case in all of its complexity. If very little is known about the case and/or it has intrinsic interest, analysis may focus more on description than interpretation.

Because cases may be persons, entities, or events, analysis plans vary depending on the nature of the "case" and the data to be collected. They also employ differing approaches depending on whether the study design is cross-sectional or chronological. Patton (2002) notes that the choice of a "case" may shift during sampling (e.g., from an entire school to selected classrooms or from classrooms to selected teachers and students). A case study may include both an entity and an event, for example, a study of a mental health agency in downtown Manhattan in the aftermath of the September 11th attacks. It can advance an argument. An example of this type of case study is Bradshaw's (1999) study demonstrating that the

closure of a military base did not produce the predicted dire consequences. A case study may also explore the causes and consequences of a
major policy change, for example, the New York City Police Department's
shift to a "broken windows" policy of quality-of-life arrests in the 1990s
(Kelling & Coles, 1996).

The term "case study" refers to the process as well as the outcome
(Patton, 2002). The key distinguishing feature of case study analyses is
that they maintain the holistic integrity of the case. A "case" is unpacked
and its contents closely examined, but the parts are ultimately viewed as a
whole and in relation to one another. A "case study-as-product" is a comprehensive description built up from immersion in multiple sources of
data. It brings in specifics but does not get bogged down in detail.

Box 7.2 discusses multiple case study analysis in the New York Services
Study with an emphasis on varied sources of data and the decision making
that cross-case comparison entails. Figure 7.1 offers an example of one
source of NYSS case data—a "life trajectory" of a 53-year- old female study
participant displaying changes in key life domains over time. Multiple case
study analysis presents special challenges to ensure that the integrity of the
case is maintained during aggregation. Ragin (1987) developed a method of
"qualitative comparative analysis" based on Boolean algebra that resolves
some of the issues, but it is not a good fit for qualitative research. Many of
the same methods for thematic analysis and pattern recognition discussed in
this chapter apply to multiple case study analyses. As a rule, similar cases
are easier to cross-case analyze than dissimilar ones.

Data Analysis in Narrative Approaches

As discussed in Chapter 2, narrative approaches bring to the surface
the tacit meanings embedded in the structure of naturally occurring
speech and talk. Individual narratives and conversations are revelatory
events when analyzed for their cadences, interruptions, intonations,
emphases, and lyrical storytelling.

Data analyses in narrative approaches draw on literary traditions while
reflecting a social science preoccupation with social and cultural meaning.
Narrative approaches fall roughly into two types: 1) analyses of stories
that naturally occur during interviews; and 2) analyses of conversational
exchanges between two or more individuals in which the study participants may be unrelated (e.g., focus groups) or members of a family
or group of friends. The first of these, narrative analysis, analyzes
storytelling, plots, and chronologies of events (Riessman, 1993). The

BOX 7.2 Multiple Case Study Analyses in the NYSS

In Phase 1 of the NYSS, we conducted case study analyses of individual life histories to ensure that the sequencing and timing of events were given center stage. To carry these out, we assembled and reviewed the data for each study participant (SP) listed below:

- Interview transcripts (two per SP).
- Interviewer feedback forms documenting observations of the SP interviews.
- Brief case summaries.
- Life trajectory graph (depicting key events; see Figure 7.1 for an example).

Writing the case summaries required an immediate decision: Would they track the person's life over time or by topical area, for example, substance use, mental illness, homelessness, and so on? We opted for topical areas, but also focused on chronologies (by topic) with a "life trajectory" chart in an Excel spreadsheet format. These life trajectories showed onsets (and endpoints) of substance abuse, homelessness, incarceration, psychiatric treatment, and the like. This color-coded visual display (we had fun discussing which colors should be assigned to marijuana, cocaine, alcohol, etc.) compressed a tremendous amount of information into several parallel trajectories. Cross-case inspection—which involved the old-fashioned act of printing and laying out the trajectories on a large seminar table for visual inspection—revealed patterns such as the early onset of substance abuse (predating psychiatric treatment) and the lack of formal substance abuse treatment for most study participants.

Case study analyses were group meetings that drew on these trajectories and the other case-specific data. With the participant's primary interviewer acting as the discussion leader and another team member acting as scribe, we sat down as a group and discussed each person with a list of questions as a guide. These questions included: 1) the sequencing of mental illness, homelessness, and substance abuse in his or her life course; 2) what appears to have "worked" and "not worked" in terms of services for these problems; 3) traumatic events in childhood

(Continued)

(Continued)

or adulthood that appeared to be turning points in their lives; 4) other positive or negative events that stand out in their recollections. Answers to these questions formed a focused narrative for each SP that was compared to the other case narratives to explore commonalities in the life histories. Echoing Patton's (2002) distinction between a *pattern* and a *theme*, we found descriptive patterns (e.g., early teen onset of substance abuse, child sexual abuse of women, and an absence of work history and job skills) that were not present in all cases but prevalent enough to be noteworthy. Themes included: cumulative adversity and loss, aging and self-reflection as precursors to cessation of substance abuse, and the "situatedness" of mental illness as one of many setbacks in a lifetime of deprivation.

second, which encompasses discourse and conversation analysis, examines dialogic aspects of human communication. Both approaches have formal procedures for data analysis.

Following Labov and Waletzky (1967), narrative analysis involves identifying six elements of a fully formed narrative: *abstract* (summary or précis of the event), *orientation* (time, place, participants, context), *complicating action* (what actually transpired), *evaluation* (meaning and significance of the event), *resolution* (conclusion of the event), and *coda* (giving closure by returning the listener to the present time). A couple of caveats are pertinent here. First, not all narratives contain all six elements and analysts may reasonably disagree about what constitutes a coda, evaluation, and so forth. Second, narrative stories may be embedded within a long interview or they can emerge over a series of interviews (Riessman & Quinney, 2005).

Analyzing naturally occurring speech can uncover social and cultural influences that structure human interaction. *Conversation analysis* does this by examining turn-taking; silences and nonverbal utterances that signal gender, age, and race; and other role-playing that is enacted when individuals speak with one another (ten Have, 1999). *Discourse analysis* is more broadly defined to include texts as well as conversation. Analytic procedures center on spotlighting how larger social influences (especially unequal power and dominance) shape modern discourse(s) (Gee, 2005).

Narrative approaches share a goal of understanding in the context of talk and verbal interaction. Whether following the arc of a personal narrative or

NYSS ID: 140 DURATION ACROSS LIFETIME | **Key2** continuous → ─ ─ ─ → intermittent | Current Age: 53

Timeline: (1957) 5 (1962) 10 (1967) 15 (1972) 20 (1977) 25 (1982) 30 (1987) 35 (1992) 40 (1997) 45 (2002) 50 (2007) 55 60 65

FIELDS	key 1	Commentary / notes
WORK HISTORY		
educational level		
commentary		Attends and Graduates from High School
vocational training		
commentary		
agency linked		
commentary		
independent employ		Works as a home attendant
commentary		Works at a bank after graduation for 2 years, until held at gunpoint in robbery.
INCARCERATION		
jail		
commentary		
prison		
commentary		
RESIDENTIAL		
street/subway		lives on streets, subways, buses 1 year
commentary		Brief period of homelessness when SP loses her room at YWCA, shifts from friend's houses, and even sleeps in father's car overnight
shelter/drop-in		
commentary		Park Slope Women's Shelter 3 years
structured residence		Adult Residence
commentary		
supported housing		
commentary		
own apartment/other		
commentary		Lived with parents up to graduation Moves to PA Returns to NYC, takes care of ailing uncle and then moves back in w/father lives with friends in Jamaica, Queens

Figure 7.1 (*Continued*)

147

NYSS ID: 140 **DURATION ACROSS LIFETIME** Current Age: 53

Key2	continuous	intermittent

FIELDS	key 1	(1957) 5	(1962) 10	(1967) 15	(1972) 20	(1977) 25	(1982) 30	(1987) 35	(1992) 40	(1997) 45	(2002) 50	(2007) 55	60	65
MENTAL HEALTH Tx														
Inpatient admission *commentary*														
outpatient treatment *commentary*									*First diagnosed as bi-polar at women's shelter and prescribed psychotropic meds.*				
other														
SUBSTANCE USE														
alcohol *commentary*					*Begins drinking and smoking marijuana at age 12 to age 54 with one year of sobriety in early 20s. Stopped for 11 months currently*								
marijuana *commentary*					*Begins drinking and smoking marijuana at age 12 to age 54 with one year of sobriety in early 20s. Stopped for 11 months currently*								
cocaine/crack *commentary*									*Begins smoking crack in early 40s. Stops using, but continues to drink and smoke pot*				
heroin/opiates *commentary*														
other			*experiments with LSD and psychedelic drugs in late 60s–early 70s*										

Figure 7.1 (*Continued*)

NYSS ID: 140 **DURATION ACROSS LIFETIME**

Key2 | continuous | intermittent | Current Age: 53

FIELDS	key 1	(1957) 5	(1962) 10	(1967) 15	(1972) 20	(1977) 25	(1982) 30	(1987) 35	(1992) 40	(1997) 45	(2002) 50	(2007) 55	60	65
SUBSTANCE Tx														
detox *commentary*														
short-term recovery *commentary*														
long-term recovery *commentary*														
day program *commentary*														
Peer Support Groups														

Figure 7.1   A Sample Life Trajectory From the NYSS

the back-and-forth of a conversation, the analyst's job is to extract meaning (Hyden & Overlien, 2004; Sands, 2004).

Phenomenological Analyses

Phenomenological studies fill an important niche by exploring the depths of human experience, whether this experience refers to living with chronic illness or winning the state lottery. Developed largely in the field of psychology (Colaizzi, 1978, Giorgi, 1985), phenomenological data analyses share a few basic activities. These include synopses of each study participant's experiences ("textural description"), examination of the context and setting of these experiences ("structural description"), and a condensation or summary of major themes with associated excerpts from the interviews (Moustakas, 1994). Before and during the analyses, the researcher explores his or her personal experience with (or opinions about) the phenomenon and seeks to "bracket" or sideline it. A step-by-step example of this is provided by Groenewald (2004) in his phenomenological study of educational programs in South Africa, a study in which, by the way, he found QDA software to be unsuitable.

Action and Community-Based Participatory Research: Analyzing Data

Action research and community-based participatory research emphasize portability and facility in data collection and analysis to accommodate community partnering and advocacy. Data analyses, which may draw on quantitative as well as qualitative data, follow the lead of the particular approach being used with the added emphasis on using time-sensitive adaptations such as Rapid Ethnographic Assessment (REA) and other Rapid Assessment Procedures (RAPs; Knoblauch, 2005; Scrimshaw & Gleason, 1992). Their low-tech, field-based applications should not be confused with greater ease of use. Indeed, RAPs work best when experienced researchers (especially ethnographers familiar with the community or region) are able to shorten the learning curve and maximize results that will make a difference.

Analysis in Longitudinal Designs

Few qualitative studies are longitudinal in the sense of prospectively collecting data in multiple waves at specified time intervals (Flick, 2004). Quantitative researchers have developed sophisticated ways of analyzing time-ordered data but qualitative methods have barely entered this arena. In the NYSS, where we had three waves of interviews over a 12-month period, we elected to open code the baseline interviews using grounded theory. The 6- and 12-month interviews were analyzed using thematic coding (Boyatzis, 1998) and were also folded into the case summary analyses. Our interest in change over time has been assessed in two ways so far: 1) quantitative analysis of change scores in measures such as the Mental Health Recovery Index; and 2) case study analyses of each person's trajectory over the 12 months in terms of social contacts, service use, and other domains.

Coding and Thematic Development

Coding and thematic development are the most commonly used analytic procedures in qualitative research. That said, there is tremendous variety in how these are carried out and described in the final report. The majority of qualitative researchers (including those using grounded theory methods) stay with description and interpretation without producing a fully developed "theory." Flick (2004) asserts that requiring theory development constitutes an excessive and unrealistic burden for many studies, especially graduate theses and dissertations. This, of course, does not preclude theoretical thinking (which should be brought to bear early and often).

Qualitative researchers have other options for coding analysis besides grounded theory, including methods developed by Boyatzis (1998) and Patton (2002). Nevertheless, grounded theory has a sacred and honored status in qualitative data analysis, inspiring qualitative researchers to strive for higher-order thinking and interpretation.

Varied Approaches to Coding

Coding occurs at several levels, from transferring chunks of text into conceptual "bins" to the more elaborate interpretive procedures associated with theory development. Ideally, coding breaks the "data apart in analytically relevant ways in order to lead toward further questions about the data" (Coffey & Atkinson, 1996, p. 31). As noted by Tesch (1990), each chunk or quotation has two contexts, one its origin in the narrative and the other a "pool of meaning" located in higher levels of abstraction. Coding sets the stage for interpretation and it is interpretation.

At the outset, coding involves close and repeated readings of the transcript (or other text) in search of "meaning units" that are descriptively labeled so that they may serve as building blocks for broader conceptualization. Somewhat like a funnel, coding starts at a descriptive level and moves upward to greater selectivity and synthesis (Charmaz, 2006).

Questions and decisions arise early on (e.g., where code labels come from, to what extent can these labels draw on a priori concepts and theories, the level of detail attending the analysis [think of a fine- versus a coarse-toothed comb]). The answers to these questions depend on the study's overall conceptual framework and design, but some basic guidelines are discussed in the following sections.

Starting Out: Identifying and Labeling Codes

Most qualitative researchers begin with open coding (Charmaz, 2006; Ryan & Bernard, 2000). For the novice, this can seem like working the trapeze without a net, but one need not approach coding as a blank slate (pardon the mixed metaphors here). Grounded theorists refer to *sensitizing concepts* (Glaser, 1978) as providing initial guidance on where to start looking. Thus, a study of persons with schizophrenia would likely consider looking for "stigma," and one examining eating disorders might look at "body image." Regardless of whether sensitizing concepts are invoked, the researcher approaches the text with as few preconceptions as possible and holds the ones she has lightly.

A qualified exception to this comes especially from evaluation research where codes may be imported directly from the interview questions, with varying degrees of openness to new information and new codes (Patton, 2002). Similar to what Crabtree and Miller refer to as a "template" approach (1999), we used this more selective format in an evaluation of foster care in New York City (Freundlich, Avery, & Padgett, 2007). Consultation with key stakeholder groups (youths, social workers, attorneys, judges) and the literature produced seven domains that structured the open-ended questions as well as the analyses. These domains were: youth involvement, transitioning, recommendations for improved services, quality of placements, safety in the placements, services in the placements, and permanency planning. Such prepackaged codes permitted us to expedite the study's data collection and analysis yet stay true to the stakeholder opinions that shaped their content. The tradeoff—losing the freshness and creativity of inductive thinking—was worth it because sponsors and study participants asked for a quick turnaround (less than 18 months) for the results and policy recommendations.

When coding, one can use the righthand margins of the transcript to bracket relevant segments and assign code labels to them. Although this may be carried out directly on the computer screen using QDA software, I prefer marking hard copies first (always using pencils with erasers!). A few important considerations arise at this point. First, every line of the transcript is not necessarily coded (or code-worthy). Second, a single passage of text may be so rich that it yields several code-worthy chunks of information. Coding can get messy in such instances—sometimes one must literally circle the relevant text with an arrow leading to the code label in the margin. (Righthand margins can look like traffic gridlock when an interview yields a lot of important material.) Third, codes need to have clear definitions to guide their usage (i.e., what belongs in and what does not). Finally, codes are provisional and subject to change, either through clarification and revision or outright elimination.

Early in data analysis—usually after three or four transcripts—a start-list of codes is compiled and applied to additional transcripts. A commonly used approach is to have two persons independently code the first few transcripts, then meet to discuss their findings and arrive at a provisional list of codes. In this way, new codes may be added and excess codes discarded.

Trimming back a proliferating code list is inevitable. Codes get dropped for two primary reasons: 1) they have too few excerpts (or their content is too thin); and 2) they become merged with or absorbed by another code. A code's staying power is not a matter of quantity. Counting the number of times something is mentioned (or the number of lines of text these items occupy) is largely the domain of content analysis.

After coding a few more transcripts (this number varies depending on the density and richness of the data), the list of codes starts to gel and no new codes emerge. The size of the final list can vary considerably, but it tends to become unwieldy when codes number more than 30 or 40. Less (or fewer) codes can be more.

At this initial stage, one should strongly resist the temptation to use professional jargon in labeling codes. Staying close to the data helps prevent this from happening because few individuals express themselves this way in normal conversation (e.g., referring to their "denial" or "repressed emotions"). Code labels should be brief but descriptive. Charmaz (2006) suggests using gerunds whenever possible to evoke dynamic processes. In the NYSS, for example, we used the code "living independently" to refer to occasions when study participants talked about the benefits of having an apartment of their own. (See more about this code in Box 7.5 on page 165.)

Code labels may be *in vivo*, emerging directly from participants' words. Interviews with case managers in the NYSS led us to use the in vivo code "working the system" to connote the various actions they use to help their clients. We could not hope to improve on this as a label. Sometimes an in vivo code is the product of jargon that has seeped into common parlance. Thus, studies of addiction might encounter the lingo of 12-step groups (e.g., "people, places, and things" or "hitting bottom").

Charmaz (2006) urges the use of compelling or interesting code labels that will grab the reader. Statements like "I take my nephews to school every day" and "I get medicines for my elderly neighbor when she gets sick" might be coded rather dryly as "altruistic actions" or more evocatively as "helping others." Codes with what Charmaz refers to as "grab" are usually in vivo or inductively derived because their graphic nature cannot (and probably should not) be anticipated in advance.

Documenting and Verifying
Coding Procedures: Independent Co-Coding

Coding is a profoundly discretionary activity; it involves painstaking sifting and sorting but it is also intellectually demanding. At the outset, it is not unusual to have dozens or even hundreds of codes. (When two or more persons are involved in coding, one person needs to be in charge of the code master list to maximize coordination.) Over time, some codes will be discarded, others may be spliced into a single code, and still others may be large enough to further divide into subcodes.

The early stages of co-coding invariably produce discrepancies. Although some positivist-oriented researchers calculate inter-coder agreement using percentages or statistics, such as Cohen's kappa (Mayring, 2004), qualitative data are rarely conducive to such precision. Areas of disagreement during co-coding center on: 1) what segments are deemed code-worthy; 2) the size of a particular segment selected for coding; 3) the choice of words or phrasing for a code label; and 4) the definition of the code including what is and is not encompassed by it. It is hard to imagine two individuals, no matter how well trained and like-minded, emerging from an exercise in independent coding with concordance along most or all of these parameters.

Coding is a process of consensual validation rather than the pursuit of unanimity implied by statistical measures of agreement (Sandelowski & Barroso, 2002). Co-coders meet to compare their results, relying on cogent arguments and persuasion grounded in the data. Although it would be naive to assume that no coder has ever used arm-twisting to prevail over a fellow coder, the ideal is a process directed toward what best fits the data. That this process is organic and iterative ensures flexibility and openness to change.

Calculating inter-coder agreement may make sense after a code list and definitions are finalized, but it is still an elusive phenomenon given the many possibilities for discrepancy. Thinking about codes, discussing and defending them, and reaching consensus are valuable aspects of the process, not something to avoid or prematurely conclude. These activities honor the richness of the data and take into account the inevitability of multiple standpoints.

Comparing and Contrasting: Memo-Writing

Coding does not take place in an analytic vacuum. Memo-writing is an offshoot of this process in which one documents thoughts and ideas that emerge through interacting with the data. Strauss and Corbin (1990) distinguish between three types of memos: *code notes, theory notes,* and *operational notes.* Code memos are the basis for definitional statements and documentation of their reason for being. Theory notes are a record of ideas and hunches about what is going on in the data. Operational notes are placeholders for logistical and other concerns. (Box 7.4 on page 163 offers some examples of operational notes.)

Memos are safety zones for discovery and creativity, a place for hunches and conjecture. They may be shared with one's advisor or collaborators but otherwise should remain private repositories of ideas. It is difficult at times to distinguish memos from codes. Codes are indexical (i.e., words or phrases that "speak for" chunks of raw data). Memos are running commentaries rooted in the data but not intended to directly represent it.

As coding proceeds, the analyst remains cognizant of similar incidents in other interviews as well as the larger context, searching for patterns but also remaining alert to negative instances and irregularities. What grounded theorists refer to as *constant comparative analysis* describes a systematic search for similarities and differences across interviews, incidents, and contexts (Strauss & Corbin, 1994). A constant comparative analysis stays close to the data, but its ultimate value comes from an ability to think abstractly and make sense of myriad comparisons, winnowing through them to note what is meaningful. In practice, comparative analysis is cyclical, beginning as inductive, then becoming deductive, and then returning to the inductive. This cycle can be repeated many times over.

Producing Categories and Themes: Differing Analytic Possibilities

It is customary to cut and paste each coded segment into a separate file linked to its respective code label. (QDA software makes this step easy once the segments have been bracketed.) Opinions differ on how much of the surrounding context should be grabbed along with the quote; the rule of thumb is to take as much as is needed to understand the quote but not to burden it with extraneous material.

A manual version of these tasks dating back to earlier days involved literally cutting an excerpt from an extra copy of the text and pasting it onto an index card with additional information like ID number, line numbers, and so on. A kind of pile sort technique was sometimes used in which the quotes/cards were spread out on a table and gradually organized by themes. "Splitters and lumpers" take different tacks to categorizing, but the former have the edge because fine-grained categories can always be aggregated later on (Ryan & Bernard, 2003). Although rarely done, thematic development may employ quantification as part of the process. Box 7.3 offers one such example.

As texts are fractured into meaning units, the resulting code files replace transcripts as the focus of analysis. In what Tesch (1990) refers to as decontextualizing and recontextualizing, analyses of code excerpts involve pattern recognition, drawing on comparisons and contrasts. While doing this, the researcher refers back to the study's research questions as well as the literature—keeping in mind what is known and not known.

There is no consensus on what terminology to use when talking about these interim phases of analysis (Walker & Myrick, 2006). Charmaz (2006) refers to *focused coding* as the time when open codes are winnowed down. Focused codes may result from aggregating a few open codes under a single label. Alternatively, an open code with high salience may become a higher-order focused code or even a theme. Driving this process is constant referencing back to the data and making adjustments to accommodate variation in participants' experiences and beliefs. As an example, Charmaz (2006) traces the origins of the code "identifying moment" as a

---

BOX 7.3   An Example of Quantified Thematic Development

Barkin, Ryan, and Gelberg (1999) describe a deductive-inductive approach to analyzing interview data from pediatricians, community leaders, and parents in South Central Los Angeles inquiring about what doctors can do to prevent youth violence. Given the narrow scope and limited time for the study, the researchers started out with three a priori themes: *potential* (for doctors to address youth violence), *barriers* (to addressing youth violence), and *resources* (for addressing youth violence). These themes were used by two team members to identify statements associated with each (numbering 84, 74, and 41, respectively) made by the 26 study participants. For subtheme identification, this deductive approach shifted to inductive as four coders separately pile-sorted the three sets of thematic statements to come up with subthemes. Three of the four coders were naive (blinded) to the study's goals. Each statement was scaled 0 to 4 depending on the number of coders who placed it in a subtheme pile. The researchers then turned to multidimensional scaling and cluster analysis to identify the final set of subthemes. The distributions of these subthemes were displayed by interview group to show how frequently pediatricians, community leaders, and parents endorsed them. Although the authors did not use the term, the early phases of data analysis resembled content analysis insofar as they were identifying previously selected phenomena and counting their frequency.

---

descriptor for pivotal incidents when persons with chronic physical illness are reminded by others of their disability. Originally defined as referring only to negative experiences, the code was broadened to include positive ones as well. Ultimately, "identifying moment" became a *category*, the grounded theory term for a theme or pattern that arcs across large swaths of the data. Herein lies an important lesson: Although most codes serve out their duty in the descriptive trenches of analysis, an occasional one will make the jump to higher levels.

In grounded theory, a third type of coding—*axial coding*—specifies the properties of the category and its subcategories (Strauss & Corbin, 1990). Just as open coding parses data into digestible bits, focused and axial coding start the process of reintegration by creating a preliminary conceptual framework. In practice, few qualitative studies use axial coding, in part because it is demanding and, according to some, overly prescriptive (Kelle & Erzberger, 2004). The same applies to *selective coding,* a process of selecting and refining "core categories" alone and in relationship to one another (Strauss & Corbin, 1990).

Grounded theorists may turn to *theoretical sampling* to tighten and extend their analyses. Unlike initial sampling, theoretical sampling involves the careful selection of additional cases or settings that will help test out emergent hypotheses. Often guided by memos, the logic of theoretical sampling dictates locating cases for a specific purpose—the refinement of the theory. Perhaps you are studying adolescents who drop out of high school and notice a pattern (e.g., that boys say their reason for leaving was bullying and intimidation and girls say their family responsibilities interfered with school). Further analyses lead to developing a provisional theory of gender differences in "push versus pull" factors and you wish to refine it further. This could entail seeking out teens who stayed in school to ascertain if gender differences in these stressors hold and if their intensity is less (hence they had stayed in school). Theoretical sampling can also involve seeking out new types of data and re-interviewing study participants with new questions.

At this stage of analysis, researchers may turn to *schemas* to display categories and relationships. Strauss and Corbin (1994) offer a template schema that includes identifying *conditions, actions,* and *consequences.* As an example, this schema could be applied to an understanding of why homeless mentally ill clients "go AWOL" from residential programs, including the conditions or circumstances surrounding this act (rule-breaking, relapsing into drug abuse, etc.), the specifics of carrying it out (when, where, with whom, etc.) and the consequences that ensue (e.g., return to the streets or shelters).

Metaphors and *analogies* are frequently drafted into service (Lakoff & Johnson, 1980; Ryan & Bernard, 2003). The example of "going AWOL" illustrates the use of an analogy in coding in the NYSS. It was also an in vivo code, its origins in military usage obscured and broadened to include a variety of conditions surrounding the sudden departure from homeless residential programs. Metaphors can be invoked by the researcher or emerge in vivo. In the Harlem Mammogram Study in which I was involved, some of the women with breast cancer used a metaphor of gardening to describe how cancerous tumors took root and spread, one even saying "I had a garden growing in there."

Bohm (2004, p. 273) adapted the work of Barney Glaser to describe several useful ways to approach qualitative data, including:

1. Process (phases, transitions, sequences)
2. Degree or intensity
3. Typologies
4. Strategies (tactics, techniques, mechanisms)
5. Interactions (mutual effects, interdependence)
6. Identity (self-concept, self-reflection)
7. Turning points (critical junctures, point of no return)
8. Cultural and social norms
9. Consensus (conformity versus conflict)

These organizing frames constitute a set of options that a researcher may draw on—they are especially useful for graduate students and others new to qualitative methods.

To allow for a consistent frame of reference that transcends grounded theory, I will henceforth use the terms "themes" and "subthemes" (rather than categories and subcategories) to describe the culminating phases of data analysis. Themes take shape as the linkages between codes are mapped out, their ultimate value dependent on return passes through the data. Patton (2002) advises looking for recurring regularities or convergences in the data and ensuring that the emergent themes have internal homogeneity (all data indexed by them dovetail closely) and clear boundaries (minimal or no overlap across categories). Ideally, the full set of themes (and subthemes) captures all salient information.

Harking back to the earlier discussion of data displays suggested by Miles and Huberman (1994), some qualitative researchers construct a pyramid-type chart displaying subcodes at the bottom level, then codes, then code clusters or focused codes, and then categories or themes at the top. Others prefer to display the themes and subthemes as nodes and networks with linkages in between. (See Figure 7.2 for an example.) Researchers who wish to go the distance and develop a grounded theory are obliged to pursue the more demanding steps of testing their model and ensuring that all connections cohere into an integrated model.

Keep in mind that field notes, interviewer observations, documents, and material items, in addition to transcripts, can be fodder for the analyst. Some of these can be coded directly and others are folded into analytic memos, their value distilled by the discerning researcher.

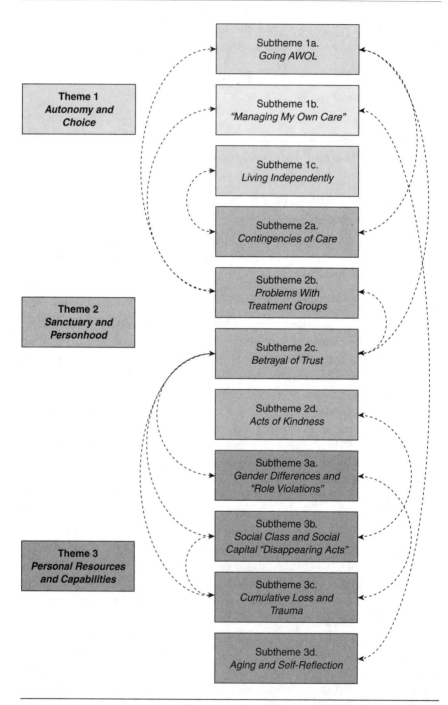

Figure 7.2   Themes and Subthemes From Phase 1 of the NYSS

Beyond Coding

As important as it is, coding is only the starting point. Wider frames of reference can be employed (e.g., examining what participants do not talk about, whether intentionally or not; Bogdan & Taylor, 1975; Levy & Hollan, 2000). In Phase 1 of the NYSS, participants were asked to tell their life stories however they saw fit. Given their diagnosis of a major mental disorder, the literature led us to expect that this would figure prominently in their narratives. For the most part, however, this did not happen. Indeed, participants focused on their family troubles, the hardships of being homeless, problems with the law, and struggles with substance abuse. Mental illness was talked about, but most often in the context of unhappy treatment experiences and medication side effects (Padgett, Henwood, Abrams, & Davis, 2008).

One can also attend to form as well as content (i.e., the way participants talk; Coffey & Atkinson, 1996). In what can resemble (or eventually become) narrative analysis, the researcher may identify stories embedded in the text and note the meaning-making they imply. He may also take note of interesting vocabulary usage or paralinguistic phenomena such as long sighs, a quavering voice, or a hostile demeanor.

Here is an example of interacting with the data in a non-coding way. While reading transcripts in the NYSS, we took note of the fact that men frequently referred to women as "females," as in "I would like to have a relationship with a female" or "Females have been a problem for me." This term of reference, common to rap and hip-hop lyrics, was not necessarily remarkable in and of itself. But it appeared to fit with other evidence that a gender divide characterized participants' life experiences. Summarized in the interpretive phrase "outlaws versus outcasts," this divide cast homeless mentally ill women in a gendered role of victim—of physical and sexual assault, of sex trading, of pimps—and de-feminized outcast. Their struggle for survival, a testimony to their resilience, was similar to that of their male counterparts but with this additional form of gendered adversity. Men, in contrast, could be "outlaws" (drug dealers, pimps, illegal vendors) in masculine roles celebrated rather than denigrated in the wider culture (Padgett, Hawkins, Abrams, & Davis, 2006).

Multitasking During Coding: An Example From the NYSS

Box 7.4 shows an excerpt of a NYSS interview with a 32-year-old Latino man. (Some facts were changed to protect his identity.) Typical of many such interviews, there are several things going on here, some of them understood only by referring to the larger context of his life as well as what is known about drug addiction, parolee status, and so on. Javier (a pseudonym) is talking about getting out of prison and returning to his old neighborhood. He also mentions an earlier incident that ensued when he had an argument with his father and stalked out of his parents' apartment. On the street, he witnessed a mugging, stepped in to help the crime victim, and was attacked and sustained a serious head wound. Woven into this narrative are brief sidebars when Javier talks about his life and his struggle with drug addiction.

The reader is invited to go to the exercises at the end of this chapter to practice open coding on this excerpt and also see how we ended up coding it. At the same time, even this small chunk of text offers several opportunities to interact with textual data in addition to coding. Here are a few general suggestions for going about this: 1) write thoughts and observations in the lefthand margin; 2) flag information that is factual; in the NYSS, we use the letter "C" in the left margin to indicate this is a factual item that belongs in the individual's case summary; and 3) highlight exemplar quotes that might come in handy later; color-coded markers can be used to highlight these excerpts. Case summary information can also be code worthy. Take, for example, a quote such as: "When I lost my two children to foster care, that was the end of the line for me." First, it indicates a "fact" (that the participant's children were removed from her custody), and second, it chronicles the profound emotional impact of that event.

Returning to Javier's interview excerpt, we might note a few case summary items, for example, the date and circumstances of his brutal attack and the neighborhood where his drug problems originated. Using Strauss & Corbin's typology (1990; mentioned earlier in this chapter), such "notes to self" might include:

1. Code note: Is the 12-step lingo of "people, places, and things" an *in vivo* code?

2. Theory notes: Javier attributes his drug abuse to earlier traumas—is this becoming a pattern in the sample? What does he mean by "I'm gonna die soon"? Is impending mortality a constant in SPs' lives? Is his worry about getting older part of a larger pattern in which SPs' awareness of advancing age and mortality push them toward recovery from substance abuse?

3. Operational notes:
   Am I (interviewer) probing enough?
   Check psychosocial records (from referring program) on when his parole ends.
   Make sure incentive is sent to his mother as he requested.

1 **BOX 7.4**   An Interview Excerpt From the NYSS

2 144A: And, anyway I came out and I went back to the same neighbor-
3 hood but I felt, "You know what, I can't stay in this house no more."

4 **Interviewer: What neighborhood was that?**

5 144A: A hundred fiftieth and Broadway, and uh, because that's
6 where my people, places and things is at. All I have to do is show my
7 face out in the front and they're already giving me stuff. And I said,
8 "Then this'll you know, make it look bad for my PO [parole officer] if
9 she finds out I got arrested again 'cause I wanted to get high." You
10 know when I was getting high it was to, to block away the, the
11 flashbacks of my violent past. And um, you know sometimes I
12 would, you know, I asked God, "Why, why do I have to go through
13 all of this? Um, what's the reason and purpose for it?" You know,
14 now I'm, I'm learning to deal and accept I'm gonna die pretty soon.

15 **Interviewer: Why do you believe that?**

16 144A: See, when that young individual hit me over the head with a
17 baseball bat, he didn't do it once, but 24 times. As you can see, my
18 hair's starting to fall out in this section [gestures to his scalp] . . . I'm
19 willing to accept death. It happens. You know, I shouldn't have gotten
20 into an argument with my father that day. But I'm going to college
21 and this guy's [SP's father] stressing me out. So I decided to leave the
22 house and I witnessed you know, a crime and um, it was, the reason
23 why I got involved because the female [mugging victim] was six
24 months pregnant. I'm the innocent bystander that got attacked.

25 **Interviewer: When was that?**

26 144A: That happened in 1998, yeah, 1998. Uh, I think about a, a, a yeah,
27 a month after my birthday which I didn't celebrate either. And um, that's
28 why life has been very difficult for me. You know and I, I keep trying, you
29 know. Thank god I've got a work history you know, that I'm not making
30 stuff up. I've really gone well beyond myself. . . . Because in my mind I'm
31 going through my mid-life crisis and what, what's gonna be happening
32 when I'm forty, fifty years old? Do I have to go through more difficulties?

These represent a small fraction of the queries, leads, and self-reflections that emerge when interacting with rich data. Staying close to the data is necessary but not sufficient. One must simultaneously frame one's observations within a larger context—whether that means constant comparisons with other interviews or with existing knowledge of the subject matter. As shown in Box 7.5, a code may have meaning both within a particular context and wider applications that "link up" to theories that were not part of the study's original conceptual framework.

Using Qualitative Data Analysis (QDA) Software Part II: Facilitating Data Analysis

As mentioned earlier, QDA software provides a highly efficient means of working with massive data files. All QDA programs enable the researcher to code-and-retrieve (i.e., divide the text into coded chunks, attach codes to the chunks, and search and display these coded chunks on demand; Weitzman & Miles, 1995). Memos can be registered and linked to sections of data. QDA software may also offer additional functions for analyzing non-text data (images, audio, and video) and for inserting hyperlinks to connect instantly to other files or data sources.

Coding on-screen is made easier by using a drop-down menu displaying the codebook and by the software's capacity to handle multiple overlapping coded sections. Auto-coding (text searching for code words) and "key word in context" (KWIC) searches can easily be performed, similar to using the "find" command in word processing. In the NYSS, for example, we used ATLAS/ti to search for all versions of the word "help" (the wildcard designation allowing recognition of multiple forms such as helped, helping, etc.) on an initial pass through the data. This type of searching yields hits as well as misses, and the researcher must scrutinize the results to weed out the latter. However, auto-coding and KWIC should not be confused with grounded theory and other types of meaning-centered coding.

Drisko (2004) describes how filters can be used to identify subsets of the data for further analysis and comparison. In addition to filtering by code label, one can select subsets of data according to participant characteristics such as sex, age, and the like. For example, men and women might be compared in their responses coded under "childhood abuse experiences." Another useful function is the ability to create concept maps and plot horizontal and/or vertical connections between the nodes (e.g., "diet" and "exercise" can be connected to the higher order code "self care"). These flexible

BOX 7.5   The Life of a Hard-Working Code: Linking "Up and Out"
to Theory

"Living independently" became a workhorse of a code in the NYSS,
ultimately becoming a subtheme. (See Figure 7.2 on page 160.)
Alternative code labels such as "need for housing" or "desire for autonomy" might have sufficed, but they did not do justice to participants'
descriptions of what it was like to have their own apartment—either in
the present or in a hoped-for future.

Examining the many coded excerpts filed under "living independently" revealed more than just material comforts being invoked (or
sought). Women talked about no longer needing to trade sex for shelter
and being able to avoid abusive male friends. Men spoke of the freedom
of having a key with a lock on the door and of having clean clothing every
day. Men and women alike noted the relief of not being under constant
surveillance and supervision. These psychological benefits extended
beyond the apartment walls, as participants noted how gratifying it felt to
go out and know they had a safe place to return where they could cook
their meals, watch television, entertain friends, or just be alone.

Glaser (2002) writes about the staying power of concepts and their
capacity to link a study's findings "up and out" to larger issues and
ideas. Attempting to better understand what "living independently"
meant in the context of housing status, I searched the public health
and urban planning literature and came across the theory of ontological
security. This produced a classic "aha" moment.

R.D. Laing (1965) wrote that ontological insecurity was a problem
for persons with schizophrenia whose mental illness deprived them
of stable functioning and identity development. Sociologist Anthony
Giddens (1990) developed a broad theory of ontological security for
the post-modern era, arguing that many persons need (but lack) the
constancy in their social and material environment that engenders self-
actualization and faith in one's future.

Interestingly, the literature revealed that empirical research on ontological security was largely confined to studies of home ownership (versus renting) in New Zealand and the United Kingdom. In this context,
the leap from sleeping on a park bench to one's own apartment
seemed especially momentous. Dupuis and Thorns' markers of ontological

(Continued)

(Continued)

security related to having a home (1998) provided sensitizing concepts for me to use as I returned to the NYSS Phase 1 data to re-code and reanalyze. These markers included: *constancy, day-to-day routines, a sense of control* due to *a lack of surveillance,* and a *secure base from which identities can be constructed* (Dupuis & Thorns, 1998).

These markers mapped onto the data beautifully. Moreover, as often happens, a new code emerged inductively from the analysis. Labeled "what's next," this code captured the anxiety felt by participants who had left behind the urgency of survival to face an uncertain future amidst the cumulative disability brought on by poverty, mental illness, and social exclusion (Padgett, 2007).

This story of a code that proved to have deep interpretive traction exemplifies how "outside" theories may be brought into the study to help illuminate and refract meaning from the data. In this instance, it also shows how the outside theory can itself benefit from the association and gain broader explanatory power. Although most codes do not have this power, vigilance is needed to discriminate the leaders from the rank-and-file.

network-making functions can display static relationships as well as flow charts. Among the various types of software, NUD*IST has the most developed capacity for theory development and supports the creation of hierarchical "tree structures." It is also the most demanding to learn.

Given the inevitable questions and confusion that accompany first-time use, there are a number of listservs and Web sites available for help in using QDA software. (See listing at the end of this chapter.) Otherwise, workshops are a good way to get a hands-on learning experience.

The advantages of QDA software include the ability to code, sort, create, reformat, and print reconstituted files with ease. Not surprisingly, these programs have their limitations. Although usually less expensive than their statistical counterparts, QDA software programs are still an added expense. Each program has its own rather quirky terminology; the time and effort needed to master its operations can be extensive even for those with computer skills.

QDA software is better suited to grounded theory as opposed to other analytic approaches (Kelle & Erzberger, 2004). The popularity of this software has raised larger concerns about the potential for over-structuring and mechanizing analyses and casting a misleading image of technological precision over what is always an untidy, iterative, and painstaking process. In reality, the hard work of data reduction and building conceptual frameworks is cerebral—once again the researcher is the instrument. Quantitative researchers have software that will manage and analyze their data. QDA software facilitates analysis, but it does not analyze the data. Computers do not allow the "simultaneous visual access to materials that makes ideas happen" (Agar, 1991, p. 193). As with the earliest days of qualitative analysis, there is no substitute for spreading out data on a large table (or the floor) to look for patterns, a panoramic view no computer can offer.

Using Numbers and Quantification in Qualitative Data Analyses

As mentioned earlier in this book, numbers may crop up during qualitative data analyses. Development of a typology, for example, could lead to reporting the number of participants associated with each type. As described in Box 7.3 on page 157, numbers and counting may be used during coding and theme development, although this is relatively uncommon.

According to Miles and Huberman (1994), counting themes via frequencies and percentages can help in identifying patterns or in verifying a hypothesis. At the same time, numbers and quantification must be approached carefully to avoid misleading the reader. Reporting the frequency of something, for example, can imply that a denominator exists when it does not. To state that 15 out of 20 adolescents mentioned going on drinking binges implies a "75% rate" of alcohol abuse, but this only makes sense if every teen was asked about drinking. Even if this was done routinely, a rate calculated from such a small number of individuals has little import (and could be misunderstood if taken out of context). As noted by Morse (2007), qualitative research favors describing "what is" rather than "how much." For most qualitative researchers, numbers can be useful for some types of description, but when it comes to interpretation, they have limited value.

Negative Case Analysis and Causation

In qualitative data analysis, the search for negative cases roughly corresponds to the quantitative researcher's reliance on a null hypothesis. In both instances, provisional theories are tested by searching for falsifying evidence (i.e., we become our own devil's advocate). This follows the logic of philosopher Karl Popper that hypotheses are not truly verified, but only supported in the absence of refuting evidence. As Popper noted, even if we see a million white swans, we can never fully conclude that all swans are white—the sight of only one black swan will falsify this thesis. As Albert Einstein said, "no amount of evidence can prove me right, and any amount of evidence can prove me wrong" (quoted in Miles & Huberman, 1994, p. 242).

Here is an example of how negative case analysis might be used. Let us say that you are interviewing depressed women and detect a pattern of childhood sexual abuse in their life stories. This leads you to theorize that childhood abuse is a contributor to depression in adulthood. At this point, you are obligated to return to the data to search for negative cases— depressed women who did not experience childhood sexual abuse. Finding a disconfirming case need not lead you to completely discard the theory but it does require serious reconsideration and caution. If the countervailing evidence becomes strong (i.e., negative cases start to pile up), it is time to let the theory go.

It is important to distinguish between *disconfirming evidence* (cases that refute an emerging theory) and *discrepant evidence* (cases that refine an emerging theory; Goetz & LeCompte, 1984). In the first instance, the exceptional case disallows the rule (e.g., the black swan). In the second instance, it proves the rule but also refines and expands it.

The line between disconfirming and discrepant cases is blurry at times (Ely et al., 1991). Theories may become so refined and spread so thin that their explanatory value begins to sag under the weight of the evidence. A researcher may also be so taken with negative case analysis that he disconfirms every theme and achieves the dreaded state of analytic paralysis. Somewhere there is a happy medium—a mixture of enthusiasm tempered by skepticism. In the meantime, it is probably better to err on the side of caution than to throw it to the wind.

Where does this leave qualitative researchers when questions of causation arise? Experts run the gamut of opinions about this, ranging from relative enthusiasm (Huberman & Miles, 1994) to serious doubt (Lofland & Lofland, 1995). On the sidelines, anti-positivist skeptics question whether the search for causation is plausible or desirable, given the postmodern premise that facts are "fictitious" (Lofland & Lofland, 1995). As with so many contested issues in qualitative research, one's position depends in large part on one's epistemological stance. My inclination is to be cautious and not make promises qualitative research cannot (and probably should not try to) keep.

Secondary Analysis and Meta-Synthesis

Given the sizeable investments of time and resources that go into a qualitative study, it makes sense that researchers are increasingly willing to share their data with others. Secondary analyses extend the life of a study and are an efficient use of resources. As a general rule, richer and complex data offer more fertile ground for secondary analyses than narrow or thin data. In the NYSS, the Phase 1 life history data have turned out to be a mother lode open to "mining" from different perspectives and with different methods of analysis. The Phase 2 interviews follow specific domains and are more circumscribed, thus narrowing analytic options.

Thorne (1998) distinguishes five types of secondary analysis beginning with *analytic expansion,* in which the researcher ventures into new topics using her own data. *Retrospective interpretation* involves going back to the database to further develop themes. *Armchair induction* applies new textual analytic techniques to existing data. *Amplified sampling* involves comparing several distinct databases for broader analysis. Lastly, *cross-validation* takes the researcher beyond her own findings to seek confirming or disconfirming evidence from other databases. From a logistical standpoint, the analysis may approach the raw data for open coding or it may work with codes developed in the earlier study.

Secondary analyses may be carried out by the original research team, by some of its members in collaboration with new researchers, or by an entirely new investigative team with minimal knowledge of the original study. The downside of the latter scenario includes the likely inability to return to study participants for validation purposes and inadequate documentation of the analytic decision trail followed earlier.

Regardless of who is involved, there is the potential problem of retrofitting new research questions to the earlier data (Thorne, 1998; Williams & Collins, 2002). Although usually more open and "raw" than quantitative datasets, qualitative data have undergone their own filtering and sorting processes unknown to subsequent investigators. The norms for maintaining audit trails are far from agreed on within qualitative research, and many investigators either avoid doing so or reject it on the principle that it is too constraining. Finally, the immersion and interconnectedness of researcher and participant, one of the most rewarding and informing aspects of qualitative research, are missing from secondary analyses. Qualitative researchers who prefer collaborative models of inquiry with their study participants would find this unsatisfying.

On the positive side, gaining Institutional Review Board approval for secondary analyses is usually much easier because interacting with "human subjects" is not involved. Yet secondary analyses are not without ethical risks. Identifying information, for example, can inhere in the data even when the names of participants are not included (Thorne, 1998). The respect for privacy and awareness of context that characterized earlier relationships may be missing on the second go-around. Data from a study of abortion among college students, for example, could become the basis for interpretations that range well beyond what the study participants believe they had signed on for in the first place.

Meta-syntheses involve aggregating the findings from several qualitative studies of the same topic to draw conclusions for comparative purposes. Like their quantitative counterpart (meta-analysis), meta-syntheses have been touted as essential for identifying evidence-based practices (Thorne, Jensen, Kearny, Noblit, & Sandelowski, 2004). They also present epistemological and methodological challenges, including the potential for repeating and even intensifying the biases and errors of the earlier studies. The small sample sizes and idiosyncratic features of many qualitative studies can produce an "apples and oranges" problem of comparing vastly different phenomena poorly suited to aggregation.

Problems of representation in meta-synthesis can become exaggerated by conveying a message that the component studies had not intended (Thorne, 1998). For example, most qualitative studies of persons with schizophrenia have relied heavily or exclusively on white or Caucasian respondents even though African Americans are disproportionately diagnosed with the illness. Synthesizing findings from these samples will almost certainly misrepresent the experience of schizophrenia.

Hybrid and Mixed Qualitative Approaches to Data Analysis

As discussed in Chapter 2, researchers often choose to mix and match qualitative approaches. This can occur at different stages of a study and unfold in differing combinations and for different purposes. It can also introduce problems in the form of method and data incongruities (Johnstone, 2004; Wimpenny & Gass, 2000). As noted by Annells (2006), mixing at the analytic level can be problematic if the underlying philosophical paradigms are in conflict—a lesser concern for pragmatists.

Arguing in favor of hybrid vigor, Fereday and Muir-Cochrane (2006) used inductive and deductive thematic analyses by mixing Boyatzis' inductive methods (1998) with Crabtree and Miller's template style of coding (1999) to study nurses in their day-to-day performance. Thus, data-driven codes from participant interviews, such as "trust and respect" were combined with theory-driven codes, for example, "reciprocity," to produce an integrated model of performance feedback and self-assessment in nursing practice. Uehara (2001) creatively blended narrative analysis with event structure analysis (Griffin, 1993) to trace the temporal sequencing of events as a Cambodian American family sought help for the "spirit invasion" experienced by their severely distressed mother.

An example of sequential use can be found in Beck's study of postpartum depression in which she conducted phenomenological analyses followed by grounded theory analyses of the data (1993). Close concordance was found between the two sets of findings, thus lending credence to her development of a substantive theory explaining the onset and course of depression shortly after the birth of a child (Beck, 1993). Agar and MacDonald (1995) used juxtaposition to compare the results of conversation analyses of focus group data (in which teens discussed drug abuse) with their ethnographic observations of adolescent drug use.

Saturation and Interpretation

Interpretation deals with the less obvious and more abstract dimensions of the data, the act of "reading into" and "extracting meaning from." All research involves interpretation, whether of numbers or narrative; quantitative studies tend to be restrained and cautious, letting the statistical findings tell most of the story. In contrast, qualitative studies operate from a premise of greater interpretive latitude, their ultimate contribution dependent on how this latitude is handled. Multidisciplinary perspectives are especially helpful in this phase because they offer diverse ideas and framing devices for understanding what is going on.

The concept of *saturation* is invoked at various stages of qualitative analysis to refer to the point at which no additional data collection is needed, no new codes are developed, and themes and subthemes have been fully fleshed out (Bowen, 2008; Morse, 1995). Saturation refers to completion or fullness. Studies with modest aims and a priori codes are likely to be saturated much sooner than more ambitious and inductive endeavors.

Saturation does not depend on word or incident counts and frequencies because fullness comes from depth rather than breadth. Perhaps not surprisingly, it is easier to assert having reached this stage than to prove it (Morse, 1995), although careful documentation and memo-writing can alleviate some concerns about premature closure. The alternatives to saturation—an endpoint set in advance or a decision based on arbitrary criteria—are a poor fit for qualitative inquiry. Box 7.6 offers a rare case example documenting how saturation is achieved. The authors (Guest, Bunce, & Johnson, 2006) conclude that fewer interviews than anticipated were needed to reach the saturation point, but they also caution that predicting this number in advance is highly risky.

Interpretation gains momentum as the analysis proceeds; memos log this process but also propel it forward. Meaning comes from the linkages or interstices as well as the building blocks which comprise the themes and sub-themes (Miles & Huberman, 1994). These relationships may be temporal (as in stages and phases) or, more commonly, conceptual networks arrayed in horizontal or vertical (hierarchical) fashion. Searching for disconfirming cases, serendipitous relationships, and paradoxes helps open up the process and keep it fresh.

Interpretation brings in the larger context (i.e., applying interpretive frames from the literature and from the realms of practice and policy). Having thorough knowledge of related research lends greater sophistication as well as wider applicability. Are the findings consistent with this literature? Do they expand on what is already known? Do they challenge the received wisdom? Qualitative research has a unique capacity for debunking the status quo. Elliott Liebow's classic work *Talley's Corner* (1967) has endured because it forced a reconsideration of stereotypes about the lives of African American men in the 1960s.

An Example of a Conceptual Schema

Figure 7.2 (on page 160) shows the conceptual model developed from Phase 1 of the NYSS. The model has a visual and schematic logic, but narrative description is needed to make it come to life. Although space limitations preclude full elaboration, certain features can be pointed out to illustrate thematic development. As shown, the three themes are: autonomy and choice (Theme 1), sanctuary and personhood (Theme 2), and personal resources and capabilities (Theme 3). The subthemes elaborate on each theme and comprise its full content (subthemes1a and 1b were in vivo codes).

BOX 7.6   Operationalizing Saturation: A Study of Sex Workers in West Africa

Guest, Bunce, and Johnson (2006) decided to explore the question of saturation empirically using data analyses from their qualitative study of sex workers in West Africa. When, they asked, would the codebook be complete and no further changes needed? Would six interviews yield as much information as 12, 30, or 60 interviews? Could coding activity slow down to a trickle after X number of interviews then suddenly yield new codes much later after "saturation" had presumably been achieved? Starting with 60 interviews, they began coding in increments of six, keeping track of the number of codes and code definitions as they proceeded. Here is what they found:

- After coding the first 30 interviews, the codebook contained 109 codes of which 80 (73%) were identified within the first six transcripts.
- Of the remaining 29 codes, 20 were identified in transcripts 6–12 (now up to 90% of all codes).
- Coding of transcripts 31–60 yielded only five new codes; four of these were spin-offs from existing codes rather than entirely new information.
- The strength or reach of a code was measured by the number of interviews in which it occurred rather than the number of coded excerpts (because talkative interviewees could easily skew the data). Of the 36 high-frequency codes, 34 had been identified within the first six transcripts.

Guest and colleagues concluded that 12 interviews would have been sufficient (rather than the 60 they conducted). However, they offered a few caveats about this finding. First, they used a standardized list of open-ended questions about beliefs and experiences surrounding sex work. Studies with more improvisational questioning would not be likely to yield such a stable list of codes early on. Second, the coders had similar backgrounds and knowledge about the phenomenon so that consensus—even when coding independently—was probably easier. Put another way, there were fewer "lumper versus splitter" disagreements that often beset co-coding comparisons. Finally, their

(Continued)

> (Continued)
>
> sample was relatively homogeneous. Response variation led more often to definitional tweaking than to coding overhauls (dropping codes, adding new ones, etc.).
>
> Commentary: Qualitative researchers naturally fear that premature closure of data collection will deprive them of vital information waiting just around the corner. Yet unnecessary interviews and diminishing returns drain scarce resources and burden respondents. The study done by Guest and colleagues is innovative for taking on the "saturation threshold" as an empirical question. Yet its findings cannot be generalized too far because they were based on several restrictive premises that do not fit many qualitative studies.

The dotted arrows show connections among the subthemes. The longest dotted arrow, for example, shows that participants desire to "manage their own care" (subtheme 1b)—as in fiddling with medication dosages and quitting drug abuse without treatment—was associated with reflections on advancing age and the need to take charge of their lives (subtheme 3d).

The model's theoretical uplinks are noteworthy. As described in Box 7.5 on page 165, the code "living independently" graduated to become a subtheme that aligned with the theory of ontological security (and expanded the theory beyond its original scope). Themes 1 and 2 in the model are emic, that is, rooted in participants' perspectives. Theme 3, on the other hand, is etic in that it captures our observations filtered through social science theories and ideas. All of the subthemes under Theme 3 had enough empirical and conceptual salience to support separate analyses and manuscripts for publication. These include: subthemes 3a and 3c on gender and trauma (Padgett, Hawkins, Abrams, & Davis, 2006), subtheme 3b on social network depletion (Hawkins & Abrams, 2007), and subtheme 3d on the effects of aging and self-reflection (Shibusawa & Padgett, in press). Theories and concepts found applicable to the data and analyses included feminist, trauma, and social capital theories as well as the life course perspective.

In Pursuit of Methodological Transparency

Qualitative reports often obscure full description of their methods. This state of affairs reflects a tradition of eliding methodological description in the absence of agreed-on procedures and the resulting scarcity of accessible role models. Not surprisingly, the contestation over qualitative methods has also had an impact, with postmodern critics deploring "methodolatry" (Janesick, 2000). Concerned about this trend, British ethnographer Paul Atkinson pointed to an American fixation with rejecting methods that "smack of formal analysis," substituting in their place "vague ideas of experience, evocation and personal engagement" (2005, p. 4). This leaves novice researchers struggling to emulate their role models from afar with inadequate instruction.

This chapter represents a modest attempt to redress this situation and to join forces with qualitative researchers who have similar commitments to transparency (Charmaz's 2006 book on grounded theory being one example). Demystifying qualitative methods makes them more accessible and it facilitates cross-disciplinary communication (Ryan & Bernard, 2003). To be sure, an over-emphasis on documentation can lead to superficiality and dampen creativity. Every activity cannot be chronicled in the report—space limitations alone mitigate against this. Yet a study's findings and conclusions inspire much greater confidence when built on methodological transparency.

Summary and Concluding Thoughts

This chapter began by offering guidelines for managing and analyzing data and strengthening the development of conceptual schemas via negative case analysis, theoretical sampling, and other strategies. Computer software facilitates these activities in a number of helpful ways, but it cannot analyze the data.

Despite a dizzying array of possibilities, most qualitative data analyses have the following in common: 1) full and repeated immersions in the data; 2) going "deep" into descriptive specificity as well as "across" with pattern recognition; 3) attending to context—temporal and environmental; and, 4) proceeding "up and out" to weave in theoretical and empirical knowledge from the literature. Analysis begins inductively, but the pathways to its completion often include deductive thinking as well. The insider perspective is an invaluable part of this process, but the ultimate contribution of a qualitative study depends on the probity and intellectual clarity of its interpretations.

Each of the six qualitative approaches has its own analytic traditions, but the emphasis in this chapter was given to what is done most often (i.e., coding and thematic development). Whether this leads to a fully developed grounded theory or, more commonly, an interpretive framework, such analytic involvement is an exercise in restraint (from becoming weighed down by a priori ideas and concepts) and creativity (comparing and contrasting, searching for what is unusual and unknown).

Despite its demands, qualitative data analysis is exciting, the necessary step to making previous efforts come to fruition. The sense of accomplishment—of producing new knowledge—can be immensely gratifying. Candid and thorough description of methods goes a long way toward making them accessible. And for those seeking mastery on their own, three words come to mind: practice, practice, practice.

EXERCISES

1. Instructors who have transcripts of qualitative interviews can share portions with their students and ask them to code the interviews. Students then meet in groups and discuss their codes and the reasoning behind them.

2. In the classroom, students focus on a common experience (such as their reasons for going to graduate school) and break up into small groups to discuss the topic and expand on it as much as possible. Next, refer to Bohm's nine organizing frames (2004) listed earlier in this chapter and choose one or two as a way to think about these experiences. Have each group discuss their "findings," stating whether they took the form of a typology, a sequencing, and so on.

3. Conduct and audiotape a brief (30-minute) interview with a colleague or classmate asking for his or her life story. Transcribe the videotape. How long did it take? Were there vocal utterances or other sounds during the interview that were meaningful but not captured in the words?

4. Read the excerpt in Box 7.4 and choose one of the following options to analyze it:
   Option A: Open code the text (using line numbers to show what segments go with what code). Discuss your codes with a colleague who has independently open-coded the same excerpt.
   Option B: Take a look at the list of NYSS codes below and assign them to the text as you see fit. (Use line numbers to identify the segments that go with each code.) Note the code abbreviation is followed by its full label or title and its definition in parentheses.

NE—refers to "neighborhood effects" (can be negative or positive, for example, drug temptations and crime dangers as well as feelings of support from neighbors and local community).

SA/U—"substance abuse/use talk" (when SP talks about drinking and illicit drug use).

SR/LP—"self-reflection/life perspectives" (reflections on one's life; includes what went right and what went wrong).

VIO/VIC—"violence and victimization" (episodes of being violently attacked or otherwise victimized; also includes perpetration of violence).

The following are suggested "answers" for Option B. Keep in mind that these are not hard and fast—coding decisions are rarely uniform. Your answers may vary somewhat, but the central meaning or idea of the code should be present in each excerpt so labeled.

NE (lines 2–9); SA/U (lines 2–11); VIO/VIC (lines 16–28); SR/LP (lines 9–14 and 27–32)

ADDITIONAL READINGS

Bernard, H. R. (Ed.). (2000). *Handbook of methods in cultural anthropology.* Walnut Creek, CA: Altamira Press.

Charmaz, C. (2006). *Constructing grounded theory: A practical guide through qualitative analysis.* Thousand Oaks, CA: Sage.

Coffey, A., & Atkinson, P. (1996). *Making sense of qualitative data.* Thousand Oaks, CA: Sage.

Dey, I. (1993). *Qualitative data analysis: A user-friendly guide for social scientists.* New York: Routledge.

Dey, I. (1999). *Grounding grounded theory: Guidelines for qualitative inquiry.* San Diego, CA: Academic Press.

Gee, J. P. (2005). *An introduction to discourse analysis: Theory and method.* London: Routledge.

Hsieh, H., & Shannon, S. E. (2005). Three approaches to qualitative content analysis. *Qualitative Health Research, 15*(9), 1277–1288.

Lofland, J., & Lofland, L. (1995). *Analyzing social settings: A guide to qualitative observation and analysis.* Belmont, CA: Wadsworth.

Miles, M. B., & Huberman, A. M. (1994). *Qualitative data analysis* (2nd ed.). Thousand Oaks, CA: Sage.

Moustakas, C. (1994). *Phenomenological research methods.* Thousand Oaks, CA: Sage.

Patton, M. Q. (2002). *Qualitative research and evaluation methods* (3rd ed.). Thousand Oaks, CA: Sage.

Riessman, C. (1993). *Narrative analysis.* Newbury Park, CA: Sage.

Smith, C., & Short, P. M. (2001). Integrating technology to improve the efficiency of qualitative data analysis: A note on methods. *Qualitative Sociology, 24*(3), 401–407.

Stake, R.E. (2005). *Multiple case study analysis.* Thousand Oaks, CA: Sage.

Strauss, A. L., & Corbin, J. (1990). *Basics of qualitative research: Grounded theory procedures and techniques.* Newbury Park, CA: Sage.

Tesch, R. (1990). *Qualitative research: Analysis types and software tools.* Bristol, PA: Falmer Press.

Thorne, S. (2000). Data analysis in qualitative research. *Evidence-Based Nursing, 3,* 68–70.

Weston, C., Gambell, T., Beauchamp, J., McAlpine, N., Wiseman, C., & Beauchamp, C. (2001). Analyzing interview data: The development and evolution of a coding system. *Qualitative Sociology, 24*(3), 381–400.

Yin, R. K. (2003). *Case study research: Design and methods* (3rd ed.). Thousand Oaks, CA: Sage.

QDA Software Resources

Readings

Drisko, J. W. (2004). Qualitative data analysis software. In D. K. Padgett (Ed.), *The qualitative research experience* (pp. 189–205). Belmont, CA: Thomson.

Fielding, N., & Lee, R. (Eds.). (1991). *Using computers in qualitative research.* Thousand Oaks, CA: Sage.

Gibbs, G. R. (2007). Media review: ATLAS/ti software to assist in the qualitative analysis of data. *Journal of Mixed Methods Research, 1*(1), 103–104.

Kelle, U. (1996). *Computer-aided qualitative data analysis: Theory, methods and practice.* Thousand Oaks, CA: Sage.

Miles, M. B., & Weitzman, E. A. (1994). Choosing computer programs for qualitative data analysis. In M. B. Miles & A. M. Huberman (Eds.), *Qualitative data analysis: An expanded sourcebook* (2nd ed.). Thousand Oaks, CA: Sage.

Richard, L. (1999). Data alive! The thinking behind NVivo. *Qualitative Health Research, 9*(3), 88–93.

Richards, T. J., & Richards, L. (1994). Using computers in qualitative research. In N. K. Denzin & Y. S. Lincoln (Eds.), *Handbook of qualitative research* (pp. 445–462). Thousand Oaks, CA: Sage.

Weitzman, E., & Miles, M. (1995). *Computer programs for qualitative data analysis: A software sourcebook.* Thousand Oaks, CA: Sage.

Software Information

An excellent independent resource (not supported by a software company) can found on the Web at: http://caqdas.soc.surrey.ac.uk

An overview of QDA software can be found at: http://www.quarc.de/overview.html

Products

General product information: www.scolari.com

ATLAS/ti: http://www.atlasti.com

CDC EZ Text (free download): http://www.cdc.gov/hiv/software/ez-text.htm

The Ethnograph: http://www.qualisresearch.com

HyperRESEARCH: http://www.researchware.com

NUD*IST: http://www.qsr.com.au

NVivo: http://www.qsr.com.au

8

Strategies for Rigor

O ne of the most vexing questions in qualitative research centers on defining what is "a good, valid, and/or trustworthy qualitative study" (Sandelowski & Barroso, 2002, p. 2). Glaser and Strauss addressed this question with a chapter on "The Credibility of Grounded Theory" in their seminal work (1967), Lincoln and Guba provided their own discussions of quality (1985), and others have followed suit (Inui & Frankel, 1991; Morrow, 2005).

Like their quantitative colleagues, qualitative researchers seek respect and legitimacy, their efforts deemed worthy of recognition and wider dissemination. Still, consensus has been elusive on how to achieve this hallowed state. Miles and Huberman (1994) wrote of this dilemma, "We have the unappealing double bind whereby qualitative studies can't be verified because researchers don't report on their methodology, and they don't report on their methodology because there are no established canons or conventions for doing so" (p. 244). Critics of qualitative methods are emboldened by this impasse. How, they ask, can one trust findings from studies where standards are shifting and subject to diverse interpretations?

The ever-changing landscape of qualitative inquiry virtually guarantees that opinions about rigor will differ, one of few areas of agreement being a rejection of traditional quantitative criteria (Altheide & Johnson, 1994; Whittemore, Chase, & Mandle, 2001). Pivotal to discussions about quality have been different ideas about the role of subjectivity, the stance of the researcher, and who has the authority and legitimacy to judge good versus bad qualitative research.

Considered anathema in quantitative research, subjectivity is the part of qualitative inquiry in which the insider perspective is valued (Ellis & Flaherty, 1992). Once distance and objectivity cease to be operating principles, the researcher's subjectivity is also acknowledged and, to varying degrees, managed through *reflexivity* or systematic self-awareness. Feminist researchers were among the first to break down traditional researcher-researched boundaries, promoting in their stead a close partnership (Fonow & Cook, 1991; Reinharz, 1992). Davies, for example, wrote that she once conducted an interview on the respondent's double bed where they talked about body image and femininity while drinking coffee (Davies & Dodd, 2002). Differing opinions about the optimal degree of researcher subjectivity are reflected in the sometimes contentious debates about what constitutes rigor. In this chapter, I will briefly review these debates, discuss some of the threats to trustworthiness in qualitative research, and end with recommendations for strategies to improve rigor.

Evaluating Qualitative Research: Debates About Standards and Strategies

Virtually all qualitative researchers reject the traditional quantitative standards of reliability and validity, but agreement usually stops there. To constructivists, a consensual set of criteria would raise the specter of intrusive oversight reminiscent of positivism. To pragmatists, standards of quality are needed but the struggle to identify and agree on them can be a difficult (although worthwhile) effort.

A critical distinction arises at this point: Evidence of quality emerging from a completed study is not the same as building into a study's design deliberate efforts to improve quality. *Evaluative standards* are applied to completed studies; *strategies for rigor* are pursued during the study. Not surprisingly, the debates have been most heated over what are (and are not) acceptable standards and the value of uniform criteria. Few (if any) qualitative researchers would argue against taking specific actions to ensure that a study is of high quality, but disagreements arise over what those actions should be.

Evaluative Criteria and External Standards

Lincoln and Guba (1985) were in the vanguard when it came to developing separate criteria applicable to qualitative methods (which they initially called naturalistic inquiry). Drawing direct parallels from quantitative research, they proposed *credibility, transferability, auditability,* and *confirmability* as alternatives to internal validity, external validity, reliability, and objectivity. Together, these connoted the *trustworthiness* of a qualitative study.

Credibility is the degree of fit between respondents' views and the researcher's description and interpretations. *Transferability* refers to generalizability, not of the sample (as in quantitative terms) but of the study's findings. External validity is not a priority because the focus is on subjective meanings and depth over breadth (Donmoyer, 1990). *Auditability* (or *dependability*) means that the study's procedures are documented and traceable—they need not lead to the same conclusions but should have a logic that makes sense to others. *Confirmability* is achieved by demonstrating that the study's findings were not imagined or concocted but, rather, firmly linked to the data.

Guba and Lincoln's criteria did not receive universal acclaim or adoption, but they served an important purpose in offering alternatives to replace ill-fitting quantitative standards. Later, additional terms were offered such as *truthfulness* (instead of validity), *consistency* (instead of reliability; Slevin & Sines, 2000), and *reflexive accounting* (Altheide & Johnson, 1994). Others have turned to literary standards of rhetoric and persuasiveness or to the humanities where elegance, consistency, and coherence are emblematic of quality (McCracken, 1988). According to Morrow (2005), an upsurge in the popularity of positive psychology could lead to the revival of Wolf's (1978) criterion of *social validity.*

In the Eye of the Beholder?

Running through the commentary on rigor is a thread of doubt concerning who is entitled to make evaluative judgments. An appraisal of quality implies having a sense of what is good and bad; this could range from the fully subjective to the application of predetermined criteria. Consider the distinction between art and science. Art critics are the guardians of aesthetic excellence, their taste and judgment intended to keep out the unworthy (Becker, 1996). Museum-goers or art buyers can make their own decisions about what is pleasing to them, but their access to the art and its market value are heavily influenced by a relatively small number of elite judges and appraisers.

The art-world distinction between expert criticism and individual consumer taste carries over to research, except that aesthetic value is replaced by the quality of knowledge generated. In research, the process of appraisal can happen in two ways. First, evaluative judgments are made by peers regarding whether a study is worthy of dissemination. Peer reviewers are the traditional gatekeepers of quality, their effectiveness dependent upon the existence of criteria that can be shared and understood. Second, a study is appraised by the wider audience of research consumers over time. Once published or otherwise disseminated, a study may disappear from view or it may have a profound impact. (The overwhelming majority of studies fall somewhere in the middle.) Many researchers consult the Social Science Citation Index to see how often their published works are cited by others and thus how they have fared in the marketplace of ideas.

Qualitative researchers also value the opinions of their study participants, referred to as *member checking* when conducted while the study is still in progress (Guba & Lincoln, 1989). Asking for input from one's respondents is empowering and it is also a form of validation by the "experts." Member checking can also be problematic—a topic to be addressed later in this chapter.

Questions of expertise and authority are not easily answered in qualitative inquiry—much depends on the study's disciplinary foundations, it immediate aims, and its intended audience. Appraisals can take place at various times and places and be carried out by differing constituencies—participants, peers, practitioners, and policymakers. Although far from perfect, professional peer review is preferable to relying on an aesthetic elite to make this determination.

The Meaning(s) of Generalizability in Qualitative Methods

Generalizability in qualitative research is subject to differing opinions. Constructivists have led the way in questioning its relevance, arguing that an emphasis on generalizing strips away the context that imbues a qualitative study with credibility. Ethnographies have been lauded for their intrinsic value—few would argue that Malinowski's (1922) classic studies of the Trobriand Islanders are deficient because they lack generalizability.

Much has changed in the world as well as in qualitative methods since the early 20th century. Qualitative studies can still have intrinsic interest, but this particular raison d'etre has lost ground as expectations have been ramped up in academic as well as applied settings where findings are expected to have wider ramifications.

Maxwell (2002) defined generalizability as having different levels of meaning, one referring to extending one's findings from the sample to others in the setting who were not included in the study and other levels referring to wider contexts for extrapolation. For example, can the findings from a study of youth gangs in Los Angeles be applied to local gang members who were not interviewed? What about youth gangs in Chicago, or gangs in general? It is reasonable to inquire about these outwardly radiating circles of inference—sometimes referred to as *transferability*—because localized knowledge without larger meaning has questionable value.

Turning the tables, it is fair to say that generalizability is often a problem in quantitative studies because many are unable to meet the assumptions of random sampling, normal distributions, and bounded sampling frames that underlie inferential statistics. Sophisticated sampling and polling techniques have had better success at this, but large-scale surveys constitute a very small part of the research agenda for researchers in the practicing professions. Most populations of interest, for example, abused women, substance abusers, immigrant families, and persons with AIDS, cannot be randomly sampled.

To their credit, the vast majority of qualitative researchers neither make extravagant claims nor try to "chew more than they bite off." Whether and how far qualitative findings can be extrapolated depends on what claims are being made. That qualitative studies do not share the inferential ambitions of quantitative research does not mean that they eschew applicability (or transferability) altogether. A qualitative evaluation of an HIV prevention program, for example, has far more impact if its results can be used to inform other HIV programs. Following Maxwell (2002), this applicability may extend to other programs in the same city, programs across the country, or HIV programs around the world. It all depends on the study's ultimate goals.

Qualitative researchers desire fame (if not fortune) as much as anyone and know full well that the farther their findings resonate the better. Findings can have transferability and resonance without being "generalizable" in a statistical sense based on how the sample was selected. The capacity for a study to stimulate thought, improve practices and policies, and incite further research is a metric of success agreeable to most anyone.

Defining Rigor in Qualitative Research

Dictionary definitions of rigor bring to mind strictness and rigidity (as in rigor mortis), but in qualitative research it is akin to self-discipline and vigilance about methods (Davies & Dodd, 2002). Thus, rigorous research is accountable even if it follows flexible guidelines.

It is often easier to talk about what the pursuit of rigor is not rather than what it is. Because qualitative research is not devoted to capturing a fixed reality, internal validity is an inappropriate goal. Nor are reliability and replication suitable criteria because they imply fidelity and repetitiveness rather than flexibility. Similarly, as discussed previously, generalizability is not a priority in qualitative studies, at least as it is understood in quantitative research (Donmoyer, 1990).

Guba and Lincoln's concept of *trustworthiness* (1985) comes closest to capturing this phenomenon of rigor and accountability in qualitative research. A trustworthy study is one that is carried out fairly and ethically and whose findings represent as closely as possible the experiences of the respondents (Steinmetz, 1991). Trustworthiness is not a matter of blind faith; it must be demonstrated.

Threats to the Trustworthiness of Qualitative Studies

Threats to trustworthiness in qualitative research fall under three broad headings: *reactivity, researcher biases,* and *respondent biases. Reactivity* refers to the potentially distorting effects of the researcher's presence on participants' beliefs and behaviors. Quantitative research uses distance and controlled conditions to protect against reactive effects, but the intensity and closeness of qualitative research relationships make this a constant concern.

Researcher biases emerge when observations and interpretations are clouded by preconceptions and personal opinions of the researcher. Thus, investigators may choose informants who are simpatico with their world view, may ask leading questions to get the answers they want, or may ignore data that do not support their conclusions. Emotional pitfalls can also contribute to researcher biases. The unwary qualitative researcher may veer too far in either direction—overly familiar or estranged—and thus lose her effectiveness.

Finally, there is the threat of *respondent bias*. This issue is a bit trickier to talk about because it implies that the respondents' subjectivity can sometimes be questioned. Respondents may withhold information and even lie to protect their privacy or to avoid revealing unpleasant truths. Inquiring about illegal drug use and sexual activity is likely to bring this about, but any topic can prompt a desire to conceal or mislead. At the other extreme, participants may try to be helpful and offer answers that they believe we (and/or the larger society) want to hear.

Rather than deliberately mislead, respondents may have faulty recall or interpret events in a way that conflicts with what the researcher "knows" from another source. What does one do, for example, if the agency records say a respondent relapsed and was in detox for a week and he does not mention this during the interview? Getting at the "truth" may be worth risking a confrontation but it is usually better left alone, at least until a more propitious time when rapport and trust have deepened. Focusing too literally on truthfulness can turn the researcher into an interrogator.

These three types of threats to trustworthiness—reactivity, researcher bias, and respondent bias—affect all studies, whether quantitative or qualitative. But the intensity of the research relationship and the pivotal role of the researcher-as-instrument place qualitative studies in greater jeopardy with regard to the first two. Fortunately, there are a number of ways to build confidence that the study's methods are, indeed, rigorous.

Strategies for Rigor in Qualitative Research

Imagine that you are writing a qualitative research proposal and must convince a dubious audience that your study will provide findings of value. Such a presumption of skepticism is not unfounded. Even when viewed favorably, qualitative methods are frequently misunderstood. I have encountered many "friendly doubts" voiced by colleagues who practice quantitative research and wonder about small sample sizes and obtuse methods.

One way to help alleviate doubts is to incorporate a section into the proposal explaining the rationale for using qualitative methods (Marshall & Rossman, 2006 ; Morse, 1994; Munhall, 1994). Although this may seem to be an unfair burden (quantitative researchers need not do this), it is an opportunity to educate the reader and convey a sense of mastery. When the topic is appropriate, this is an easy argument to make.

Defending one's choice of methods is not the same as taking specific actions over the course of the study. In the following paragraphs, I will discuss six strategies for enhancing rigor and trustworthiness in qualitative research. Although not all are relevant or feasible for any given study, they represent an array of techniques consonant with the aims of qualitative research. Culled from the literature on qualitative methods, each strategy addresses one or more of the threats to trustworthiness described earlier.

Prolonged Engagement

Arising from the early days of anthropological fieldwork, prolonged engagement has come to be a defining characteristic of qualitative studies regardless of where they take place. As shown in Figure 8.1, prolonged engagement helps to ameliorate reactivity and respondent bias. Thus, the effects of the researcher's presence dissipates considerably when she spends long periods of time in the field and becomes accepted (or at least tolerated).

Prolonged engagement makes withholding information or lying by respondents less likely. As Eliot Liebow (1993) noted in his study of home-less women, "lies do not really hold up well over long periods of time" (p. 321). A trusting relationship between researcher and respondents reduces the motivation as well as the opportunity for deception. An experienced researcher can often tell when respondents are shading the truth or lying, but it usually takes more than one encounter to do so. For interview-based studies, prolonged engagement may not be possible. (However, as discussed in Chapter 6, conducting more than one interview is a step toward accomplishing this goal.)

One drawback of prolonged engagement is the risk of researcher bias. Researchers can go too far in either direction—they can "go native" and lose all interpretive distance or experience the "familiarity breeds contempt" problem. Nevertheless, the advantages far outweigh the disadvantages.

Triangulation

The term triangulation, borrowed from navigational science and land surveying, originally referred to using two or more sources to achieve a comprehensive picture of a fixed point of reference. Four types of triangulation were outlined by Denzin (1978):

1. *Theory triangulation:* The use of multiple theories or perspectives to interpret a single set of data.

2. *Methodological triangulation:* The use of multiple methods to study a single topic.

3. *Observer triangulation:* The use of more than one observer in a single study to achieve inter-subjective agreement.

Threat to trustworthiness

Strategy	Reactivity	Researcher Bias	Respondent Bias
Prolonged Engagement	+	−	+
Triangulation	+	+	+
Peer Debriefing/ Support	0	+	0
Member Checking	+	+	+
Negative Case Analysis	0	+	0
Audit Trail	0	+	0

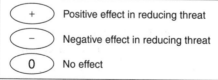

(+)   Positive effect in reducing threat

(−)   Negative effect in reducing threat

(0)   No effect

Figure 8.1   Strategies for Enhancing Rigor and Trustworthiness

4. *Data triangulation:* The use of more than one data source (interviews, archival materials, observational data, etc.).

Valerie Janesick (2000) added a fifth type of triangulation: *interdisciplinary triangulation,* or using more than one discipline in a single study.

A social work researcher, for example, might collaborate with a psychologist, sociologist, anthropologist, or historian.

From its earliest use solely as a means of confirmation, triangulation has expanded in definition to include *completeness* and the *enlargement of perspectives* (Flick, 2004). Triangulation by theory and triangulation by discipline are a good fit with this new definition. In contrast, triangulation by observation implies validation or corroboration. An example of this can be found in Snow and Anderson's (1991) study of the urban homeless in which they used multiple observers to enhance the reliability of their observations.

Triangulation by method most often refers to using qualitative and quantitative approaches in tandem. This can be done for confirmation or completeness depending on the study's purposes. Known as "mixed methods," this type of triangulation has many iterations and possible designs (more on this in Chapter 10).

Having multiple coders could be considered a form of *analytic triangulation*. As discussed in Chapter 7, independent coding and comparison are valuable safeguards against bias in data analysis. Although sometimes treated as calculable (as in coder agreement rates and Cohen's kappas), independent coding is better understood as triangulation for completeness rather than for accuracy.

Triangulation by data source—the most common type—is typically used for corroboration or confirmation. When data from field notes, interviews, and/or archival materials are convergent, one has greater confidence that the observations are trustworthy. As shown in Figure 8.1, triangulation helps to counter all of the threats to trustworthiness. Yet, inconsistencies and contradictions are common (Bloor, 1997). When this happens, one must decide whether to favor one source over another or view discrepancies as an opportunity for new insights. Riessman's study of divorcing partners (1990) found that men and women gave very different accounts of their marital problems. Their conflicting stories became a jumping-off point for an insightful discussion of the ways that men and women make sense of divorce. Just as negative case analysis may open the door to refining one's interpretations, disagreement among data sources may lead to new and expanded perspectives.

Peer Debriefing and Support

It is abundantly clear by now that carrying out a qualitative study can be hard on the researcher. Debriefing and support often go unheralded as a means of keeping the "instrument" sharp and true. Such support often comes from an academic advisor or a mentor, but one of the most effective means is peer debriefing and support (PDS; Padgett, Mathew, & Conte, 2004).

PDS groups can be a lifeline for qualitative researchers (Steinmetz, 1991). Members get and give feedback, offer fresh ideas, and simply recharge their batteries. Attending a PDS group meeting gives the researcher a chance to share the emotional ups and downs of fieldwork and data analysis. However, the role of these groups in qualitative research is not simply socioemotional. They are also a mechanism for keeping the researcher honest (Lincoln & Guba, 1985). To this end, PDS groups contribute to the rigor of a qualitative study by reducing researcher bias (see Figure 8.1).

PDS group members may present ideas or hunches for feedback. They may read portions of their coding memos along with relevant chunks of data to see if the codes make sense. Group members may read passages from their field notes and journals to get reactions from others about their observations and their ability to be self-reflexive. Some group members may become reciprocal co-coders. There are rarely any set rules as long as confidentiality is maintained and the focus stays on constructive criticism.

PDS groups work best when they meet on a regular schedule (monthly or bimonthly) and rotate leadership roles among group members. Their composition can be homogeneous by discipline or they may be multidisciplinary. Homogeneity allows members to draw on common interests, communicate in a common language, and reduce time spent negotiating disciplinary boundaries. Heterogeneous groups drawn from diverse fields can be intellectually invigorating. For qualitative researchers who do not have access to a PDS group, acquiring even one peer can be helpful.

In addition to their rigor-enhancing qualities, PDS groups perform instrumental functions. Group members give helpful hints, for example, remembering to take extra batteries to interviews. They share news of the latest in QDA software and tips on how to use it. They encourage each other to set and meet deadlines in completing the project. They might offer suggestions on how to negotiate with an unhappy partner feeling neglected by the researcher's time spent in the field. Where else can one go for this kind of help? Come to think of it, a quantitative researcher could also benefit from a PDS group!

PDS groups have a few risks. They can collectively veer off course, either by fostering a sort of "group think" atmosphere of enforced conformity or by becoming hypercritical and intolerant. New ideas are fragile creations and can get crushed even by well-meaning colleagues (Wolcott, 2001). When done properly, however, peer support is an invaluable addition to the repertoire of rigor enhancement.

Member Checking

As data collection segues into analysis and interpretation, qualitative researchers may seek verification of preliminary findings by going back to the study participants. *Member checking* (Lincoln & Guba, 1985) can be an important step in guarding against researcher bias. It also represents a logical extension of the close relationship between the researcher and the respondent. However, it also raises a number of questions, making it one of the more problematic of rigor strategies both in theory and practice.

Member checks shift authority toward participants, thereby properly challenging the status of researcher as infallible observer. Two problems emerge from this, however. First is the basic issue of what exactly members are checking. If asked to review their own interview transcript or personal case summary, participants' authority is rarely challenged. But member checks often refer to cross-case interpretation; it is reasonable to wonder if an individual respondent can (or should) be expected to pass judgment on findings involving many hours of immersion and synthesis. Second, member checking (as with triangulation) implies that a single "reality" can be captured (albeit this time by participants rather than by peers or others; Sandelowski, 1993). Thus, respondents may disagree with a study's findings not because the findings are inaccurate but because respondents have their own standpoints and realities, all of which may change over time (Rolfe, 2006).

The practicalities of member checking can be daunting. Some respondents do not want to be bothered or will hastily "rubber stamp" whatever is in front of them. Others may not wish to revisit their earlier statements and emotions. An agency director, for example, may have second thoughts about what she has told you about mismanagement by mid-level administrators. For some studies, logistical barriers or gatekeeper issues prevent going back—frail elders, recalcitrant adolescents, and busy executives come to mind. Member checks also fall into a gray area when it comes to human subjects committee oversight. Can they be considered part of the approved interview protocol and thus not require additional consent? What happens if and when member checking verges into new data collection? This is a fine line that cannot often be predicted or managed in advance.

As with triangulation, it is when member checking produces conflicting perspectives that problems arise. This can prompt revisiting the data and generating new interpretations, but the researcher may wish to stick to her viewpoint (and explain why she feels this way). Novice qualitative researchers should take heart: Non-negotiable disagreements during member checking are rare. In any event, the act of consulting with respondents—regardless of the outcome—affirms their dignity as research partners.

Negative Case Analysis

Although discussed in Chapter 7, the importance of negative case analysis bears repeating here as a strategy for rigor (see Figure 8.1). Just as the PDS group challenges a researcher to explore personal biases, negative case analysis puts the onus on the researcher to operate in a critically self-reflective way. As such, it enhances fairness (i.e., giving equitable attention to differing viewpoints and avoiding favoritism and lopsided interpretations; Morrow, 2005).

Auditing—Leaving a Decision Trail

Leaving an audit trail means adopting a spirit of openness and documenting each step taken in data collection and analysis (Lincoln & Guba, 1985). The components of an audit trail include raw data as well as memos noting decisions made during data collection, coding, and analysis. Although it is not intended for exact replication, an audit trail does enhance *reproducibility*, that is, another researcher is able to use it to verify the findings (Schwandt & Halpern, 1988). Imagine for the moment that your study is being audited by the research equivalent of the Internal Revenue Service—a Bureau of Rigor in Research (BRR). Could you defend your report and the decisions you made with actual documentation? Or do you find yourself shrugging helplessly and asking the auditor to have faith in your good intentions? The notion of a BRR may sound far-fetched, but similar scrutiny comes when submitting a manuscript for peer review or one's dissertation for committee review. In a sense, auditing is a meta-strategy for enhancing rigor because it documents that the other strategies—prolonged engagement, peer support, member checks, triangulation, and negative case analysis—have been used appropriately. Box 8.1 provides an exemplary article in which the authors (Morrow & Smith, 1995) successfully applied (and wrote about) all six strategies for rigor.

BOX 8.1   Strategies for Rigor in Action: An Exemplar Study

A sure sign of the maturity of qualitative methods is the growing number of rigorous *and* transparent studies in the published literature. One of these, a study of women who survived childhood sexual abuse, offers particularly thorough description. Conducted by Susan Morrow and Mary Lee Smith (1995), the study is one of few that used—and reported on—all six strategies for rigor. Here is what they tell the reader:

Prolonged Engagement—The authors report multiple interviews and more than 16 months of varied encounters with participants.

Peer Debriefing—Morrow met weekly with an interdisciplinary qualitative research collective where members shared feedback on their data collection and analysis procedures.

Triangulation—The authors used multiple sources of data including in-depth interviews with 11 survivors; videotapes of a 10-week focus group consisting of a subset of seven interviewees; documents such as participants' journals; and field notes and a self-reflective journal kept by Morrow.

Member Checking—At the conclusion of the focus group, all seven members were invited to become participant coresearchers; four accepted and received a brief introduction to grounded theory analysis. Over the course of a year, they worked with the authors on member checking, analyzing videotapes of their respective group sessions, and developing codes and categories.

Auditing—The authors kept detailed analytic and self-reflective memos to document their progress. Large poster boards with movable tags were used to arrange and rearrange codes and categories. The audit trail consisted of chronological narratives of their activities as well as a complete list of the 166 codes that formed the basis of the analyses.

Negative Case Analysis—Acknowledging a "human cognitive bias toward confirmation" (1995, p. 26), the authors report that they actively searched for disconfirming evidence, including consulting with participants on discrepant findings.

In addition, Morrow and Smith (1995) address *evidentiary adequacy* by reporting on the breadth of the data: 220 hours of audio- and video-taping, 165 hours of interviews, 24 hours of group sessions, and 25 hours of follow-up interactions over a period of 16 months. Data for analysis exceeded 2,000 pages of transcriptions, field notes, and documents.

Questions of Rigor in Community-Based Research

For most researchers, community-based participatory research (CBPR) requires adjusting to a new ethos of sharing control with community members (Israel et al., 2005; Minkler & Wallerstein, 2003). This can introduce a potential loss of methodological rigor (Allison & Rootman, 1996). Community members rarely have knowledge of research methods or the inclination to accept all of the demands incurred by research protocols. Moreover, the fact that CBPR prioritizes community empowerment can conflict with the researcher's orientation to drawing conclusions that are empirically based (regardless of whether they conform to advocacy goals).

Enthusiasm for social change and community development can produce rhetoric and emotion that threaten a study's trustworthiness. This tension between rigor and relevance, found in all research, is front and center in CBPR. Although researchers' career advancement depends on rigor far more than relevance, community members understandably may not share this point of view. Dichotomous thinking should be avoided here. Too often viewed as a zero-sum game—more community involvement equals less scientific rigor—CBPR is more appropriately viewed as a balancing act than an "either-or" proposition.

CBPR is not inherently qualitative, but many of its proponents feel comfortable with qualitative (or mixed) methods as the optimal means of working in community contexts. All six of the strategies for rigor can be applied in qualitative CBPR and some, for example, member checks, hew closely to its values. In contrast, quantitative researchers have much more difficulty achieving the varied forms of reliability and validity while in the field.

Although ultimate resolution of the rigor versus relevance balancing act depends on the particular circumstances of a study, a few recommendations can be made. First, rigor in CBPR takes dedication, time, and patience. Community members have a right to know and question the study's methods, if not actively participate in their development and implementation. If and when community members seek to veto some aspect of the proposed study, the researcher must find a way to either dissuade them respectfully or accede to their wishes and try another route. Second, the most demanding and distancing research designs are a difficult fit with CBPR, especially in the early stages when community buy-in is critical. Thus, an experimental trial to test an innovative program is far more likely to be successful if implemented after a period of community involvement and collaboration. Finally, threats to the rigor of a CBPR study are greatest when time is short and results are needed quickly. Given the need for flexibility and options, researchers in a hurry should probably not go the CBPR route. As discussed in Chapter 2, rapid assessment procedures (RAPs) have been developed to meet the needs of CBPR as well as those of more traditional community-development programs. Rigorous RAPs are not impossible achievements, but the onus on the researcher is that much greater.

Strategies for Rigor in Differing Qualitative Approaches

Some types of rigor strategies are a better fit than others, depending on the type of qualitative approach being used. Ethnographic research depends first and foremost on prolonged engagement, but it obviously does not preclude using the other strategies. Case study and grounded theory analyses can also benefit from using any of the six strategies, with data triangulation leading the way in case studies and negative case analysis historically allied with grounded theory. A reliance upon texts among narrative approaches makes data triangulation unlikely (given the absence of need for alternative sources of data) and negative case analysis inappropriate (since such approaches are not intended to produce explanation), but member checking plausible. In phenomenological approaches, peer debriefing and auditing are considered potentially contaminating influences that interfere with the search for deep structures of meaning.

Guidelines for Appraising the Quality of a Study: Adequacy Is Key

Appraising the quality of a study goes beyond documenting which strategies for rigor will be (or were) pursued and how. As shown in Box 8.2, skeptical reviewers, whether one's colleagues or "outside" experts, often pose questions that the qualitative researcher would be wise to anticipate. Over the years, a number of checklists for quality have emerged to guide discerning readers (Inui & Frankel, 1991; Patton, 2002; Sandelowski & Barroso, 2002). Cutting across these guidelines are a few central concerns: Are the findings grounded in the data? How were the inevitable intrusions of bias addressed? Were decisions about sampling and analysis reasonable and logical? How systematic and auditable were the study's procedures? Are the interpretations strong and insightful?

BOX 8.2   Addressing Questions From Skeptical Reviewers

Experienced qualitative researchers are accustomed to answering questions from colleagues, many well-meaning but nonetheless persistent in their skepticism. The following are some common queries. The more you can anticipate these, the better prepared you will be to explain not only your study but also all qualitative studies.

- "How can this study be generalizable with that sample size?"
- "Where are your hypotheses?"
- "Why isn't this more objective?"
- "Will sample attrition be a problem with so few in the study?"
- "Why can't you be more forthcoming about what your findings will look like in advance?"
- "How is this different from journalism?"

Erickson (1986) summed it up as *adequacy*—of data richness, data variety, disconfirming evidence, and interpretations. Existing as a kind of transcendent criteria, adequacy is not about quantity but, rather, sufficiency. Its achievement is rarely predictable in advance but is enhanced considerably by taking the actions described in this chapter.

The "before and after" distinction is important here. Although qualitative researchers might include strategies for rigor in their description of methods before the study begins, equally if not more important is the documentation of what actually transpired in the study. Unlike quantitative studies where "what you see is what you get," qualitative studies entail an obligation to report what happened, why, and how. Box 8.3 features brief descriptions of studies in which the authors did just this.

Summary and Concluding Thoughts

This chapter has revolved around a few main points: 1) methodological rigor and evaluative standards are needed in qualitative research; 2) evidence of quality emerging from a completed study is not the same as building into a study's design deliberate efforts to improve quality; 3) achieving rigor can be enhanced by using one or more of six strategies developed explicitly for qualitative studies; and 4) a study's trustworthiness depends on fairness and ethical conduct as well as rigor. Peer

BOX 8.3   Some Examples of Methodological Transparency

What actually takes place during a study may be more rigorous than its description implies. Space limitations and confusion over what to include or exclude often lead researchers to shortchange their methods descriptions. Some have published articles devoted to explicating their methods so that others can learn from their experiences. A few journals feature methodological articles, including *Qualitative Social Work, Qualitative Health Research,* and the *International Journal of Qualitative Methods.* The following are a few concrete examples of transparency in methods descriptions.

- Beeman (1995) gave an account of how she addressed rigor in her study of social support and child neglect among low-income African American mothers. She described how steps in the data analysis were documented in a journal and in memo form to external auditors so that the reasoning behind the codes could be assessed and potential biases uncovered and addressed.
- Chiovitti and Piran (2003) used their grounded theory study of psychiatric ward nurses to illustrate the step-by-step process of generating a theory, checking it with study participants, and establishing auditability and transferability.
- Correll (1995) carried out an ethnographic study of an online "lesbian cafe" and candidly discussed the challenges of doing research in cyberspace, including what "observation" means, the ethical challenges of maintaining anonymity in an open-access site, and the creative use of emoticons and other text notes unfamiliar in traditional data analyses.
- Bowen (2006) wrote of the challenges of using grounded theory in a community-based anti-poverty project in Jamaica. Following a constructivist paradigm, he applied sensitizing concepts such as empowerment and social capital while developing a grounded theory of stakeholder collaboration in development work. Bowen used hindsight to reflect on his study and the ways in which *a priori* concepts blended with emergent findings.

reviews serve the primary gatekeeping function in determining rigor and trustworthiness. By implication, such reviews are dependent on a set of criteria that serve as guideposts rather than stringent prescriptions. That there is no consensus on what these criteria should be constitutes an ongoing conundrum for qualitative researchers.

By now, the reader may be wondering if any stone has been left unturned in the search for rigor. On the plus side, this pursuit is a decidedly "low-tech" enterprise, requiring neither technical savvy nor fancy software (nor footwork). On the challenging side, there can be difficulties along the way. Setting up peer debriefing groups can tax the resources of a researcher, school, or department. The time commitment necessary for prolonged engagement requires shifting one's life around to support absences from work and home. Miles and Huberman (1994) estimate a 20% increase in time expenditures imposed by documentation for an audit trail. Finally, member checking and triangulation can bring out discrepancies and interpretive conflicts that are not easily resolved.

Despite these complicating factors and demands, rigor is essential to all forms of empirical research, whether quantitative or qualitative. However the evaluative standards are defined and applied, it is difficult to justify a nonrigorous study as having relevance.

EXERCISES

1. This can be done alone or in a group. Select and read a qualitative study from one of the following journals: Qualitative Health Research, Qualitative Social Work, or Qualitative Sociology. Note what (if any) strategies for rigor the authors mention in discussing their methods and findings.

2. Read the article titled "Reading Qualitative Studies" by Sandelowski and Barroso (available online in the *International Journal of Qualitative Methods*, 1(1), 2002, http://www.ualberta.ca/~iiqm/backissues/1_1Final/1_1toc.html). Following their guidelines, choose a published study or a dissertation and critique it. What are some of the topics most often neglected by authors?

3. Develop an idea for a study you would like to conduct in the future. Which strategies for rigor would be most appropriate?

4. In a group, discuss the three threats to trustworthiness (reactivity, researcher bias, and respondent bias) and how they differ in quantitative versus qualitative studies. Are quantitative studies more vulnerable to some threats than others? What about qualitative studies?

ADDITIONAL READINGS

Altheide, D. L., & Johnson, J. M. (1994). Criteria for assessing interpretive validity in qualitative research. In N. K. Denzin & Y. S. Lincoln (Eds.), *Handbook of qualitative research* (pp. 485–499). Thousand Oaks, CA: Sage.

Davies, D., & Dodd, J. (2002). Qualitative research and the question of rigor. *Qualitative Health Research, 12*(2), 279–289.

Kidd, P. S., & Parshall, M. B. (2000). Getting the focus and the group: Enhancing analytical rigor in focus group research. *Qualitative Health Research, 10*(3), 293–308.

LeCompte, M. D., & Goetz, J. P. (1984). Problems of reliability and validity in ethnographic research. *Review of Educational Research, 52*, 31–60.

Leininger, M. (1994). Evaluation criteria and critique of qualitative research studies. In J. M. Morse (Ed.), *Critical issues in qualitative research methods* (pp. 95–115). Thousand Oaks, CA: Sage.

Lincoln, Y. S. (1995). Emerging criteria for quality in qualitative and interpretative research. *Qualitative Inquiry, 1*(3), 275–289.

Marshall, C. (1990). Goodness criteria: Are they objective or judgment calls? In E. G. Guba (Ed.), *The paradigm dialog* (pp. 188–197). Newbury Park, CA: Sage.

Maxwell, J. A. (1992). Understanding and validity in qualitative research. *Harvard Educational Review, 62*(3), 279–300.

Morrow, S. L. (2005). Quality and trustworthiness in qualitative research in counseling psychology. *Journal of Counseling Psychology, 52*, 250–260.

Morse, J. M., Barrett, M., Mayan, M., Olsen, K., & Spiers, S. (2002). Verification strategies for establishing reliability and validity in qualitative research. *International Journal of Qualitative Methods 1*, Article 2.

Sandelowski, M. (1993). Rigor or rigor mortis: The problem of rigor in qualitative research revisited. *Advances in Nursing Science, 6*, 1–8.

Sandelowski, M., & Barroso, J. (2002). Reading qualitative studies. *International Journal of Qualitative Methods, 1* (1), Article 5.

Seale C. (2002). Quality issues in qualitative inquiry. *Qualitative Social Work, 1*(1), 97–110.

Whittemore, R., Chase, S. K., & Mandle, C. (2001). Validity in qualitative research. *Qualitative Health Research, 11*(4), 522–527

9

Telling the Story

Writing Up the Qualitative Study

Qualitative researchers who have a talent for writing are fortunate souls. For most, however, writing up a qualitative study takes a good deal of effort—it is a craft to be learned and honed over time. Susser (1997) drew an interesting distinction between "authoring" and "writing" when discussing authorship in the burgeoning research literature. Many journal articles and books are authored (and coauthored), but few of the authors actually write. Writing is not merely reporting, it requires systematic thought and creativity. To illustrate this point, consider how most quantitative reports look. Full of tables and graphs, their readability takes second place to numerical precision. The terminology of statistical analyses, embedded within a standardized reporting format, produces a writing style that informs but rarely captivates.

There are advantages to quantitative reporting. First, one need only follow the standard rules and conventions (of which there are thousands of examples in journals and elsewhere). Thus, producing a quantitative report is possible for someone who is not able to write well. Second, peer reviews and revising for publication follow consensual standards and leave less room for arbitrariness, editorial whims, and outright confusion.

If the act of writing up quantitative research is pro forma and somewhat anticlimactic (a well-conducted study can usually survive a poor write-up), it is the climactic event in qualitative research (Padgett, 2004b). Studies are "vast conversations with dispersed others" (Flaherty, 2002, p. 510) and qualitative researchers have an obligation to ensure the conversation is lively and thought-provoking.

The ideal scenario in writing up a qualitative study involves maintaining a clear alignment between one's choice of method and the explicit terminology used to describe the study and its procedures. (If invoked, epistemology should also be compatible.) Sandelowksi and Barroso (2003) examined a number of qualitative studies and found this ideal was rarely attained. Instead, authors obscured the diversity of their approaches through generic description, many relying on what appeared to be variations of content analysis. For studies that offered specifics, there was frequently a disconnect between self-labeling and reality, for example, a study that was ostensibly phenomenological used a watered-down version of grounded theory.

Two rather obvious suggestions can help you prepare for writing. First, read as many good qualitative studies as possible. Exemplary articles have been cited throughout this book, and several suggestions for full-length monographs are listed at the end of this chapter. Reading and absorbing both the form and substance of qualitative studies will expose you to the many options available for the study write-up and help you to develop your own style. Second, begin writing early and build in plenty of time for editing and polishing your writing. To employ a sports analogy, if reading is like being a spectator, writing is like being a player (Lofland & Lofland, 1995). It is better to write even when you do not feel like it than to wait for a lightning bolt of inspiration to strike (Wolcott, 2001). Start with an outline and flesh it out as you go. Difficulties in writing are less often due to "writer's block" than to "idea block" (Lofland & Lofland, 1995, p. 205). The self-selection process leading individuals toward qualitative research tends to favor creative, abstract thinkers. The challenge is to keep those ideas and abstractions firmly grounded in the data.

Deciding on an Approach

Many qualitative researchers have shared their own strategies for writing, including Gilgun (2005), Richardson (2000), van Manen (2006), Weiss (1994), and Wolcott (2001). In reviewing their works and through my own writing experience, I have identified five key decisions facing the qualitative researcher approaching the write-up phase. These are (1) the audience for the study, (2) whether the study is diachronic or synchronic, (3) the researcher's role in the report, (4) whether and how to use numbers, and (5) coauthorship.

Targeting the Audience

Qualitative reports have the potential to reach broad audiences with their accessible, almost literary content. Some of the best qualitative studies began as research reports but crossed over to gain wide and lasting public appeal. Eliot Liebow's *Talley's Corner* (1967) is a case in point—his portrayal of the daily lives of African American men in a Washington, DC, neighborhood continues to captivate readers with its scholarly yet readable format.

Qualitative studies may be written up for a number of purposes and audiences. For academic audiences—doctoral dissertation committees, journal editors, and conference attendees—the write-up is pitched at a high level to ensure that new knowledge is produced, not merely described. Evaluative reports are usually written in more pragmatic language (less academic-speak) and are structured to provide concrete suggestions for improving policies and practices. When a study is commissioned and funded, the sponsoring organization usually wants the researcher to assess problems and recommend solutions. As a target audience, the sponsor may also try to influence how the study is written. It is always a good idea to consult with key stakeholders, but the researcher must assume ultimate responsibility for producing a report that is as balanced and accurate as possible.

The widest possible audience—the general public—is one that some researchers scorn and others long for. The benefits of reaching a wider audience lie in providing an accessible entrée to rigorous research. (The royalties on sales do not hurt either.) Problems can arise when a researcher is tempted to abbreviate, dilute, or distort findings to make them marketable, but otherwise this outlet for dissemination can be powerfully influential. Several of the monographs listed at the end of this chapter have enjoyed wide distribution and have had such an impact.

Diachronic Versus Synchronic Reports

A fundamental decision centers on the element of time. How the writer chooses to deal with "time" depends on the study's goals and design.

This, in turn, structures the presentation of the findings (Weiss, 1994). A *diachronic report* tells a story through time. The most obvious example of this is life history, but the study may also pivot around a single event. Examples include the birth of a child, a cancer diagnosis, or the aftermath of a natural disaster. Here, the thrust of the report is on change over time. In contrast, *synchronic reports* collapse months or years of study into a static (but rich) description and interpretation.

The distinction between synchronic and diachronic is not always clear-cut. In their study of hospital-based physicians and social workers, Mizrahi and Abramson (1994) developed a typology to explain how health professionals approached collaboration with one another—traditional, transitional, and transformational. This typology represented a continuum of accommodation (or resistance) to social workers' autonomy in their collaborative roles with physicians. Taken at face value, this typology is an informative but static description of the working relationships of physicians and social workers. However, Mizrahi and Abramson took a step toward diachronic reporting by pointing out the dynamic nature of these collaborative styles, how physicians and social workers can adopt differing approaches over time in response to new exigencies.

Weiss (1994) suggests that diachronic reports have the advantage of a built-in storyline. This is true as far as it goes, but both diachronic and synchronic reports run the risk of *under-conceptualization*. This rather unwieldy term describes a study that is more impressionistic than idea-driven (i.e., the absence of a conceptual framework renders the study unconnected to the world of ideas).

The Researcher's Role in the Report

The de facto stance for a qualitative researcher up to the 1970s was largely that of an omniscient but invisible outsider. Characterized as "Realist Tales" by Van Maanen (1988), these earlier studies took scant notice of the researcher's role—to use first-person pronouns was an unthinkable breach of etiquette. Authors of Realist Tales spent many private hours regaling colleagues and students with stories of their experiences in the field but then edited such stories out of the final report as unseemly self-indulgence (Van Maanen, 1988).

The rise of constructivism and postmodernism directly challenged this state of affairs. To critics, the human emotions stirred by fieldwork were squeezed out of the report by a "Doctrine of Immaculate Perception" (Van Maanen, 1988, p. 73) that obscured the vividness and ambiguity of qualitative research. In the meantime, academic and general audiences have come to accept the use of first-person pronouns (at least in qualitative studies). In some quarters, the pendulum has swung all the way to the researcher as the focus of interest with auto-ethnographies, memoirs, and other "Confessional Tales" (Van Maanen, 1988) taking center stage.

It is abundantly clear that the researcher is a key actor in the qualitative study and should not be hidden or edited out of the final report. What remains open to question is how prominently the researcher's role should be featured. If taken too far, reflexivity produces tedious self-absorption. However, much of one's experience in the field—failures as well as successes—can be pertinent to the credibility of the study.

The decision about how much personal information and experience to include in the final report is influenced not only by one's epistemological stance but also by the intended audience and the outlet for the report's dissemination. Whereas some audiences might appreciate full reflexivity, practitioners and policymakers are likely to find it self-indulgent and distracting. The form reflexivity takes can range from brief mention of one's stance at the report's outset to a thorough description of how the researcher entered the field, interacted with participants, and grappled with potential intrusions of bias. The latter, often drawn from the personal journal or diary kept during the study, situates the author as an active participant in the study.

Journal articles tend to be less evidently self-reflexive in part due to the shortage of space and the need to give the methods and findings their full due. Full-length reports (e.g., dissertations and books) may have the researcher's role threaded throughout or they may place it in a separate section or appendix. A candid and lengthy appendix can be found in Mitch Duneier's book *Sidewalk* (1999), in which he discusses the origin and evolution of his study of homeless men in Greenwich Village, New York. Too much emphasis on confessionalism can give rise to "more reflexive than thou" positions (Marcus, 1994, p. 568) that lead to intellectual dead ends rather than accumulation of new knowledge. In their write-ups, most qualitative researchers give the lion's share of space to the data and findings without trying to hide their role. Harking back to the previous chapter, including a section on strategies for rigor used during the study is an excellent vehicle for addressing the latter.

Using Numbers in the Report

Perhaps less weighty is the decision about whether and how to use numbers in writing the final report. Few qualitative studies give much credence to numbers, but some findings can be amenable to quantifying.

In a study of care-giving daughters and their elderly mothers, Walker and Allen (1991) identified three relationship types (intrinsic, ambivalent, and conflicted) and the percent of mother–daughter pairs for each type (45%, 34%, and 21%, respectively). Providing these proportional indices helps the reader to understand how the types were distributed among the mother–daughter pairs who were studied.

As discussed in Chapter 7, a few caveats pertain to using numbers in qualitative studies. First, given nonrepresentative and small sample sizes, numerical findings can give a false impression of precision where none exists. Sometimes, using "most" or "some" is sufficient (Weiss 1994). Thus, "most of the women in the study expressed satisfaction with their medical care" sounds better than "80% were satisfied with their medical care" when "80%" refers to 8 out of 10 women and "satisfaction with medical care" was not measured or calibrated. At the same time, numbers are sometimes useful when presenting findings that are clear-cut, for example, "10 agency directors (40% of those who participated in the study) lost their jobs during the course of the study."

Another caveat: Many important findings in qualitative studies were not routinely elicited but emerged serendipitously and voluntarily. As such, any count of the number of respondents who gave certain information is probably an undercount and is thus misleading for those who assume it is a "true" measure of frequency. These caveats do not mean that all numerical indicators should be banned from qualitative reports—at a minimum demographic characteristics usually get reported in frequencies and percents. They do, however, draw attention to the risks of using numbers.

Coauthorship in Qualitative Studies

Qualitative research has a long tradition of solo work. A trend toward team-work, however, has made coauthorship a common endeavor (with the obvious exception of doctoral dissertations). This trend has been especially evident in professions such as social work and nursing where research collaboration was already a common byproduct of working in multidisciplinary settings.

Qualitative collaborations present challenges that quantitative researchers do not normally encounter. They are multifaceted and interwoven—almost every phase informing and being informed by every other. Viewed as a spiral or series of feedback loops, qualitative designs unfold in ways that are not always predictable. Skill sets need to overlap rather than complement one another (e.g., during co-coding). This seamless quality carries over into writing the report. In contrast, quantitative studies and reports can usually be broken down into discrete tasks and assigned to team members according to their role on the project and their individual strengths.

Deciding on authorship in any type of study can be tricky. For example, do the most senior members of the team have first dibs on authorship (especially the rank of first author)? Or should authorial rank be strictly a matter of who did what and how much? Research and professional ethics dictate that the first author has done the most work, including writing the study report. Coauthorship down the line is apportioned according to relative contribution. To deal with the inevitable confusion, many journals publish guidelines and require coauthors to sign off on what they did to earn their place in the hierarchy.

The egalitarian ethos of qualitative inquiry affects the teamwork, making leadership roles less foreordained and subverting attempts to impose decisions based on seniority alone. Fellow team members on the NYSS would probably agree that my "lone ethnographer" training often gets in the way and leads me to monopolize some analyses and write-ups. (Being graduate students, their relative inexperience has made this a little less problematic.) At the same time, each NYSS team member has made strong contributions to the study and has an open invitation to take the lead on a particular area of analysis and write-up of interest to them (an invitation that was accepted and successfully carried out). It is a testimony to their excellent skills that the data are rich enough to allow multiple analyses and write-ups to be done.

The conundrums of coauthorship in qualitative inquiry will not soon or easily go away. Meanwhile, single-authored works are in no danger of disappearing. Dissertations alone will ensure their continuation.

Organizing the Report—Key Components

The amount of creative latitude in writing up a qualitative report depends on its purpose and intended audience. Still, most qualitative reports roughly follow the same format as quantitative ones, as described here:

1. *Background and Theoretical Context.* Here, the author describes the phenomenon of interest including a rationale for the study and its use of qualitative methods. The literature review that follows places the study

within a theoretical and empirical context. The review may separately cover qualitative studies to further situate the study and its potential contribution. Theoretical influences and conceptual frameworks are presented along with the requisite caveat that they are not driving (or confining) the study. This section is a sustained argument explaining the study. Arguing does not mean constant criticism of other studies (Silverman, 2006). Critiquing the methods and conclusions of empirical work is fair game, but the argument and rationale is more about gaps in knowledge than errors or incompetence in previous research. This section usually ends with an overarching study question or two and the study's research questions.

2. *Methods.* The first part introduces the reader to the specific method (grounded theory, ethnography, narrative analysis, etc.) with liberal citations of methodologists' published work in the area. The second part gives a detailed description of how the study's goals were accomplished (which often diverges from the original proposal or plan). Here, the author describes the hows, whens, and whys of the study: its site and sample selection; entering the field and establishing rapport; data-collection procedures; storing and managing data; data analyses; human subjects and ethical considerations; and strategies used to enhance rigor. The author should be candid about the limitations of the study and his or her role as the instrument of data collection and analysis.

3. *Findings.* This section goes to the heart of the matter. Qualitative researchers may use a variety of means to report findings, ranging from graphic displays such as charts, matrices, and maps to lists or schemas of codes and themes (usually illustrated by selected quotes from the transcripts). They may also present case vignettes or typologies to illustrate major categories or themes. There are many choices available; the only requirement is that the findings are understandable and rigorous.

4. *Conclusions and Recommendations.* Highlights of the study bear repeating here to remind the reader of the study's goals, to summarize how these goals were achieved, and to candidly discuss the study's limitations. The implications of the findings are also important. How do they advance knowledge? What are their applications to practice and policy? Finally, what are suggested directions for future research?

Here are a few additional pointers: 1) make clear distinctions between content under these four sections, for example, do not introduce new findings in the conclusion section; 2) use headings and subheadings to structure the report and to serve as signposts leading the way; 3) cite your sources liberally and often—it is far better to over-cite than to risk even the appearance of plagiarism; 4) carefully choose your title (see Box 9.1 for some suggested guidelines); and 5) aim for maximum transparency. As discussed in Chapter 7, transparency and thoroughness in describing one's methods and findings enhance confidence in the study and help with the larger and much-needed task of demystifying qualitative research.

Qualitative Reports Across the Diverse Approaches

Each of the qualitative approaches may have its own writing conventions that represent variations on this format previously described, but the overwhelming majority of qualitative reports rely on narrative with the option of including tables, figures, photographs, and other illustrative graphics. Grounded theory reports typically follow the architecture of the theory or conceptual framework that emerged from the analyses. Thus, categories or themes are listed along with selected quotes to illustrate them. In some instances, the theoretical schema is diagrammed to visually depict the categories, using arrows to indicate the relationships between them. Charmaz wisely recommends that grounded theorists do not shy away from ambiguities and uncertainties in the report (2006).

Phenomenological reports tend to be prestructured based on their analytic structure. Colaizzi (1978) suggests including tables of themes and significant statements, a format that Beck (1993) followed in her phenomenological study of postpartum depression. Moustakas (1994) gives a detailed set of guidelines for phenomenological reports, including recommending an autobiographical account at the beginning to bracket the researcher. The *Journal of Phenomenological Psychology* contains many examples of this approach.

Ethnographic studies have a tradition of book-length reports, their length deemed necessary to capture the scope of the inquiry. Although many have an engaging storytelling quality, others tend toward the encyclopedic in their amassing of details about cultural beliefs and practices. Early ethnographies had missing or severely truncated sections on methods, but much has changed over the past 20 years as prominent researchers have stepped forward to offer suggestions (LeCompte & Schensul, 1999; Tedlock, 2000).

BOX 9.1   Choosing the Right Title

Ideally, the study's title is catchy but not frivolous. Anthropologists have a long tradition of two-part titles, one phrase seriously descriptive and the other intended for broader appeal. Here is a partial listing of article titles from the NYSS:

- *In Their Own Words: Trauma and Substance Abuse in the Lives of Formerly Homeless Women with Serious Mental Illness*
- *Disappearing Acts: The Social Networks of Homeless Individuals with Co-occurring Disorders*
- *There's No Place Like (a) Home: Ontological Security in the Third Decade of the "Homelessness Crisis" in the United States*
- *Engagement and Retention in Care Among Formerly Homeless Adults with Serious Mental illness: Voices from the Margins*

The phrases such as "in their own words" and "voices from the margins" indicated that the study was qualitative (to readers in the predominantly quantitative journals to which they were submitted for publication). Putting the term "qualitative" in the title and/or in the study's key words (we chose to do the latter) is important—otherwise it will never be retrievable through database searches for qualitative studies (a problem that many scholars of knowledge dissemination bemoan). We were able to use wordplay, for example, "there's no place like (a) home" and "disappearing acts," to emphasize two critical points being made in the studies. Note the use of irony and sarcasm in putting the phrase "homelessness crisis" in quotations after noting its 30-year (and counting) duration in the title. Ending this title with "in the United States" was a nod to the international focus of the journal to which it was submitted (*Social Science & Medicine,* one of my personal favorites).

Some authors like to use participant quotes in their titles. Boeri's study titled "Hell I'm an Addict, but I Ain't no Junkie": An Ethnographic Analysis of Aging Heroin Users" (2004) is one example of an *in vivo* inspired title (albeit a rather long one). Of course, one does not need a snappy phrase every time. Some journals prefer more subdued titles and some studies are better suited to catchiness than others.

Narrative approaches often use the *zoom in/zoom out technique* (Czarniawska, 2004) of spotlighting portions of annotated texts and then interpreting their meaning according to the study's specific method (narrative analysis, conversational analysis, or discourse analysis). Published examples of narrative reports show how the authors alternate interpretation with annotated excerpts (Hyden & Overlien, 2004; Riessman, 1993; Sands, 2004). By way of contrast, grounded theory and phenomenological reports place greater emphasis on interpretive structures and use illustrative excerpts.

Case studies may vary considerably in format depending on their design (single versus multiple case) and aims. Stake (2005) describes the basics of a case study report including a description of the study's purpose (especially the significance of the case or cases), methods, and setting. Because many case studies are used for evaluative purposes or to critically analyze an issue, their write-ups typically include vignettes, quotes, and graphic displays to illustrate the main points and prevent the reader from getting lost in the minutiae of the case.

Balancing Description and Interpretation

The reader has probably surmised by now that a prime source of variation in qualitative reports is how they balance description versus interpretation. Box 9.2 describes a typology of studies based on how they address this "balancing" act. Although "analytic excess" (Lofland, 2002, p. 158) robs the report of the rich detail on which it is based, too little analysis severely reduces its impact. Concerned about the latter, anthropologist Clifford Geertz (1973) introduced the term *thick description* to invigorate ethnographic interpretation. The phrase has since been widely invoked (and sometimes misunderstood as "more description" rather than "more insightful interpretation"). Whereas description is localized, interpretation is abstraction, conceptualization, and meaning-making. In interpretation, theoretical lenses can be (re)introduced to refract the data and findings.

Description plays a key role in qualitative reports, especially when the topic is new and unfamiliar. Of course, the decision about what to describe (and how to describe it) can be seen as a tacit form of interpretation. The anthropologist Margaret Mead, for example, was accused of selectively reporting what she "saw" while in Samoa in order to fit her preconceived notions about free-wheeling adolescent sexuality (1928).

Ethnographies tend to blend description with interpretation in a seamless manner, but most qualitative reports present the interpretive structure of the findings interspersed with excerpts of raw data. Creswell, for example, discusses ratios of 70/30 or 60/40 favoring description (2007). Lofland (2002) settles on roughly the same balance. For several exemplars of presentational style followed by behind-the-scenes accounts of the studies, I refer the reader to a compendium of qualitative studies in social work research (Padgett, 2004a), including the following: ethnography (Floersch), case study (Drisko), narrative (Hyden & Overlien; Sands), grounded theory (Oktay), mixed methods (Gioia), and evaluation (Barr).

Writing Stance and Style

Rhetorical Devices Suited to Qualitative Studies

Successful qualitative reports give readers a new perspective and challenge them to think differently. A favorite approach is to debunk or refute cherished notions such as stereotypes and outdated beliefs. Qualitative researchers are justifiably proud of their record of probing beneath the carefully constructed facade and coming up with findings that challenge the status quo. Carol Stack's (1974) study of African American women living in the projects struck home because she chronicled the resilience and resourcefulness of these women. This portrait directly countered the "black family as pathology" viewpoint among policymakers during the 1960s (and unfortunately continuing today). Similarly, Eric Klinenberg's *Heat Wave* (2002) reports on Chicago's disastrous summer of 1995 as a slow-motion nightmare of public policy failures resulting in the deaths of 700 of the city's most vulnerable and isolated citizens.

Some qualitative researchers embrace subtle (and not so subtle) irony in framing the findings, thereby drawing attention to gaps between what was observed and what is widely assumed or "known" (Lofland & Lofland, 1995). (An example of this can be found in Box 9.1.) As noted by Fine and Martin (1990), Erving Goffman was a master at using irony and sarcasm in his *Asylums* (1961). In contrast, quantitative reports are manifestly not ironic and appear earnest in their avoidance of rhetorical flare.

Demystification is about enlightenment and clarification. Describing the intricacies of human behavior takes in-depth probing and a willingness to take risks and be open-minded. Reji Mathew, a former doctoral student of mine, chose to study arranged marriage among her fellow

BOX 9.2   Degrees of Data Transformation: Sandelowski and
Barroso's (2003) Classification of Findings

Uniformity and consistency in describing the study—from epistemology
through data analysis to findings—is a rarity in the literature (Dixon-
Woods, Booth, & Sutton, 2007). While conducting a meta-synthesis
of 62 qualitative studies of women with HIV/AIDS, Sandelowski and
Barroso (2003) discovered sketchy description and little consistency in
the presentation of these studies. A "phenomenological" study, for
example, might actually use content analysis in its approach to the data.
This discordance made it nearly impossible to cross-classify studies by
type of approach, so they decided to focus only on categorizing the
findings. Their synthesis produced a five-part typology ranged along a
continuum from the least to the most data transformation, as follows:

1. **No Findings (not research):** Studies that were self-labeled as "nar-
    rative case studies" and contained only description, no interpreta-
    tion. Staying rigidly true to the axiom of "giving voice to study
    participants," these studies presented data as findings

2. **Topical Survey (research but not qualitative research):** Studies
    that used a form of content analysis to identify and count topics
    raised by participants. Often the product of focus group or prestruc-
    tured questions, such studies were descriptive but not interpretive.

3. **Thematic Survey:** Studies that considered the latent as well as the
    manifest aspects of the data. Such studies might have incorporated
    theoretical concepts into the interpretation but they stayed fairly
    close to a topical approach. From here on, the studies were deemed
    "qualitative research."

4. **Conceptual/Thematic Description:** Studies that synthesized as well
    as categorized, and searched for themes and concepts that arced
    across the data. Themes were not simply nominal but also interpretive
    in nature. These studies may have been *in vivo* or theory-influenced.

5. **Interpretive Explanation:** Studies that used the maximum
    amount of data transformation. They did not shun description but
    placed a premium on producing a grounded theory, ethnography,
    or other fully integrated explanation of some phenomenon.

(Continued)

(Continued)

Here, in a nutshell, is how the five types were considered to differ: "Whereas a topical or thematic survey might list or detail a set of concerns HIV-positive women expressed, and a conceptual/thematic description reframe these concerns as rationalizations, an interpretive explanation might show how each of these concerns was a condition for distinctively different defensive strategies, only some of which succeeded in allaying those concerns." (Sandelowski & Barroso, 2003, p. 914)

The authors' expert panel classified the 62 studies as follows: Type 1 (3 studies), Type 2 (30 studies), Type 3 (16 studies), Type 4 (10 studies), and Type 5 (3 studies). Sandelowski and Barroso cautioned that this typology is far from perfect—members of the panel frequently disagreed (I personally have difficulty discerning between Types 3 and 4). It is, however, a useful heuristic for understanding the analytic possibilities in data transformation—and for emphasizing the need to present one's research activities clearly and consistently. Last but not least, the distributions gave a rough sense of how few qualitative studies go all the way to full explanation in their ambitions.

South Asians living in the United States. Her in-depth interviews with immigrant women yielded a nuanced portrait of this tradition that belied some of the harsher stereotypes. Rather, these interviews revealed how "arranged introductions" emerged to meet the needs of these modern young women and their families (Mathew, 2008).

Qualitative research is tailor-made for rhetorical devices such as *debunking, irony,* and *demystification.* The politician who touts family values and privately cheats on his wife, the mother who confesses to loathing her children as much as she loves them, and the "lazy" men on the street corner who are really furloughed construction workers—all are stories that need to be told. By doing so, qualitative researchers expose the incongruities and inequities taken for granted in social life.

There is one more thing for which qualitative reports are ideally suited—giving voice to study participants. More often than not, these individuals and groups have had few opportunities to express themselves in their own words. One of the easiest arguments to make for conducting the NYSS was to urge that the opinions of the homeless mentally ill were worth listening to—and that such firsthand accounts were largely missing from the voluminous literature on the problems of homelessness and serious mental illness.

Writing Style: Creating Rhythm and Flow

Most successful qualitative reports have a rhythmic quality, weaving excerpts from the data into a seamless exposition of the study's themes and interpretation. Such reports are confident, but not pompous, compelling but not argumentative. Quantitative researchers eschew presenting raw data, but qualitative researchers typically use it to illustrate their main points.

The length of the raw excerpt depends on the approach taken by the researcher; care should be taken to avoid breaching confidentiality when making this decision. Most qualitative studies juxtapose small chunks of data—verbatim quotes or brief vignettes—with interpretation. Narrative analyses use lengthier excerpts so that the arc of the story can be presented from beginning to end (Riessman, 1993). Excerpts should push the narrative forward, not be a diversion. McCracken (1988) likened this process to a small plane practicing takeoffs and landings. The plane gains altitude (interpretation and exposition of study themes), but it also repeatedly touches down on the landing strip (excerpting of raw data). The researcher should aspire to flawless takeoffs and landings.

Jargon, especially of the academic type, is ill-suited for qualitative reports. Professionals in a variety of fields have their own vernacular and idioms, whether it is arcane medical terminology or the latest psychological argot. Yet jargon-laden writing conceals meaning and sets the writer apart from the reader. Scholarship dependent on obfuscation loses its impact.

Use of Metaphors and Other Tropes

One of the more enjoyable aspects of writing (and reading) qualitative reports is the use of metaphors. Erving Goffman (1961) described the "careers" of mental patients and Sandelowski and Jones (1995) told of the "healing fictions" that pregnant women devise to explain a diagnosis of fetal anomalies. Other examples of metaphoric invocations include Riessman's divorcing couples who "mourn different dreams" (1990) and Liebow's portrayal of the "little murders of everyday life" endured by homeless African American women (1993).

Respondents may use metaphors, whether commonplace ("walking on thin ice") or highly imaginative. Metaphors have been used to describe qualitative research in general (e.g., a "journey of discovery") as a way of capturing its excitement and uncertainty. Less uplifting (but no less graphic) is the muddy boots imagery invoked by Schön (1983). In this word picture, scientists in their pristine white lab coats occupy the "high, hard ground" overlooking the swamp and qualitative researchers slog around in the swampy muck below. Although I find this contrast over-stated, it has served a purpose in provoking debate among qualitative researchers about their role vis-à-vis quantitative researchers (Ely et al., 1991; Guba & Lincoln, 1989).

Other tropes used to spice up a qualitative narrative include *turning points* and *epiphanies* (Denzin, 1989), each calling to mind those critical moments when events converge to alter a person's life. Such figures of speech give a transcendent quality to the study and its interpretations. Their appeal is at once familiar and unfamiliar, bringing the reader into the story.

The Ultimate Goal—Dissemination of the Study Findings

Dissemination has to be the ultimate goal of all studies. Researchers have a number of reasons (excuses?) for not disseminating. Some apply unreal-istic standards to their own work and become paralyzed by them. There is also the fear of failure. As Robert Weiss (1994) noted, "writing is expo-sure" (p. 205), and few exposures are more humbling than submitting manuscripts for publication.

Three basic formats exist for disseminating qualitative research: oral pre-sentations, books, and journal articles. Primary outlets or venues include hardcopy publishing, conferences and workshops, and the Internet. With the exception of peer-reviewed online journals, the Internet is generally a less reliable source. Oral presentations at conferences, workshops, and sem-inars are usually more easily attained than publication.

Qualitative reports are especially suited for publication in book form because of their length—virtually all of the "classic" works were in book form. Regrettably, the days when academic presses offered small press runs of scholarly books are virtually over in this era of market-driven competition. Meanwhile, book publishers have increasingly turned to peer reviews (in addition to the traditional standard of marketability) in determining the worthiness of a manuscript for publication.

Writing up research for peer-reviewed journal publication is the most challenging form of dissemination. For some qualitative researchers, squeezing findings into 25 or fewer pages compromises the study's integrity and is too much to ask. For most, however, the prestige and career enhancement make it worth the effort. Of course, the greatest challenge comes from meeting the standards of these peer-reviewed journals. Problems come from the fact that reviewers and journal editors are predominantly quantitative and have difficulty accepting the norms of qualitative scholarship. Small sample sizes and a purported lack of generalizability are among the most common objections.

Even qualitative-friendly journals and reviewers must grapple with the lack of consensus on standards for quality and rigor. Submitting a manuscript for review can feel like trying to hit a moving target (or one hidden entirely from view). I have experienced one set of journal reviewers complaining about too many direct quotes without interpretation and another set critiquing the amount of interpretation vis-à-vis direct quotes. I have also had grounded theory purists express dissatisfaction that a fully developed grounded theory model was not in the manuscript, even though the majority of such studies do not reach this pinnacle nor is it always appropriate (Flick, 2004).

On a more upbeat note, "quantitative" journals are open to qualitative studies as never before. The growth in qualitative-specialty journals has also been remarkable, leading to diversity in topical area as well as approach. *Qualitative Inquiry,* for example, is heavily tilted toward the postmodern, *Qualitative Social Work* is aimed at a specific profession (social work), and *Qualitative Research* is for international audiences and multidisciplinary dialogue. Several journals feature articles about qualitative methods, including *International Journal of Qualitative Methods, Field Methods, Qualitative Social Work, Qualitative Health Research, The Qualitative Report,* and the *Journal of Contemporary Ethnography.* Would-be authors are well-advised to scrutinize a journal closely to get a sense of what successful entries look like and to ensure that they can meet the required space limitations. To remedy length concerns, online appendices are often available so that addenda can be posted, including audio or video clips (Drisko, 2004).

The over-riding message here is tenacity and hope. I like to think that every worthwhile study has a place somewhere in the universe of dissemination options. Journals nowadays have impact scores and rejection rates available to would-be submitters so that they can compile a list of potential outlets based on degree of difficulty as well as fit. If I feel I have an "A-list" manuscript, I go for it (and let the reviewers decide). If they do not approve, I go to Plan B or Plan C as the occasion demands.

At other times, I may have a more modest effort and will start out with a B- or C-list journal.

Unless explicitly told not to resubmit, I consider rejection letters accompanied by reviewers' comments as open invitations to try again. (I learned this lesson from a more experienced colleague who congratulated me when I dejectedly showed him my first rejection letter.) Unlike my doctoral advisee, Ben Henwood (who had his first-ever manuscript submission accepted without revisions), I have never had a manuscript accepted on the first try. I have also been soundly rejected. (One can usually tell when an editor does not want you back.) Most often, the verdict is "revise and resubmit" with no guarantee of publication. Assuming the suggested revisions are reasonable, I faithfully make them and resubmit. If a suggestion appears unreasonable, I politely counter-argue that it does not work for the study. Revisions may have to go a second or even third round, but take heart that the editor usually wants you to succeed after investing so much effort mediating between you and those picky reviewers.

Morse (2007) offers some helpful hints from her long-time position as editor of *Qualitative Health Research,* including making sure that the introduction and discussion sections are not lengthy when compared to the results (which should be the longest section of a manuscript). She also urges authors to include interpretation along with quotations and ensure that confidentiality is maintained (e.g., demographic characteristics are presented only in the aggregate). Last but far from least, strong manuscripts must make new and compelling contributions to the literature that are stated explicitly and without reservation. Hubris should not be overweening, but writing the report is "no time to be humble" (Morse, 2007, p. 1164) when stating one's claims.

Even when a manuscript is rejected, peer reviewers' comments offer helpful tips for revising and resubmitting it elsewhere. As difficult as it may seem at times, a willingness to roll with the punches is the best survival mechanism. This is especially important advice for researchers early in their careers because peer-reviewed publications are the most valued and trusted forums of scholarly productivity. Regrettably, qualitative researchers must contend with the same problems afflicting journal publication in general, including slow turnaround times (in which manuscripts are essentially held hostage for months at a time) and the uneven quality of reviews.

A final note on dissemination: The growth in online publishing has made qualitative research more widely accessible. Noteworthy examples include

The Qualitative Report, Forum: Qualitative Social Research (Forum: Qualitative Sozialforschung), and the *International Journal of Qualitative Methods*. Electronic access will undoubtedly grow in the future, although the challenges of providing rigorous peer reviews will remain.

Summary and Concluding Thoughts

Qualitative reports are written, not authored. This chapter has offered a number of suggestions for writing the qualitative report, all proffered in the spirit of "take what is useful and applicable for your needs." Much depends on the structure, format, and style of the writing. At the same time, writing for show rather than substance belies a lack of seriousness and purpose.

The decisions start early and pivot around questions of audience, researcher reflexivity, diachronic versus synchronic approaches, use of numbers, and divvying up authorship responsibilities. Most write-ups follow the conventional outline (introduction, methods, findings, and conclusions) but can vary depending on which qualitative approach is used and how much space is available for the report.

Stylistically, a qualitative report is an extended argument that also tells a story. In a rhythmic fashion, it blends description and interpretation. To enliven the argument and make it more compelling, qualitative writers use a number of rhetorical devices including metaphors, irony, and other tropes. With the exception of method-specific terminology such as "constant comparative analysis" or "bracketing," the writing should have minimal jargon and be understandable to a broad audience. Intense scholarly works such as dissertations have to employ a higher level of discourse, but they need not be obscurantist. Successful qualitative studies are rigorous, but they are also a good read, spirited and thought-provoking. The researcher's capacity to be surprised and to present serendipitous findings in an engaging manner can make the difference between a ho-hum report and one that grabs an audience and stays with them.

Finally, it is imperative that researchers disseminate their work. Every well-conducted qualitative study has a home out there, whether it is in a top-tier journal or one farther down the prestige hierarchy. It may be presented as a plenary talk at an international conference or as part of an in-service training at a local agency (or both). Without dissemination, all of the hard work that came before and all of the cumulative growth of knowledge that can come after are imperiled.

EXERCISES

1. Go to one or more of the qualitative journals mentioned in this chapter. Using key word search techniques, select an article of interest to you that represents one of the qualitative approaches and bring the article to class for discussion.

2. In class discussion, present your selected article, highlighting the style of writing used in the article. Does it follow standard conventions? Do the authors use metaphors or other narrative techniques to get their point across? Do they use tables or figures? If so, how?

3. Locate the journal's guidelines for authors submitting manuscripts. Do they include adequate description regarding what the journal expects? Is information provided on the journal's rejection rate or other aspects of its impact?

4. From the list of monographs at the end of this chapter, check one out from the library and answer the following questions. Is there a chapter or appendix on methods? Does the author talk about his or her role in the study? If so, how much detail is offered? Are figures, tables, and/or photographs used? If so, how do these visual displays help tell the story?

ADDITIONAL READINGS

Gilgun, J. F. (2005). "Grab" and good science: Writing up the results of qualitative research. *Qualitative Health Research, 15,* 256–262.

Janesick, V. J. (2004). *"Stretching" exercises for qualitative researchers* (2nd ed.). Thousand Oaks, CA: Sage.

Padgett D. K. (2004b). Spreading the word: Writing and disseminating qualitative studies. In D. K. Padgett (Ed.), *The qualitative research experience* (pp. 285–295), Belmont, CA: Thomson.

Prendergast, C. (2004). The typical outline of an ethnographic research publication. *Teaching Sociology, 32*(3), 322–327.

van Manen, M. (2006). Writing qualitatively, or the demands of writing. *Qualitative Health Research, 16,* 713–722.

Wolcott, H. F. (2001). *Writing up qualitative research* (2nd ed.). Thousand Oaks, CA: Sage.

SELECTED MONOGRAPHS

Early Classics

Becker, H., Geer, B., Hughes, E., & Strauss, A. (1961). *Boys in white: Student culture in medical school.* Chicago: University of Chicago Press.

Bosk, C. L. (1979). *Forgive and remember: Managing medical failure.* Chicago: University of Chicago Press.

Estroff, S. (1981). *Making it crazy.* Berkeley: University of California Press.

Gans, H. (1962). *The urban villagers: Group and class in the life of Italian-Americans.* New York: Free Press.

Goffman, E. (1961). *Asylums: Essays on the social situation of mental patients and other inmates.* Garden City, NY: Basic Books.

Humphries, L. (1970). *Tearoom trade: Impersonal sex in public places.* Chicago: Aldine.

Liebow, E. (1967). *Talley's corner: A study of Negro street corner men.* Boston: Little, Brown.

Lynd, R. S., & Lynd, H. M. (1956). *Middletown: A study in modern American culture.* New York: Harcourt Brace.

Myerhoff, B. (1978). *Number our days: A triumph of continuity and culture among Jewish old people in an urban ghetto.* New York: Simon & Schuster.

Nash, J. C. (1979). *We eat the mines and the mines eat us: Dependency and exploitation in Bolivian tin mines.* New York: Columbia University Press.

Painter, N. I. (1979). *The narrative of Hosea Hudson: His life as a Negro communist in the south.* Cambridge, MA: Harvard University Press.

Powdermaker, H. (1966). *Stranger and friend: The way of an anthropologist.* New York: Norton.

Scheper-Hughes, N. (1981). *Saints, scholars and schizophrenics: Mental illness in rural Ireland.* Berkeley, CA: University of California Press.

Stack, C. (1974). *All our kin. Strategies for survival in a black community.* New York: Harper Colophon.

Whyte, W. F. (1955). *Street corner society* (2nd ed.). Chicago: University of Chicago Press.

Later Examples

Anderson, E. (1999). *Code of the street: Decency, violence, and the moral life of the inner city.* New York: W. W. Norton and Company.

Bourgois, P. (1995). *In search of respect: Selling crack in El Barrio.* New York: Cambridge University Press.

Chan, S. (Ed.). (1994). *Hmong means free: Life in Laos and America.* Philadelphia: Temple University Press.

Duneier, M. (1999). *Sidewalk.* New York: Farrar, Straus & Giroux.

Floersch, J. (2002). *Meds, money and manners.* New York: Columbia University Press.

Gourdine, A. K. (2002). *The difference place makes: Gender, sexuality, and diaspora identity.* Columbus: Ohio State University Press.

Hall, T. (2001). *Better times than this: Youth homelessness in Britain.* London: Pluto Press.

Hays, S. (2003). *Flat broke: Women in the age of welfare reform.* New York: Oxford University Press.

Hochschild, A. (with Machung, A.). (1989). *The second shift: Inside the two job marriage.* New York: Avon.

Iversen, R. & Armstrong, A.L. (2006). *Jobs aren't enough: Toward a new economic mobility for low-income families*. Philadelphia, PA: Temple University Press.

Karp, D. A. (1996). *Speaking of sadness: Depression, disconnection and the meaning of illness*. New York: Oxford University Press.

Klinenberg, E. (2002). *Heat wave: A social autopsy of disaster in Chicago*. Chicago: University of Chicago Press.

Liebow, E. (1993). *Tell them who I am: The lives of homeless women*. New York: Penguin.

Luhrman, T. M. (2000). *Of two minds: The growing disorder in American psychiatry*. New York: Random House.

Martin, E. (2007). *Bipolar expeditions: Mania and depression in America*. Princeton, NJ: Princeton University Press.

Moller, W. D. (2004). *Dancing with broken bones: Portraits of death and dying among inner-city poor*. New York: Oxford University Press.

Newman, K., Fox, C., Roth, W., & Mehta, J. (2005). *Rampage: The social roots of school shootings*. New York: Basic Books.

Oktay, J. (2005). *Breast cancer: Daughters tell their stories*. Binghamton, NY: Haworth Press.

Rhodes, L. (2004). *Total confinement: Madness and reason in the maximum security prison*. Berkeley, CA: University of California Press.

Riessman, C. K. (1990). *Divorce talk*. New Brunswick, NJ: Rutgers University Press.

Scheper-Hughes, N. (1992). *Death without weeping: The violence of everyday life in Brazil*. Berkeley, CA: University of California Press.

Venkatesh, S. A. (2006). *Off the books: The underground economy of the urban poor*. Cambridge, MA: Harvard University Press.

Young, A. A. (2004). *The minds of marginalized black men*. Princeton, NJ: Princeton University Press.

10

Mixed Methods

T his chapter is about a topic that has become very popular in recent years—mixed methods. The "new era" of method integration (Tashakkori & Creswell, 2007, p. 3) is attributable in large part to the unprecedented acceptance of qualitative methods within quantitative circles. This newfound appreciation for mixed methods can also be seen as a pragmatic response on the part of researchers wanting to maximize their understanding of a particular problem (Johnson & Onwuegbuzie, 2004; Morgan, 2007). Some research topics (such as public opinions about mental illness) are manifestly quantitative; others (such as gang initiation rites) are undoubtedly qualitative. In the vast middle ground lie many opportunities to use both approaches for synergistic ends.

At the same time, mixed methods designs are complicated and sometimes messy affairs. Integrating the quantitative and qualitative "sides" poses logistical challenges that few research courses address (Tashakkori & Teddlie, 2003). That said, the momentum behind this trend is unlikely to slow down anytime soon.

The Rise of Mixed Methods and Their Rationale(s)

Just as the term "qualitative methods" came of age in the 1970s, "mixed methods" is a fairly recent addition to the research lexicon (Tashakkori & Teddlie, 2003). Formerly (and sometimes still) referred to as "multi-method," "multistrategy," or "triangulation by method," mixed method studies currently offer a wide and at times confusing array of options (Bryman, 2006; Creswell, 2007; Tashakkori & Teddlie, 2003).

As discussed in Chapter 1, ethnographers and others have a long history of including quantitative data and analyses. This unheralded "mixing" lost favor as the methods became more interview-based with the rise of grounded theory and narrative approaches. In addition, mixing on the qualitative side was derogated in critiques asserting the incompatibility of positivist assumptions of realism with constructivist assumptions of multiple interpretations (Lincoln & Guba, 1985; Morgan, 2007).

On the quantitative side, the soaring dominance of quantification and statistics by the mid-20th century cast doubt on the value of qualitative data with its small samples and presumed lack of generalizability. Lazarsfeld and Barton (1955), for example, viewed qualitative data as useful only when transformed into descriptive statistics for exploratory or preliminary studies. Pioneering quantitative methodologists (Campbell & Stanley, 1963; Cook & Campbell, 1979) acknowledged the utility of qualitative data, but only in a supplementary or minor role. Interestingly, Campbell recanted some of his earlier criticisms of case studies and went further to state that conflicting results in mixed methods studies should cast the quantitative results as suspect "until the reasons for the discrepancy are well understood" (1979, p. 52).

Three basic reasons for carrying out mixed methods studies include: *triangulation, complementarity,* and *expansion* (Greene, Caracelli, & Graham, 1989). Triangulation, the earliest and most widely invoked of rationales, refers to comparisons for purposes of corroboration (Morse, 1991). Because triangulation presumes a fixed point of reference waiting to be converged, its use has been criticized as naïve and sometimes misleading (Flick, 2004; Sandelowski, 2000). Complementarity refers to enhancement or clarification. Thus, the quantitative and qualitative substudies represent different pieces of the puzzle. Expansion refers to the broadened theoretical understanding that can come from juxtaposing qualitative and quantitative perspectives.

Types of Mixed Methods Research

All research designs operate from a premise of intentionality. An experiment, for example, promises random assignment and one or more comparison groups. The study design may not work out as planned, but it is presented as an obligation the researcher(s) intend to fulfill. Mixed methods designs point to the desire to link or integrate. As such, they portend specific procedures to carry this out (Haase & Myers, 1988). If a quantitative study follows a qualitative study in sequence, this is not "mixed method" research per se. I previously used the term *concatenation* to refer to the sequential linking of multiple studies' findings that falls short of intentional mixing (Padgett, 2004c). The NYSS, for example, used findings from the earlier New York Housing Study as a starting point, but it was not part of an intentionally planned design.

As shown in Table 10.1, two primary axes of combinations are available—*sequential versus concurrent* and *dominant/subdominant versus equal* (Creswell, 2003; Miller & Fredericks, 2006). "Dominant" refers to which method is given more weight and prominence in the study. When examining a study's written report, this can be glaringly obvious or deeply ambiguous, depending on the study's design and how clearly it is described.

Using established notations of capital letters (for dominance or priority), arrows (for sequencing), and plus signs (for simultaneity; Morse, 1991), Table 10.1 shows various possibilities for the sequential and concurrent designs. As might be expected, QUAN-dominant designs are more common than QUAL-dominant designs and dominant/less-dominant designs are more common than equally weighted designs. Both of these observations are a reflection of the way the research world is organized and the tendency to conserve resources and/or favor one method over another. A caveat before we go further: These design types are offered primarily as a heuristic device. In practice, mixed methods studies are complicated and not so easily categorized (Miller & Fredericks, 2006).

Table 10.1   Mixed Methods Designs Arranged by Timing and Dominance

	Sequential	Concurrent
Dominant– Less Dominant	CELL 1 QUAL → quan Qual → QUAN QUAN → qual Quan → QUAL	CELL 2—*"Nested"* QUAL+quan QUAN+qual
Equal Weighting	CELL 4 QUAL → QUAN QUAN → QUAL	CELL 3—*"Fully Integrated"* QUAL+QUAN

Sequential Designs

In sequential designs, how the study's segments are prioritized and integrated depends on its priorities. As shown in Cells 1 and 4 of Table 10.1, this can occur in six different ways. Among the dominant/less-dominant designs, the most common (qual→QUAN and QUAN→qual) typically involve using focus group or individual interviews to prepare for the "main event" (survey, instrument development, experimental trial, etc.) or to better understand it after the fact. Wackerbarth, Streams, and Smith, for example, used individual and focus group interviews to generate items for a broad-based survey of Alzheimers' caregivers (2002).

The rationale for a post-hoc qualitative segment can emerge from a quantitative study's findings of statistical significance or the lack thereof—it all depends. The New York Housing Study began as an all-quantitative experiment of four years' duration, but shifted to a mixed QUAN→qual design as the mid-course statistical analyses revealed a puzzling lack of group differences on several key outcomes (Padgett, Gulcur, Tsemberis, 2006). The "small qual" segment of the study entailed appending several open-ended questions to the final interview. These questions were audiotaped and analyzed for patterns and themes that could shed light on the earlier quantitative findings.

The ecological validity of a quantitative study can be enhanced considerably by grounding the study in qualitative interviews and observation before and/or after. Conducting focus groups with students and teachers before implementing a safe sex education program is one example of this approach; positioning the focus groups afterward is another example, albeit for a different purpose.

QUAL→quan and quan→QUAL studies position their quantitative segments as less-dominant. An example of the first would be an intensive qualitative case study of an innovative program for individuals with multiple sclerosis that is used to develop questions for a brief online survey of agencies serving MS patients. In the reverse sequence (quan→QUAL), a telephone survey of parents in a school district might be used to select a subsample willing to be interviewed in-depth about their experiences with the district's new zero-tolerance policy on bullying.

Although less common, equal weighting in sequential designs (Cell 4 of Table 10.1) means that both qualitative and quantitative segments receive sufficient allocations of resources to meet their respective sampling and data quality needs.

Concurrent Designs

In concurrent designs, one method may be dominant over the other (QUAN+qual or QUAL+qual) or they may be given equal weight (QUAN+QUAL). As mentioned earlier, "dominant-less dominant" or nested designs (Cell 2 of Table 10.1) are much more common (Creswell, 1994). Box 10.1 offers an example of a QUAN+qual study carried out in different nations.

In QUAN+qual designs, researchers typically collect qualitative data to enliven or illustrate their quantitative findings, for example, excerpts from responses to open-ended questions or case vignettes (Morgan, 1997). In the reverse QUAL+quan approach, qualitative researchers might collect some quantitative data via standardized measures or they might use supplementary quantitative data from documents or archives. Snow and Anderson (1991) made use of tracking data from various agencies to supplement their intensive interviews and ethnographic observation of the homeless. The resulting depictions contained both statistical and ethnographic descriptions of their lives. As another example, we decided in Phase 2 of the NYSS to include an index of mental health recovery so that our observations of change over time would not be entirely dependent on qualitative data.

Using quantitative data can be risky with small samples, but if done judiciously it need not detract from the inductive, emergent nature of a qualitative study. Similarly, the inclusion of ancillary qualitative data does not challenge the primacy of a "big QUAN" study. A fully integrated QUAL+QUAN study (Cell 3) is among the rarest of mixed method types due to aforementioned demands on time and resources.

Mixed Methods: Ways of Going About It

Structural and Design Decisions: What, When, Where, and How?

Leaving the abstract realm of design types for real-world decisions about mixing methods requires that we unravel the research process and

BOX 10.1   A Mixed Method Study (QUAN+qual) Testing a
Measure of Social Capital in Peru and Vietnam

Mixed methods have an intrinsic appeal for instrument development and testing because most measures' underlying constructs are complex and open to differing meanings and interpretations. One such concept, that of *social capital,* has become widely used as an indication of the ways that social relationships may confer health benefits, from fostering a sense of belonging to providing links to valuable resources. The measurement of social capital at the individual level is seen as a potential indicator of health in general and access to health care in particular (Szreter & Woolcock, 2004).

DeSilva and colleagues (2006) developed a measure of social capital (the SASCAT), translated it into Spanish and Vietnamese, and administered it to a large sample of children's caregivers (3,000 in Peru and 2,771 in Vietnam). In addition to psychometric tests of the measure's validity, the researchers criterion-sampled 20 Peruvian and 24 Vietnamese respondents for in-depth interviews. These "cognitive interviews," lasting from one to two hours, elicited further thoughts and ideas related to each SASCAT item. An example of an item is: "In the past 12 months have you joined together with other community members to address a common problem or issue?" The interviews were audiotaped and content analyzed to see if (and how often) open-ended comments diverged from the authors' original intention regarding each item's meaning.

The findings were revealing. Although the quantitative factor analysis results from the two countries were strikingly similar, the qualitative interviews brought several cultural misunderstandings to the surface. The concept of "community," for example, was readily accepted in Vietnam but not understood by many Peruvians (who defined it as one's social support network, not the surrounding area). In both Peru and Vietnam, "trust" was not considered something one can impute to the "community" in general but only to known individuals. Similarly, "help from others" was largely defined as economic support—contrary to the measure's inclusion of emotional support within the definition. The authors understandably concluded that cognitive validation needs to precede instrument development (DeSilva, Harpham, Tuan, Bartolini, Penny, & Huttly, 2006).

> **Commentary:** This study's QUAN+qual design was an ambitious and successful application of mixed methods. The two methods were used for corroboration as well as completeness (i.e., the researchers did not posit a single meaning for each item but instead sought out multiple meanings to improve the measure). The findings demonstrate the critical importance of qualitative methods in cross-cultural research in which subjective meanings can vary along cultural lines. If this is not taken into consideration, quantitative data collection will be prone to error and misunderstandings.

decide which phases will (or should) intersect and which will remain intact. Are there constraints on doing this or can one mix and match at will? Consider the following series of statements:

- Paradigms (post-positivist, constructivist, critical) do not dictate methods (grounded theory, phenomenological, experimental/quantitative, surveys, etc.).
- Methods do not dictate data-collection techniques (interviews, questionnaires, observation).
- Techniques of data collection do not dictate data analyses.

Such assertions are strongly opposed by postmodern contentions that one cannot mix positivist and constructivist epistemologies (Lincoln & Guba, 2000). But such objections have not slowed the movement toward mixing below the paradigmatic level (Morgan, 2007). (The reader might want to return to Figure 1.1 in Chapter 1 (on page 14), which shows the downward line or spiral of a study). Thus, a grounded theory study can be carried out using post-positivist or constructivist epistemologies; some studies appear to do both simultaneously). At a lower level, many a study has transformed qualitative data into numbers. To be sure, some combinations do not work, for example, narrative analysis and quantitative data. Moreover, one should not mix and match willy-nilly without considerations of fit and appropriateness.

According to Sandelowski (2000), most mixing takes place "on the shop floor of research" (p. 246) during sampling, data collection, and data analysis. Tashakkori and Creswell (2007) discuss dual dimensions to sampling (probability and purposive), data collection (quantitative and qualitative), data analysis (statistical and thematic), and presentation of the findings (numeric and narrative).

The points of contact between the quantitative and qualitative sides can be many or few. Sequential designs leave open the opportunity for each substudy to remain intact (assuming a reasonable connection is made). In concurrent designs, the parallel processes, or "strands" (Tashakkori & Creswell, 2007, p.3) may intersect at one or more phases. The lowest level of mixing intensity is when the two sides stay separate and come together only at the end when findings are juxtaposed.

Mixing at the data analysis level, according to Tashakkori and Teddlie (2003) may include "qualitizing" quantitative data and its opposite process of "quantitizing" qualitative data. The latter of these, which refers to converting qualitative data into numbers or variables, has a long history in content analysis. (An example of "quantitizing" is provided in Box 10.2.) Sandelowski (2000) "qualitized" her quantitative data by creating profiles or categorical types from scores on standardized measures.

With regard to the "what" question, Bryman reports that the concurrent mixing of standardized surveys and qualitative interviews is most common (2006), the latter often based on a purposively selected subsample from the larger survey sample. From the qualitative side, focus groups are a popular choice for mixing—life history interviews and ethnographic observation are much less amenable to mixing. From the quantitative side, randomized clinical trials offer less fit for mixed methods compared to standardized interviews and surveys.

Some Examples of Mixed Methods Studies

The following are a few iterations of mixed methods designs with hypothetical examples.

- A sequential design in which scores on an instrument administered during a survey are subsequently used for criterion sampling of a small subsample for qualitative interviews. For example, a study of depression in college dormitories might use scores on the depressive symptom scale to identify students at highest and lowest risk. These students could then be interviewed in depth about their college experiences and life stressors.

- A concurrent design at the data-collection stage in which in-depth interviews are paired with Likert-type survey questions. For example, a study of South African women that administers measures of exposure to partner violence in a community meeting along with post-meeting focus groups for volunteers willing to discuss the issue at greater length.

BOX 10.2 "Quantitizing" Data in a Grounded Theory Study of Breast and Prostate Cancer Online Discussion Boards

Online chat rooms and discussion boards offer an abundance of narrative data for qualitative analysis. Gooden and Winefield (2007) used grounded theory and a "quasi-numeric" (p. 103) approach to examine gender differences in language styles and communication among cancer survivors communicating online. They started with a hypothesis positing greater use of emotional communications by women and greater use of informational communications by men. They examined online communications among 69 women with breast cancer and 77 men with prostate cancer by using open, axial, and selective coding conducted independently by two readers. The number of codes per message (or posting) and the frequency with which individuals posted were calculated and displayed in tables in the published article.

From these analyses, two selective codes ("information support" and "emotional support") were identified along with their respective axial and open codes. Examples of axial codes included "facts about the disease" (under information support) and "coping philosophies" (under emotional support). Instances of open codes were counted in each database and categorized proportionately under each of these two main headings. As a result, Gooden and Winefield found that information communication comprised 60% of women's communications and 64% of men's communications. Thus, there were modest (and probably nonsignificant) gender differences in the frequency of emotional (versus informational) communication. Virtually all of the results section of the article was devoted to describing the codes, thereby revealing subtle but meaningful aspects of gender. Under "information support," for example, men were likely to offer detailed factual information compared to briefer informational summaries supplied by women. Under "emotional support," women used warm dialog and affectionate phrasing while men suggested to their peers that they "keep their chin up" and "beat the bastard." In other code domains, such as use of humor and group spirit, men and women did not differ.

Commentary: This study's use of a hypothesis and a QUAL+quan design set the stage for the "quantitizing" that followed. However, the quantitative findings comparing men and women were modest and anticlimactic. In the study's write-up, the numbers told a small story but the qualitative themes and interpretations were the main event.

- A concurrent design at the data-analysis stage in which qualitative data are "quantitized" and converted to categorical variables and tested using chi-square statistical analysis. In the NYSS, for example, we could hypothetically categorize participants by whether they are "high" or "low" in terms of their mental health recovery. This dichotomous variable could be cross-tabulated with their housing status (stably versus non-stably housed) and a non-parametric Fisher's exact test (for small sample studies) could be conducted to detect if there is a statistically significant relationship between housing status and level of recovery.

- A sequential design in which quantitative data are "qualitized" (i.e., statistical analyses are used to produce profiles or clusters that set the stage for qualitative interviews with study participants within each cluster to corroborate these analyses). A standardized interview of gay male adolescents might, for example, be used to create a typology of HIV risk based on scores on measures of substance abuse, depression, and social support. Respondents who fit the "high-risk" profile could be interviewed in depth and contrasted with those who fit the "low-risk" profile to inquire about risky sexual behaviors and related stressors in their lives.

- A longitudinal concurrent design in which the quantitative and qualitative sides mutually inform one another. An example is shown in Figure 10.1 for a hypothetical community-based intervention. As shown, focus groups with key stakeholders in the community help guide the content for a household needs assessment survey. Findings from the survey help shape the intervention (e.g., a nutrition program for low-income parents) that is pilot-tested then implemented. Throughout the intervention, ethnographic observation is used to help evaluate process and fidelity aspects of the implementation, identify problem areas, and collect data from participants (children, parents, school officials) assessing effectiveness. Depending on the study's aims, the ethnographic data may be confined to informing the quantitative work or it may be separately presented as findings and compared (or triangulated) with the quantitative outcome data.

- A longitudinal sequential design oscillating between the quantitative and qualitative sides. In contrast to the previous example, this design involves alternating between sides over time. As depicted in Figure 10.2, such oscillation could take the form of ethnographic observations on an American Indian reservation that are used to inform a community survey on needs of children and families. The survey's findings then lead to criterion-sampled focus groups of adolescents, the results of which inform a targeted intervention to prevent adolescent suicide.

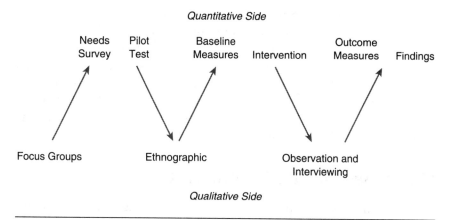

Figure 10.1   A Longitudinal Mixed Methods Design

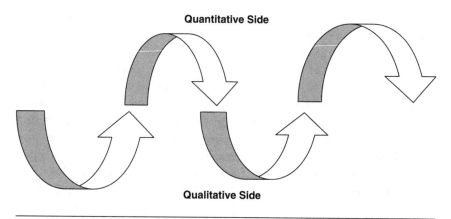

Figure 10.2   An Oscillating Mixed Methods Design

Writing the Mixed Method Report

As illustrated in the boxed inserts in this chapter, findings from mixed methods studies can be presented in a number of ways. Assuming the two sides were kept intact, the findings are presented side by side, numerical and thematic. Usually some attempt is made to interpret them in tandem and discuss the degree to which they converge or diverge. Gioia, for example, provided a descriptive summary of her quantitative findings along with a presentation of the qualitative themes and then ended with a graphic display showing how the two "sides" were related (2004). If the mixing occurred earlier such that the data analyses followed one approach, the findings are usually presented in one format. Perhaps not surprisingly given the motivation to mix methods in the first place, researchers tend to favor the multiple findings option to give each side its due.

Challenges for Mixed Methods Studies

Carrying out mixed methods studies poses challenges of various and sundry kinds. Among the logistical hurdles, most researchers are trained in one or the other method (most often quantitative), but not both. Having dual competencies in a team effort can overcome this drawback, but the lone investigator is at a disadvantage. Mixed method studies also require dual outlays of time and resources to ensure that both "sides"—quantitative and qualitative—are given sufficient attention to be rigorous (Stange, Miller, Crabtree, O'Connor & Zyzanski, 1994).

Another logistical challenge accompanies oversight of the two sides when their rhythms and phases unfold in different ways. Qualitative data analyses, for example, start early in data collection and may result in going back out into the field for further sampling and data collection. Meanwhile, the quantitative side is proceeding in linear fashion, waiting out the data collection before beginning statistical analyses. The qualitative side, even though working with a smaller sample, takes considerable amounts of time and resources for transcription and data analysis not matched on the quantitative side. Given these tensions, the temptation to use a dominant-less dominant design is strong, and the quantitative side often comes out ahead in these situations.

Because mixed methods imply combining within the confines of a single study, questions can arise regarding when and where one study ends and another begins. In sequential designs, too much time elapsed may lead to the conclusion that two separate studies were conducted. In concurrent designs, the "sides" may have few or no interactions and integration is minimal, thus giving the appearance of two unrelated side-by-side studies.

There are also questions about the adequacy and provenance of the data. Are answers to a few open-ended questions on a questionnaire sufficient to be considered qualitative data? Will a scale or index administered during in-depth interviews yield meager descriptive statistics of limited value? Collecting qualitative data under heavily quantitative auspices raises serious doubts about its authenticity and richness (Morse, 2005). Moreover, qualitizing quantitative data is not the mirror image of quantitizing qualitative data (this sentence is an admitted mouthful). With the former, quantitative data are aggregated and clustered and the resulting categories are based on decontextualized data that are hardly comparable to categories inductively derived from in-depth interviews and/or extensive observation. Similarly, a disservice is often done to deep and rich data when they are quantitized. Perhaps the best lesson to come from all this is that qualitizing and quantitizing should be done with great caution and transparency regarding the reasons for doing so.

The conundrum posed by triangulation also affects many a mixed methods study. When results from both sides are in accord, the researcher concludes (perhaps prematurely) that her findings are confirmed. As discussed in Chapter 8, the meaning of triangulation has been expanded beyond corroboration to include completeness. Ethnographers, for example, often use quantitative and qualitative analyses for comprehensiveness rather than for validation. The problem arises over what to do when the qualitative and quantitative findings are neither convergent nor complementary. Some researchers present the two sets of findings, acknowledge the conflict, and ask the reader (and future researchers) to resolve the differences. Others use the discrepancy as an opportunity to inquire further, first to ensure that each of the "sides" is not flawed or biased in some way and then to examine and even use the discrepancy as an opportunity to broaden or revise the study.

Box 10.3 gives an example of a mixed method study in which serendipitous findings from the qualitative "side" broadened the study and extended its impact to include new perspectives on barriers to breast cancer screening.

Mixed Method Approaches to Program and Practice Evaluation

The shared pragmatism of program evaluation and mixed methods makes for a productive synergy. Qualitative evaluators may grapple with the same epistemological issues as other qualitative researchers. Yet theirs is a task that must remain grounded in the reality of a specific program, practice, or policy. They must also balance using theories in general with "program theory" specifically (Rallis & Rossman, 2003).

BOX 10.3   Serendipitous Findings and Mixed Methods: An Example From the Harlem Mammogram Study

The Harlem Mammogram Study was a mixed method (QUAN+qual) study examining why African American women delay in responding to an abnormal mammogram (Kerner, Yedidia, Padgett, Muth, Washington, Tefft, Yabroff, Makariou, Freeman & Mandelblatt, 2003). Interviews included measures of health locus of control, fear of cancer, beliefs about racism, insurance status, and psychological distress. The less-dominant qualitative portion consisted of questions about their mammogram experiences and discussions of aging, racism, body image, and female sexuality.

Data analyses were carried out separately by the quantitative and qualitative members of the team who had the requisite expertise. Both "sides" shared an interest in understanding delay (or timeliness) and maintained close contact as the analyses proceeded. The quantitative side used a multivariate logistic regression model to predict time to diagnostic resolution (within 3 months or longer). The qualitative side used a modified grounded theory approach to identify codes and themes.

The qualitative data were intended to bring greater depth and understanding (a supplementary role), thus corresponding to "completeness" as a goal of triangulation. As it happened, they also contributed two serendipitous findings that would not have emerged otherwise. The first of these (mentioned in Box 6.2 in Chapter 6) was the "air theory" of cancer which was subsequently noted in the literature (Freeman, 2004). This folk belief, which holds that opening the body surgically exposes it to air that can cause dormant cancer cells to grow and spread, was volunteered by several women during the qualitative interviews. Its relevance to our interest in delay was obvious because a surgical biopsy posed just such a threat. The second unexpected qualitative finding was about the physical and psychological toll of repeated diagnostic tests among women who had had multiple abnormal mammograms. A significant minority of women in the study had to undergo repeated and painful needle biopsies and other procedures (Padgett, Yedidia, Kerner, & Mandelblatt, 2001).

The qualitative results were significant in ways that our multivariate model did not (and probably could not) take into account. How, after all, could we have anticipated or measured "air theory"? The results also turned out to have more grab than the statistical analyses that proved to be disappointingly thin. Contrary to our hypothesized expectations, the effects of income, insurance coverage, and systemic barriers were not found to be statistically significant. Among 30 predictor variables tested in the multivariate model, only the degree of mammogram abnormality and whether the patient was given information were significant (Kerner et al., 2003). Had we omitted the qualitative portion of the study, the under-performing quantitative model would have been the study's only finding for dissemination.

In a fundamental sense, evaluation is "finding the value" (Ruckdeschel, Earnshaw, & Firrek, 1994; Scriven, 1967), making judgments according to societal priorities in light of the program's mission. Evaluation researchers must work under constraints of time, resources, and competing ideas regarding what is of "value." Even when vested interest groups—policymakers, administrators, staff, and clients—agree on a program's goals, the evaluator must work under close scrutiny and risk offending one or another of the stakeholders.

There are several ways that qualitative research can contribute to a mixed method evaluation (Greene & Caracelli, 1997; Padgett, 2005; Rallis & Rossman, 2003). Quantitative evaluations are good at establishing what works, but qualitative evaluations help to understand *how* a program succeeds or fails. Although admittedly more time consuming, qualitative methods are less intrusive and less demanding than an experimental trial (Perreault, Pawliuk, Veilleux, & Rousseau, 2006). Qualitative researchers can fade into the woodwork and respond nimbly to the ebb and flow of organizational life. The addition of qualitative methods to a quantitative evaluation adds flexibility and depth (Drake, Bebout, Quimby, Teague, Harris, & Roach, 1993).

Qualitative research is particularly well suited to *formative* and *process evaluation*. Hong and colleagues used ethnography to conduct a formative evaluation of an HIV prevention program with injection drug users. Their findings regarding miscommunications and cultural relevance were used to inform and improve the intervention that resulted (Hong, Mitchell, Peterson, Latkin, Tobin, & Gann, 2005). Program or treatment fidelity studies are also amenable to qualitative inquiry (Blakely, Mayer, Gotterhalk, Schmitt, Davidson, Roitman & Emshoff, 1987). The inner workings of many programs—the dynamic interplay of the actors, their differing perceptions of events, and the effects of culture and gender—are difficult to anticipate and measure. Indeed, there is no substitute for what can be learned from extended ethnographic observation of a program and its day-to-day operations (Felton, 2005).

Qualitative approaches also mesh well with social advocacy values in evaluation—they empower less powerful stakeholders (clients, lower level staff, etc.) by giving their voices greater prominence in "finding the value" of the program. A mixed method approach cannot guarantee a successful evaluation, but it is likely to enhance the depth and relevance of the findings.

Summary and Concluding Thoughts

The popularity of mixed methods is higher than ever before. Mixed method approaches can bring unprecedented synergy, but they are not a panacea. A number of methodological and logistical barriers stand in the way of integrating quantitative and qualitative approaches, not the least of which are the additional outlays of expertise, time, and resources needed to do justice to both "sides."

This chapter began with the archetypal possibilities based on sequencing and dominance. It also offered several examples of the complicated, even messy, mixed methods designs that characterize applications in real-world settings. The devil, as they say, is in the details. Determining what to mix from the qualitative and quantitative sides, when to mix them, and how to make the linkages takes careful advance planning. Notwithstanding these challenges, mixed methods open the door to illuminating contrasts, whether done to corroborate, complement, or expand knowledge into new frontiers.

EXERCISES

1. *The Journal of Mixed Method Research* debuted in 2007 as a reflection of the burgeoning interest in method integration. Browse this journal (or another of your choice) and locate a mixed methods study of interest to you. Using the notational system from Table 10.1, how would you characterize the study's design?

2. In class discussion groups, take a look at Table 10.1. Which designs are most common and which are least likely to be used? Why?

3. Choose a program or practice of interest to you or your class discussion group and talk through how it could be evaluated using mixed methods. Choose a design from Table 10.1 and then specify how you would carry out the proposed evaluation. What types of quantitative and qualitative methods, techniques, or analyses would you use?

4. Think of a topic for which mixed methods would not be a good fit. Why is this so?

ADDITIONAL READINGS

Creswell, J. W. (2003). *Research design: Qualitative, quantitative, and mixed methods approaches* (2nd ed.). Thousand Oaks, CA: Sage.

Greene, J. C., & Caracelli, V. J. (Eds.). (1997). *Advances in mixed-method evaluation: The challenges and benefits of integrating diverse paradigms*. San Francisco: Jossey-Bass.

Johnson, P. J., & Onwuegbuzie, J. A. (2004). Mixed methods research: A research paradigm whose time has come. *Educational Researcher, 33*(7), 14–26.

Miller, S. I., & Fredericks, M. (2006). Mixed-methods and evaluation research: Trends and issues. *Qualitative Health Research, 16,* 567–579.

Sandelowski, M. (2000). Combining qualitative and quantitative sampling, data collection, and analysis techniques in mixed methods studies. *Research in Nursing & Health, 23,* 246–255.

Tashakkori, A., & Teddlie, C. (Eds.). (2003). *Handbook of mixed methods in social and behavioral research*. Thousand Oaks, CA: Sage.

Appendix:
Writing a Qualitative Methods Proposal for External Funding

W ith their flexible and rather unpredictable nature, qualitative methods present special challenges when put into proposal form (Morse, 1994). The bar is raised the highest when it comes to external funding, where intense competition combines with a review process steeped in (and thus more favorable to) quantitative methods. Qualitative researchers have reason to bemoan this state of affairs and the requisite need to anticipate skeptical or uninformed reviewers (Ungar, 2006). And yet qualitative research has attracted external funding for a long time and will continue to do so. The trick is to know how to optimize the chances of success.

Because this entire book has been dedicated to conducting the type of rigorous qualitative research that can meet the standards of external funders, I will focus in this appendix on the particulars of proposal-writing and submission. (Readers are urged to revisit Chapter 3 on design, Chapter 7 on analysis, and Chapter 8 on rigor for detailed advice.) This discussion is largely based on my own experience in collaboratively obtaining grants from the National Cancer Institute, the Centers for Disease Control (CDC), and most recently the National Institute of Mental Health (NIMH). I also draw on my experience in reviewing proposals and the experiences of successful colleagues known to me. I acknowledge at the outset a bias toward NIH funding because this is where most of my experience lies. Foundations and other non-governmental sources are equally valuable supporters of high-quality research.

Having sufficient funding for a large-scale qualitative study is rare. Getting to this level, neither a requirement in one's career nor a guarantee of high-quality research, depends on having the right combination of expertise and a strong team of collaborators. It also involves more than "mere" hard work and dedication—professional contacts, timing, and personal passions also play a role.

There is good news to start out with. First, more funders than ever before are welcoming qualitative and mixed methods proposals. Their reviews may be strenuous and success hard to come by, but at least the door is open wider nowadays. Second, qualitative studies can be low-cost enterprises. (A researcher armed with an audio recorder, a computer, and plenty of time is all that is needed.) Smaller grants can go a long way.

Third, training is available to assist researchers in writing proposals. The Office of Behavioral and Social Science Research (OBSSR), part of NIH, has been offering summer institutes for junior researchers in social work and other health professions since 2004. The first (which I was fortunate to lead) was on qualitative and mixed methods, and the 2007 institute was on community-based participatory research (CBPR). The annual conference of the Society for Social Work and Research (SSWR) is full of helpful workshops and summer intensives that are sponsored by the Institute for the Advancement of Social Work Research (IASWR). IASWR also sends out a weekly listserv announcing funding opportunities (www.iaswresearch.org). The International Institute for Qualitative Methodology at the University of Alberta offers annual conferences featuring workshops as well as lectures on qualitative methods (http://www.uofaweb.ualberta.ca/iiqm/thinking.cfm). Finally, research infrastructure supports within schools and departments are on the rise, including workload reductions, small grants for training or pilot studies, and staff assistance in preparing grant proposals.

Obtaining funding offers the "luxury" of having more resources such as personnel, participant incentives, the latest software, and transcription services. It usually brings indirect costs (or overhead) and prestige to one's institution and career advancement for the investigator. The ability to succeed in the highly competitive arena of external funding has become a common expectation of faculty, graduate students, evaluators, and program administrators. One can assume that a proposal will receive close (near-brutal) scrutiny, so thorough preparation should begin months in advance.

Writing a research proposal is an extended effort in persuasion and confidence building in the researcher as well as the methods. Poorly written and poorly argued proposals will not survive the review no matter how worthy the ideas and methods. Typos and grammatical errors raise concerns that the study will be as sloppy as the proposal itself. I have participated in grant application reviews in which reviewers threw up their hands in frustration over proposals riddled with inconsistencies and errors.

Finding the Right Fit With Funding Priorities: Emerging Opportunities

All of the points made in Chapter 1 apply here regarding reasons for doing qualitative research and the need to choose methods based on one's topic (not the other way around). Here, there is an additional layer of consideration: the potential funder's interests. Foundations tend to be up front about their current priorities, and a check of their Web site can usually provide this information. A very helpful clearinghouse on foundation support is the Foundation Center at: http://foundationcenter.org.

The choice of topic for the proposal may come from personal experience, intellectual curiosity, a passion to change the world, or all of these. What matters most is the ability to shape the topic in such a way that it will attract attention and gain support. Making the case is easier when the study fits with funding priorities. The following discussion is admittedly limited to resources in the United States (although many of these are open to non-U.S. researchers and to research topics not confined to the United States).

The U.S. National Institutes of Health is one of the largest funders of research, but NIH priorities exclude many studies in child welfare, poverty, and other non-health-related topics. It is useful to distinguish between research that is theory driven and knowledge-generating and applied research such as program evaluation. The actual difference between these two, which is often murky, can hinge on how a study is framed and the funder's overriding interest. Government agencies in child welfare, housing, mental health, addictions, and so forth tend to be interested in applied or evaluation research and may contract for it rather than invite competitive proposals. Many innovative programs and demonstration projects incorporate an evaluative component with funding allocated for research.

NIH funded research can range from DNA sequencing and laboratory experiments to services research; a thread running through these is the need to be theory driven. In contrast, the federal entity known as SAMHSA (Substance Abuse and Mental Health Services Administration) and its constituent units such as CMHS (Center for Mental Health Services) and CSAT (Center for Substance Abuse Treatment) is devoted to program development and evaluation. A quick glance at their Web site (www.samhsa.gov) reveals their interests in assessing a variety of programs from jail diversion to suicide prevention.

Community-based participatory research (CBPR) has recently attracted the interest of large-scale funders including NIH. Areas of particular interest and suitability include HIV/AIDS prevention, cancer prevention and control, nutrition, and environmental contamination. The following are some recent examples of CBPR funding opportunities from the NIH:

- National Institute for Environmental Health Sciences (NIH) Research on Environmental Justice and CBPR (http://www.niehs.nih.gov/research/supported/programs/justice/index.cfm)
- Community Participation in Research (http://grants2.nih.gov/grants/guide/pa-files/PAR-06-247.html)
- National Center on Minority Health Disparities (NIH) Community-Based Participatory Research Initiative in Reducing and Eliminating Health Disparities (http://grants.nih.gov/grants/guide/notice-files/NOT-MD-07-002.html)

These Web sites are provided as a sampling of opportunities. Most such initiatives are time-limited and the reader is cautioned to check the relevant NIH Web sites at www.nih.gov for updates and new funding announcements. The Centers for Disease Control and Prevention (CDC) is also keenly interested in community-based research in similar areas.

Various professions are understandably drawn to their own targeted funding sources even though few if any impose restrictions on what type of researchers can apply. Thus, nursing researchers turn to the National Institute of Nursing Research (NINR) at NIH. In education and disability studies, the options include the U.S. Department of Education and the National Institute on Disability and Rehabilitation Research (NIDRR) at NIH. Similarly, proposals on criminal justice research would likely go to the National Institute of Justice (NIJ). Social scientists not interested in health-related topics might go to the National Science Foundation (NSF) or the Social Science Research Council (SSRC). Being diverse in interests, social work researchers reach out to a wide variety of potential funders in child welfare (the W. T. Grant Foundation, Casey Foundation) cancer (American Cancer Society, CDC, National Cancer Institute), and poverty and public health (Bill and Melinda Gates Foundation, Ford Foundation, Kellogg Foundation, Robin Hood Foundation, Rockefeller Foundation). Although lacking a NIH institute or center of its own, social work has received more attention at NIH with the recent release of a Program Announcement titled "Research on Social Work Practice and Concepts in Health" (http://grants1.nih.gov/grants/guide/pa-files/PA-07–292.html).

Getting Past the Catch 22

Seasoned researchers usually do better at obtaining external funding than their less experienced counterparts (although seniority is no guarantee of success). Two simple reasons account for this. First is the Catch 22 that comes when review committees give higher ratings to experienced, proven researchers (on the reasonable assumption that their qualifications will enhance the study's probability of success). Second, mature researchers are usually better able to put together a credible, strong proposal drawing on their experience and knowledge of what it takes.

How does a novice overcome these drawbacks? There is obviously nothing that can be done about the Catch 22 problem, but new investigators can succeed by taking a few strategically planned actions. First, they can seek the mentorship of senior researchers in their area who have successful funding track records. (Ideally, one's mentors are included in the proposal as a co-investigator, consultant, etc.) Second, they should seek out successful proposals in their areas of interest and emulate them. There are many things that can be learned this way, including how the "argument" is made (see Box A.1 for an example), how much emphasis to place on methods, what a budget should look like, how to handle ethical issues, proper use of terminology, and so forth.

I am convinced that I could not have written the successful proposal that led to the New York Services Study without having fortuitously gained access to an all-qualitative proposal previously funded by NIMH (one of the side benefits of being asked to review proposals). The topic and population were different but the structure and tone of the proposal were revelatory for me, giving me confidence that it

---

BOX A.1   Making a Compelling Argument: Rhetoric and Reason

Proposals seeking funding must address a huge "so what?" question designed to ensure that funds are expended wisely. Here are the opening paragraphs of the grant proposal I submitted to the National Institute of Mental Health in 2004. I am grateful to my erudite co-investigator Dr. Kim Hopper for supplying most of the compelling rhetoric embedded in this excerpt:

> Psychiatrically disabled homeless adults lead complex, troubled lives struggling to meet basic survival needs and cope with serious mental illness. Their lives often complicated by substance abuse, such individuals present a standing challenge to a resource-strapped service system designed with more stable clients, more discretely packaged needs, and more predictable trajectories of service use in mind. Patient-centered care is problematic, seeming to pit wary veterans of street and shelter life against systems concerned about scarce resources and public safety. In community debates, these apparently conflicting priorities are often portrayed as weary providers confronted by recalcitrant men and women who seem to prefer the dangerous freedom of street life to the security, structure and self-discipline of rehabilitation.

> While doubtless over-simplified, it is difficult to fault this portrait since available research has brought precision at the cost of narrowed scope, i.e., it has provided a 'top down' perspective on the gap between need and use of services among psychiatrically disabled homeless adults. Studies have been *thorough* in measuring the prevalence of problems and *focused* in testing interventions for their resolution, but they have also been *partial* in perspective. In this contested arena of competing interests, *the service user's perspective remains poorly documented and understood.*

Notice a few things about these two paragraphs: 1) the judicious use of italics for emphasis (not recommended for dissertations and scholarly reports); 2) the argument is made for conducting a qualitative study, but its rhetorical power depends on the sad realities of life for homeless mentally ill adults; 3) the paragraphs are densely packed and touch on several key issues—comorbid substance abuse, public safety concerns, the lack of "fit" between the service system and consumers, and the limitations of extant research; 4) this sets the stage for the study that is specified in greater detail in the next 25 pages of the proposal. In other words, rhetoric must sooner or later be linked to substance.

could be done. Short of having such unusual access, researchers can go to the NIH CRISP (Computer Retrieval of Information on Scientific Projects) database (http://crisp.cit.nih.gov) and examine abstracts from successfully funded proposals to get both inspiration and information.

Setting the Stage

For site-specific studies, the researcher needs to have good working relationships for a variety of reasons, as discussed previously in this book. In terms of seeking external funding for a study, good working relationships help to ensure that necessary forms of cooperation will be forthcoming. This can range from posting a recruitment flyer in a waiting area to allowing full access to an agency or clinic's operations, staff, and clients (as with an ethnography). Sampling needs should be met within a reasonable time period and verified by the cooperating agency or program if they are to be involved. The principal investigator may want to establish consortium agreements among sites if a significant level of involvement is being sought.

Pilot or preliminary study findings enhance confidence in the researcher's commitment and the study's feasibility. The more this preparatory work can be incorporated into the proposal, the better.

Finally, although it may seem obvious, the researcher should corral all necessary proposal materials as early as possible. These can include support letters, appendices, departmental approval letters, bio-sketches of key personnel, and so forth. Waiting until the last minute will add enormous strain to the nail-biting process of assembling all of the proposal's parts and getting them in on time.

Questions From Reviewers Regarding Qualitative Methods Proposals

A qualitative methods proposal has a better chance than ever before, but it is still likely to arouse concerns about lack of rigor (Munhall, 1994; Ungar, 2006). Here, more than ever, transparency and specificity are needed.

The review of grant proposals varies somewhat depending on the funding source (foundation, government, private donor, institutional funds, etc.), but it invariably involves evaluating the study's overall significance and its methods. Typically, a panel of experienced researchers review and rate the proposals, then meet to discuss their merits and recommend those deemed worthy of funding. The following are some of the questions reviewers might put to the proposal (and to the researcher if she were present in the room):

- How can we be sure that the findings will justify the amount of money requested?
- Do the principal investigator and the research team have enough experience to make this study a success?
- Is this study really filling a gap in knowledge?
- Is this study innovative?
- Are there ethical problems created by asking people sensitive questions?
- Is this study feasible given the time and money being requested?
- How do we know that the methods are rigorous?
- Is the sampling strategy biased?
- Do the study findings have implications for practice/policy/future research?
- Will the findings be generalizable?
- How will this study contribute to theory development?
- Qualitative studies seem to rely more on faith in the researcher than in the methods. Does this proposal counteract this impression?

The researcher would do well to anticipate and answer these questions in the proposal. Most if not all of the answers can be found elsewhere in this book. Box A.2 gives a detailed description of how reviews of grant proposals take place at NIH, a process that is similar to that at other funding venues.

Budgeting Time and Resources

Forecasting the required amount of time and resources—and their associated costs—imposes a degree of precision all too rare in qualitative

---

BOX A.2   The Review Process at the National Institutes of Health
(NIH)

Few would argue that NIH funding is among the most prestigious and competitive of research funding sources. Primary advantages to NIH funding are the ample budgets that are possible and the high rates of indirect costs, or the percent allocated to the researcher's institution to cover facilities and administration expenses (often well over 50%). By comparison, private foundations usually fund at lower levels and pay indirect costs at lower rates (or not at all). Of course, a topic must fit NIH priorities regarding health (however broadly defined). Much of the following information is transferable to other funding venues.

Among the 27 institutes and centers at NIH, a few are the most receptive to social and behavioral research and to qualitative methods: NIMH (National Institute of Mental Health), NIDA (National Institute on Drug Abuse), NCI (National Cancer Institute), NICHD (National Institute on Child Health and Development), NIDRR (National Institute on Disability and Rehabilitation Research), and NINR (National Institute of Nursing Research). Total budgets differ (NINR's budget is a tiny fraction of NCI's) and review panels across the institutes (as well as among each institute's internal study sections) vary in their expectations and rigor.

Although NIH sometimes makes minor changes in its extramural funding procedures (recently going to all-electronic submission), the process unfolds in a predictable, if poorly understood, fashion. After the proposal has been submitted, a program officer is assigned. The proposal is then usually sent to the CSR (Center for Scientific Review) where an administrator identifies the correct study section and assigns it to three reviewers (at least one of whom ideally has qualitative methods expertise). The reviewers are assigned as primary, secondary, and tertiary; the first two expected to write a more detailed critique (including a summary of the proposal in the primary review) and the tertiary review is much shorter.

The reviewers consider the following in their critiques: *significance* (why is this study needed and important?), *approach* (what are the study's methods, are they appropriate to the aims, and how rigorous are they?), *innovation* (does the study use novel approaches and ideas?), *investigators* (do the investigators have the necessary qualifications for

(Continued)

(Continued)

the study?), *environment* (does the home institution offer an appropriate platform for the study?), *protection of human subjects* (are there any ethical concerns?), *inclusion of women, minorities, and children* (a federal requirement), and *budget* (is the proposed budget sufficient to carry out the study but not excessive or inappropriate?).

Reviewers, who receive a CD-ROM of the proposals around six weeks in advance of the panel meeting, are expected to submit their critiques and a suggested score on a secure Internet site before the meeting. Some reviewers may attend via speakerphone but most attend in person (their travel costs are covered) and convene at a hotel near NIH headquarters in Maryland. At or right before the meeting, the aggregate scores are reviewed and the bottom 50% of the proposals is recommended for tabling from full-panel discussion. (Submitters still receive the reviewers' written critiques along with an "unscored" verdict.) Scores may range from 1.0 (near-flawless) to 5.0 (not worthy, to say the least).

For the fortunate upper 50% of proposals, the next two days involve an intense discussion of each proposal in which the primary, secondary, and tertiary reviewers present their critiques amidst panel discussion of its merits. The Study Section chair, a senior researcher, must keep everyone on topic and moving along (not unlike herding cats). Each proposal is ultimately given a score by all members of the panel (influenced no doubt by the three reviewers), and the aggregate score and a percentile ranking is sent to the researcher within a few days. The synthesized critique, or Summary Statement, arrives a bit latter.

Although the cut-point for funding is unfortunately sliding lower (the top 20% of proposals used to be assured of success), a score under 2.0 and a percentile ranking of 15 **or lower** is very good reason for hope. Even a 1.1 score is no automatic guarantee—the actual funding decision is made by the institute's council (a group of eminent researchers) who are charged with enacting that institute's funding priorities. It is the rare council, however, that stands in the way of an excellent score.

The vast majority of proposals to NIH are not funded on the first round and researchers have two additional opportunities to revise and resubmit. Each revision is expected to follow the previous critiques

closely and highlight changes made. Contacts with one's program officer can help immeasurably in deciphering the review and deciding on
revisions.

A few additional pointers:

- Go to: http://cms.csr.nih.gov/AboutCSR/OverviewofPeerReviewProcess
  .htm for more information.
- Contact the appropriate institute program officer in advance and get his
  or her advice on shaping the proposal. Keep in mind, however, that
  program officers do not make funding decisions. They must sit silently
  while the panel does its work.
- Attach a cover letter to ensure that your proposal goes to the right
  review committee. Many a researcher has taken this for granted then
  found the proposal sent to a committee with little understanding or sym-
  pathy for the topic and methods.
- Don't give up . . . even the most senior researchers get rejected.

inquiry. Yet formulas can be calculated based on desired sample sizes and
generally known information on the time it takes to conduct and transcribe interviews, equipment and software costs, incentive payments, and
so forth. Ultimately, research budgets must reflect the study's proposed
reach and available resources.

Budget categories include: *personnel salaries and fringe benefits* (investigators, interviewers, research assistants, etc.), *equipment* (audio
recorders, laptops, desktop computers), *research supplies* (software, batteries, CD-ROMs, flash memory drives, postage, etc.), *transportation
costs* (subway/bus fares), *participant incentives and services* (transcription, expert consultant fees), and *travel to conferences* for presentations.
Site fees may be paid to compensate for staff assistance (in recruitment
and data collection). If allowed, *indirect costs* (also called overhead) are
computed as a percentage of the direct costs (office rent, clerical help,
utilities, etc.). Allocations within and across these categories must reflect
a realistic appraisal of what is needed (i.e., neither wildly inflated nor
unrealistically underbudgeted).

Researchers should adhere to extant norms about incentive payments,
consultant pay rates, and transcription costs. When budgeting for digital
audio recorders, go for a mid-range price (the acuity of the recording will

pay for itself). In the NYSS, we went with cheaper recorders initially and found the quality of transcription suffered as did the transcribers (who strained to catch every word).

Budgeting for interviews starts from the ground up. As a hypothetical example, assume that the study involves two 90-minute interviews with 50 participants and transcription costs are $15 an hour. This amounts to 100 interviews × 1.5 hours or 150 hours of audio needing transcription. Because the ratio of recording-hours to transcription-hours is anywhere from 1 to 3 to 1 to 8, it would be reasonable to allocate funds for 150 (recording) hours × 5 (transcription) hours, or 750 hours total for transcription time. At a rate of $15 per hour, this equals $11,250 for transcription. Incentives at $25 per interview (50 participants, each having two interviews) equals $2500, and so forth.

These calculations should be fully detailed in the *budget justification*. As such, they vividly illustrate the backstage labors involved in qualitative studies and offer a rationale for generously funding even a "small sample" study. Indeed, the budget justification can help a proposal considerably by demonstrating how intense and time-consuming rigorous qualitative studies can be.

Twenty Tips for Writing the Proposal

The following guidelines or tips can be turned into a handy checklist for planning and writing the proposal.

1. Start with compelling, unanswered study question(s) that will impress the reviewers.

2. Make sure the study begins with specific aims and research questions that present a clear road map for where you plan to go.

3. Write a concise but comprehensive abstract. (Remember that this may be the only description of your study widely disseminated later on.)

4. Include a rationale for use of qualitative methods and their requisite strengths.

5. Ground the study in a coherent, strong theoretical framework.

6. Make sure that ethical guidelines are followed and all potential threats to human subjects are minimized or eliminated.

7. If the budget allows, include expert consultants who can provide guidance on methods or other specialized study needs.

8. Be direct and explicit about research design, including an explanation for why qualitative designs need to be flexible and iterative.

9. Describe in detail the sampling and recruitment plans.

10. Build in a pilot study to ensure that protocols get a trial run-through.

11. Describe procedures for retaining study participants (contact information, payment of incentives, etc.). This is critical for longitudinal designs.

12. Structure the data analysis section around each specific aim or study goal and describe step-by-step how the analyses will be carried out.

13. Include in each data analysis section a subsection titled "Strategies for Rigor" and indicate which will be used (as appropriate).

14. Include a table in the proposal with some version of the following columns: Specific Aims (or Research Questions), Sample Size and Source, Sampling Criteria and Recruitment, Sources of Data, Type of Data Analysis, Timeframe. Reading across, each row is a specific aim followed by its requisite information.

15. Include a timeline showing the length of the study (in months) on the x axis and each task stacked up along the y axis. Lines and arrows show each task's beginning and ending point.

16. If appropriate (and this is often the case), build a community advisory board (CAB) into the proposal. CABs provide valuable input and are an indication that the study is (and will be) responsive.

17. Make sure the budget is reasonable but not skimpy—feasibility and credibility matter.

18. Observe page limitations, font sizes, and margins carefully. Ignoring these might result in a returned (or discarded) proposal.

19. If appropriate, include plans for dissemination of the study findings. Funders might want to be a part of this process to varying degrees, but all have a vested interest in seeing the study's conclusions influencing practice, policy, and future research. Conference and other presentations are excellent venues, but the ultimate impact comes from publication in peer-reviewed, respected outlets.

20. Be patient and prepared to submit again (or somewhere else)!

ADDITIONAL READINGS

Locke L., Spirduso, W., & Silverman, S. (1993) Preparation of proposals for qualitative research: Different assumptions. In L. Locke, W. Spirduso, and S. Silverman (Eds.), *Proposals That Work: A Guide for Planning Dissertations and Grant Proposals* (3rd ed., pp. 96–118). Newbury Park, CA: Sage.

Morse, J. M. (1994). Designing funded qualitative research. In N. K. Denzin and Y. L. Lincoln (Eds.), *Handbook of qualitative research* (pp. 220–235). Thousand Oaks, CA: Sage.

Munhall, P. L. (1994). *Qualitative research proposals and reports: A guide.* New York: National League for Nursing Press.

National Association of Deans and Directors of Schools of Social Work Task Force on Administrative Research Infrastructures Within Social Work Education Programs. (1997). *Challenges and opportunities for promoting federally funded research in social work programs.* Washington, DC: Institute for the Advancement of Social Work Research.

National Institutes of Health. (1999). *Qualitative methods in health research: Opportunities and considerations in application and review.* (2001). Office of Behavioral and Social Science Research (OBSSR). Available at: http://obssr.od.nih.gov/Documents/Publications/Qualitative.PDF

Ungar, M. (2006). "Too ambitious": What happens when funders under-estimate the strength of qualitative research design. *Qualitative Social Work, 5*(2), 261–277.

References

Abbott, A. (1997). Of time and space: The contemporary relevance of the Chicago School. *Social Forces, 75*(4), 1145–1182.

Agar, M. H. (1980). *The professional stranger: An informal introduction to ethnography.* New York: Academic Press.

Agar, M. H. (1991). The right brain strikes back. In N. G. Fielding & R. M. Lee (Eds.), *Using computers in qualitative research* (pp. 181–194). Newbury Park, CA: Sage.

Agar, M. H., & McDonald, J. (1995). Focus groups and ethnography. *Human Organization, 54*(1), 78–86.

Allison, K. R., & Rootman, I. (1996). Scientific rigor and community participation in health promotion research: Are they compatible? *Health Promotion International, 11*(4), 333–340.

Altheide, D. L., & Johnson, J. M. (1994). Criteria for assessing interpretive validity in qualitative research. In N. K. Denzin & Y. S. Lincoln (Eds.), *Handbook of qualitative research* (pp. 485–499). Thousand Oaks, CA: Sage.

Anfara, V. A., & Mertz, N. T. (Eds.). (2006). *Theoretical frameworks in qualitative research.* Thousand Oaks, CA: Sage.

Annells, M. (1996). Grounded theory method: Philosophical perspectives, paradigm of research, and postmodernism. *Qualitative Health Research, 6*(3), 379–393.

Annells, M. (2006). Triangulation of qualitative approaches: Phenomenology and grounded theory. *Journal of Advanced Nursing, 56*(1), 55–61.

Atkinson, P. (1997). Narrative turn or blind alley? *Qualitative Health Research, 7*(3), 325–344.

Atkinson, P. (2005, September). Qualitative research—Unity and diversity [25 paragraphs]. *Forum Qualitative Sozialforschung/Forum: Qualitative Social Research, 6*(3), Article 26. Retrieved August 18, 2007, from http://www.qualitative-research.net/fqs-texte/3–05/05-3-26-e.htm

Atkinson, J. M., & Heritage, J. (Eds.). (1984). *Structure of social action: Studies in conversation analysis.* Cambridge: Cambridge University Press.

Atkinson, P., & Silverman, D. (1997). Kundera's immortality: The interview society and the invention of the self. *Qualitative Inquiry, 3*, 304–325.

Baker, C., Wuest, J., & Stern, P. N. (1992). Method slurring: The grounded theory/Phenomenology example. *Journal of Advanced Nursing, 17*, 1335–1360.

Barkin, S., Ryan, G., & Gelberg, L. (1999). What pediatricians can do to further violence prevention: A qualitative study. *Injury Prevention, 5,* 53–58.

Barnes, D. B., Taylor-Brown, S., & Weiner, L. (1997). "I didn't leave y'all on purpose: HIV-infected mothers' videotaped legacies for their children. *Qualitative Sociology, 20*(1), 7–32.

Beck, C. T. (1993). Teetering on the edge: A substantive theory of postpartum depression. *Nursing Research, 42*(1), 42–50.

Becker, H. (1996). The epistemology of qualitative research. In R. Jessor, A. Colby, & R. Schweder (Eds.), *Ethnography and human development* (pp. 53–72). Chicago: University of Chicago Press.

Becker, H., Geer, B., Hughes, E., & Strauss, A. (1961). *Boys in white: Student culture in medical school.* Chicago: University of Chicago Press.

Beebe, J. (2002). *Rapid assessment process.* Landham, MD: Altamira Press.

Beeman, S. (1995). Maximizing credibility and accountability in qualitative data collection and data analysis: A social work research case example. *Journal of Sociology and Social Welfare, 22,* 99–114.

Berelson, B. (1952). *Content analysis in communication research.* Glencoe, IL: Free Press.

Berger, P., & Luckmann, T. (1967). *The social construction of reality.* New York: Doubleday.

Bernard, H. R. (1994). *Research methods in anthropology: Qualitative and quantitative approaches* (2nd ed.). Walnut Creek, CA: Altamira.

Bernard, H. R. (Ed.). (2000). *Handbook of methods in cultural anthropology.* Walnut Creek, CA: Altamira Press.

Blakely, C. H., Mayer, J. P., Gotterhalk, R. G., Schmitt, N., Davidson, W. S., Roitman, D. B., et al. (1987). The fidelity-adaptation debate: Implications for the implementation of public sector social programs. *American Journal of Community Psychology, 15,* 253–268.

Bloor, M. (1997). Techniques of validation in qualitative research: A critical commentary. In G. Miller & R. Dingwall (Eds.), *Context and method in qualitative research* (pp. 37–50). London: Sage.

Boeri, M. W. (2004). "Hell I'm an Addict, but I Ain't no Junkie": An ethnographic analysis of aging heroin users." *Human Organization, 63*(2), 236–246.

Bogdan, R. C., & Taylor, S. J. (1975). *Introduction to qualitative research.* New York: John Wiley.

Bohm, A. (2004). Theoretical coding: Text analysis in grounded theory. In U. Flick, E. von Kardorff, & I. Steinke (Eds.), *A companion to qualitative research* (pp. 270–275). London: Sage.

Bowen, G. A. (2006). Grounded theory and sensitizing concepts. *International Journal of Qualitative Methods, 5*(3), Article 2.

Bowen, G. (2008). Naturalistic inquiry and the saturation concept: A research note. *Qualitative Research, 8,* 137–152.

Boyatzis, R. E. (1998). *Transforming qualitative information: Thematic analysis and code development.* Thousand Oaks, CA: Sage.

Bradshaw, T. K. (1999). Communities not fazed: Why military base closures may not be catastrophic. *Journal of American Planning Association, 65,* 193–206.

Brainerd, J. (2003). Federal agency says oral history is not subject to rules on human research volunteers. *Chronicle of Higher Education, 50*(10): A25.

Bryman, A. (2006). Integrating quantitative and qualitative research: How is it done? *Qualitative Research, 6*(1), 97–113.

Butler, A., Ford, D., & Tregakis, C. (2007). Who do we think we are? Self and reflexivity in social work practice. *Qualitative Social Work, 6*(3), 281–299.

Campbell, D. (1979). Degrees of freedom and the case study. In T. D. Cook & C. S. Reichart (Eds.), *Qualitative and quantitative methods in evaluation research* (pp. 49–67). Beverly Hills, CA: Sage.

Campbell, R., & Arens, C. E. (1998). Innovative community services for rape victims: An application of multiple case study methodology. *American Journal of Community Psychology, 26*(4), 537–571.

Campbell, D. T., & Stanley, J. C. (1963). *Experimental and quasi-experimental designs for research.* Boston: Houghton-Mifflin.

Carlson, E. D., Engebretson, J., Chamberlain, R. M. (2006). Photovoice as a social process of critical consciousness. *Qualitative Health Research, 16*(6), 836–852.

Chambers, E. (2000). Applied ethnography. In N. K. Denzin & Y. S. Lincoln (Eds.), *Handbook of qualitative research* (pp. 851–869). Thousand Oaks, CA: Sage.

Chambon, A., & Irving, A. (1994). *Essays on postmodernism in social work.* Toronto: Canadian Scholars' Press.

Charmaz, K. (2006). *Constructing grounded theory.* Thousand Oaks, CA: Sage.

Cherryholmes, C. H. (1992). Notes on pragmatism and scientific realism. *Educational Researcher, 14,* 13–17.

Chiovatti, R. F., & Piran, N. (2003). Rigour and grounded theory research. *Journal of Advanced Nursing, 44*(4), 427–435.

Christians, C. G. (2000). Ethics and politics in qualitative research. In N. K. Denzin & Y. S. Lincoln (Eds.), *Handbook of qualitative research* (pp. 133–155). Thousand Oaks, CA: Sage.

Clarke, A. (2005). *Situational analysis: Grounded theory after the postmodern turn.* Thousand Oaks, CA: Sage.

Clifford, J., & Marcus, G. E. (Eds.). (1986). *Writing culture: The poetics and politics of ethnography.* Berkeley: University of California Press.

Coffey, A., & Atkinson, P. (1996). *Making sense of qualitative data.* Thousand Oaks, CA: Sage.

Colaizzi, P. F. (1978). Psychological research as the phenomenologist views it. In R. Valle & M. King (Eds.), *Existential-phenomenological alternatives for psychology* (pp. 48–71). New York: Oxford University Press.

Cook, T. D., & Campbell, D. T. (1979). *Quasi-experimentation: Design and analysis issues for field settings.* Boston: Houghton-Mifflin.

Cook, T. D., & Reichardt, C. S. (Eds.). (1979). *Qualitative and quantitative methods in evaluation research.* Beverly Hills, CA: Sage.

Cooney, K. (2006). Mothers first, not work first: Listening to welfare clients in job training. *Qualitative Social Work, 5*(2), 217–235.

Cornwall, A., & Jewkes, R. (1995). What is participatory research? *Social Science & Medicine, 41*(12), 1667–1676.

Correll, S. (1995). The ethnography of an electronic bar: The lesbian café. *Journal of Contemporary Ethnography, 24*(3), 270–294.

Crabtree, B. F., & Miller, W. L. (1999). *Doing qualitative research* (2nd ed.). Thousand Oaks, CA: Sage.

Creswell, J. W. (2003). *Research design: Qualitative, quantitative, and mixed methods approaches* (2nd ed.). Thousand Oaks, CA: Sage.

Creswell, J. W. (2007). *Qualitative inquiry and research design* (2nd ed.). Thousand Oaks, CA: Sage.

Creswell, J. W., & Maietta, R. (2002). Qualitative research. In D. C. Miller & N. J. Salkind (Eds.), *Handbook of social research* (pp. 143–184). Thousand Oaks, CA: Sage.

Czarniawska, B. (2004). *Narratives in social science research.* Thousand Oaks, CA: Sage.

Davies, D., & Dodd, J. (2002). Qualitative research and the question of rigor. *Qualitative Health Research, 12*(2), 279–289.

Denzin, N. K. (1978). *The research act: A theoretical introduction to sociological methods* (2nd ed.). New York: McGraw-Hill.

Denzin, N. K. (1989). *Interpretive interactionism.* Newbury Park, CA: Sage.

Denzin, N. K. (1994). The art and politics of interpretation. In N. K. Denzin & Y. S. Lincoln (Eds.), *Handbook of qualitative research* (pp. 500–515). Thousand Oaks, CA: Sage.

Denzin, N. K. (2002). Confronting ethnography's crisis of representation. *Journal of Contemporary Ethnography, 31,* 482-490.

Denzin, N. K., & Lincoln, Y. S. (Eds.). (1994). *Handbook of qualitative research.* Thousand Oaks, CA: Sage.

Denzin, N. K., & Lincoln, Y. S. (Eds.). (2000). *Handbook of qualitative research* (2nd ed.). Thousand Oaks, CA: Sage.

Denzin, N. K., & Lincoln, Y. S. (Eds.). (2005). *Handbook of qualitative research* (3rd ed.). Thousand Oaks, CA: Sage.

DeSilva, M. J., Harpham, T., Tuan, T., Bartolini, R., Penny, M. E., & Huttly, S. R. (2006). Psychometric and cognitive validation of a social capital measurement tool in Peru and Vietnam. *Social Science & Medicine, 62,* 941–953.

Dick, H. P. (2006). What to do with "I don't know": Elicitation in ethnographic and survey interviews. *Qualitative Sociology, 29*(1), 87–102.

Dickson-Swift, V., James, E. L., Kippen, S., & Liamputtong, P. (2007). Doing sensitive research: What challenges do qualitative researchers face? *Qualitative Research, 7*(3), 327–353.

Dixon-Woods, M., Booth, A., & Sutton, A. J. (2007). Synthesizing qualitative research: A review of published reports. *Qualitative Research, 7*(3), 375–422.

Donmoyer, R. (1990). Generalizability and the single-case study. In E. W. Eisner & A. Peshkin (Eds.), *Qualitative inquiry in education: The continuing debate* (pp. 175–200). New York: Teachers College Press.

Drake, R. E., Bebout, R. R., Quimby, E., Teague, G. B., Harris, M., & Roach, J. P. (1993). Process evaluation in the Washington D.C. Dual Diagnosis Project. *Alcoholism Treatment Quarterly, 10,* 113–124.

Drisko, J. W. (2004). Qualitative data analysis software. In D. K. Padgett (Ed.), *The qualitative research experience* (pp. 189–205). Belmont, CA: Thomson.

Duneier, M. (1999). *Sidewalk* (p. 43). New York: Farrar, Straus, & Giroux.

Dupuis, A., & Thorns, D. C. (1998). Home, home ownership, and the search for ontological security. *The Sociological Review, 46*(1), 24–47.

Ellis, C., & Bochner, A. P. (2000). Autoethnography, personal narrative, reflexivity: Researcher as subject. In N. K. Denzin & Y. S. Lincoln (Eds.), *Handbook of qualitative research* (2nd ed., pp. 733–768). Thousand Oaks, CA: Sage.

Ellis, C., & Flaherty, M. G. (1992). An agenda for the interpretation of lived experience. In E. Ellis & M. G. Flaherty (Eds.), *Investigating subjectivity: Research on lived experience* (pp. 1–16). Newbury Park, CA: Sage.

Ely, M., Anzul, M., Friedman, T., Garner, D., & Steinmetz, A. M. (1991). *Doing qualitative research: Circles within circles.* London: Falmer.

Emerson, R. (2001). *Contemporary field research: Perspectives and formulations.* Long Grove, IL: Waveland Press.

Emerson, R. M., Fretz, R. I., & Shaw, L. L. (1995). *Writing ethnographic fieldnotes.* Chicago: University of Chicago Press.

Eng, E., Moore, K. S., Rhodes, S .D., Griffith, D. M., Allison, L. L., Shirah, K., & Mebane, E. M. (2005). Insiders and outsiders assess who is "the community." In B.A. Israel, E. Eng, A. J. Schulz, & E. A. Parker (Eds.), *Methods in community-based participatory research for health* (pp. 77–100). San Francisco: Jossey-Bass.

Erickson, F. (1986). Qualitative methods in research on teaching. In M.C. Wittrock (Ed.), *Handbook of research on teaching* (3rd ed., pp. 119–161). New York: Macmillan.

Esposito, N. (2001). From meaning to meaning: The influence of translation techniques on non-English focus group research. *Qualitative Health Research, 11*(4), 568–579.

Estroff, S. (1981). *Making it crazy.* Berkeley: University of California Press.

Fals-Borda, O. (Ed.). (1998). *People's participation: Challenges ahead.* New York: Apex.

Fals-Borda, O., & Rahman, M. A. (Eds.). (1991). *Action and knowledge: Breaking the monopoly with participatory action research.* New York: Intermediate Technology/Apex.

Farnell, B., & Graham, L. R. (2000). Discourse-centered methods. In H. R. Bernard (Ed.), *Handbook of methods in cultural anthropology* (pp. 411–454). Walnut Creek, CA: Altamira Press.

Feagin, J. R., Orum, A. M., & Sjoberg, G. (Eds.). (1991). *A case for the case study.* Chapel Hill: University of North Carolina Press.

Felton, B. J. (2005). Defining location in the mental health system: A case study of a consumer–run agency. *American Journal of Community Psychology, 36,* 373–386.

Fereday, J., & Muir-Cochrane, E. (2006). Demonstrating rigor using thematic analysis: A hybrid approach of inductive and deductive coding and theme development. *International Journal of Qualitative Methods, 5*(1), Article 1.

Fetterman, D. M. (1989). *Ethnography step by step.* Newbury Park, CA: Sage.

Fine, G. A., & Martin, D. D. (1990). A partisan view: Sarcasm, satire, and irony as voices in Erving Goffman's Asylums. *Journal of Contemporary Ethnography, 19,* 89–115.

Firestone, W. A. (1990). Accommodation. Toward a paradigm-praxis dialectic. In E. G. Guba (Ed.), *The paradigm dialog* (pp. 105–124). Newbury Park, CA: Sage.

Flaherty, M. G. (2002). The "crisis" in representation: Reflections and assessments. *Journal of Contemporary Ethnography, 31*(4), 508–516.

Flick, U. (2004). Triangulation in qualitative research. In U. Flick, E. von Kardorff, & I. Steinke (Eds.), *A companion to qualitative research* (pp. 178–183). London: Sage.

Flick, U., von Kardorff, E., & Steinke, I. (Eds.) (2004). *A companion to qualitative research.* London: Sage.

Fonow, M. M., & Cook, J. A. (Eds.). (1991). *Beyond methodology: Feminist scholarship as lived research.* Bloomington: Indiana University Press.

Fontana, A., & Frey, J. H. (1994). Interviewing: The art of science. In N. K. Denzin & Y. S. Lincoln (Eds.), *Handbook of qualitative research* (pp. 361–376). Thousand Oaks, CA: Sage.

Foster-Fishman, P., Berkowitz, S. L., Lounsbury, D. W., Jacobson, S., & Allen, N. (2001). Building collaborative capacity in community coalitions: A review and integrative framework. *American Journal of Community Psychology, 29*(2), 241–261.

Freeman, H. P. (2004). Poverty, culture and social injustice: Determinants of cancer disparities. *A Cancer Journal for Clinicians, 54,* 72–77.

Freire, P. (1973). *Pedagogy of the oppressed.* New York: Seabury Press.

Freundlich, M., Avery, R. J., & Padgett, D. K. (2007). Care or scare: The safety of youth in congregate care in New York City. *Child Abuse and Neglect, 31*(2), 173–186.

Gair, S. (2002). In the thick of it: A reflective tale from an Australian social worker/qualitative researcher. *Qualitative Health Research, 12*(1), 130–139.

Gee, J. P. (2005). *An introduction to discourse analysis: Theory and method.* London: Routledge.

Geertz, C. (1973). *The interpretation of cultures: Selected essays.* New York: Basic Books.

Geertz, C. (1988). *Works and lives: The anthropologist as author.* Stanford, CA: Stanford University Press.

Gergen, M. M., & Gergen, K. J. (2000). Qualitative inquiry: Tensions and transformations. In N. K. Denzin & Y. S. Lincoln (Eds.), *Handbook of qualitative research* (pp. 1025–1046). Thousand Oaks, CA: Sage.

Gibbs, L., & Gambrill, E. (2002). Evidence-based practice: Counter-arguments to objections. *Research on Social Work Practice, 12*(3), 452–476.

Giddens, A. (1990). *Consequences of modernity.* Oxford: Polity Press.

Gilgun, J. F. (2005). "Grab" and good science: Writing up the results of qualitative research. *Qualitative Health Research, 15,* 256–262.

Gioia, D. (2004). Mixed methods in a dissertation study. In D. K. Padgett (Ed.), *The qualitative research experience* (pp. 119–146). Belmont, CA: Thomson.

Giorgi, A. (Ed.). (1985). *Phenomenology and psychological research.* Pittsburgh, PA: Duquesne University Press.

Glaser, B. (1978). *Theoretical sensitivity.* Mill Valley, CA: The Sociology Press.

Glaser, B. (1992). *Basics of grounded theory analysis.* Mill Valley, CA: Sociology Press.

Glaser, B. G. (2002). Conceptualization: On theory and theorizing using grounded theory. *International Journal of Qualitative Methods, 1*(2), Article 3.

Glaser, B. G., & Holton, J. (2004, March). Remodeling Grounded Theory [80 paragraphs]. *Forum Qualitative Sozialforschung/Forum: Qualitative Social Research,*

5(2), Article 4. Retrieved June 8, 2007, from http://www.qualitative-research.net/fqstexte/2–04/2–04glaser-e.htm

Glaser, B. G., & Strauss, A. L. (1967). *The discovery of grounded theory: Strategies for qualitative research.* Chicago: Aldine.

Goetz, J., & LeCompte, M. (1984). *Ethnography and qualitative design in educational research.* Orlando, FL: Academic Press.

Goffman, E. (1959). *The presentation of self in everyday life.* Garden City, NY: Basic Books.

Goffman, E. (1961). *Asylums: Essays on the social situation of mental patients and other inmates.* Garden City, NY: Basic Books.

Goleman, D. (2007, February 20), Flame first, think later: New clues to email misbehavior. *The New York Times,* p. F5.

Gooden, R. J., & Winefield, H. R. (2007). Breast and prostate cancer online discussion boards: A thematic analysis of gender differences and similarities. *Journal of Health Psychology, 12*(1), 103–114.

Greene, J. C. (2000). Understanding social programs through evaluation. In N. K. Denzin & Y. S. Lincoln (Eds.), *Handbook of qualitative research* (2nd ed., pp. 981–1000). Thousand Oaks, CA: Sage.

Greene, J. C., Caracelli, V. J., & Graham, W. F. (1989). Toward a conceptual framework for mixed-method evaluation designs. *Educational Evaluation and Policy Analysis, 11*(2), 255–274.

Greene, J. C., & Caracelli, V. J. (Eds.). (1997). *Advances in mixed-method evaluation: The challenges and benefits of integrating diverse paradigms.* San Francisco: Jossey-Bass.

Gregory, D., Russell, C. K., & Phillips, L. R. (1997). Beyond textual perfection: Transcribers as vulnerable persons. *Qualitative Health Research, 7*(2), 294–300.

Griffin, L. J. (1993). Narrative, event-structure analysis, and causal interpretation in historical sociology. *American Journal of Sociology, 98,* 1094–1133.

Groenewald, T. (2004). A phenomenological research design illustrated. *International Journal of Qualitative Methods, 3*(1), Article 4.

Guba, E. G. (Ed.). (1990). *The paradigm dialog.* Newbury Park, CA: Sage.

Guba, E. G., & Lincoln, Y. S. (1981). *Effective evaluation.* San Francisco: Jossey-Bass.

Guba, E. G., & Lincoln, Y. S. (1989). *Fourth generation evaluation.* Newbury Park, CA: Sage.

Guba, E. G., & Lincoln, Y. S. (1994). Competing paradigms in qualitative research. In N. K. Denzin & Y. S. Lincoln (Eds.), *Handbook of qualitative research* (pp. 105–117). Thousand Oaks, CA: Sage.

Gubrium, J. F., & Holstein, J. A. (2000). Analyzing interpretive practice. In N. K. Denzin & Y. S. Lincoln (Eds.), *Handbook of qualitative research* (pp. 487–508). Thousand Oaks, CA: Sage.

Guest, G., Bunce, A., & Johnson, L. (2006). How many interviews are enough? An experiment with data saturation and variability. *Field Methods, 18*(1), 59–82.

Haase, J. E., & Myers, S. T. (1988). Reconciling paradigm assumptions of qualitative and quantitative research. *Western Journal of Nursing Research, 10,* 128–137.

Hall, A. L., & Rist, R. C. (1999). Integrating multiple qualitative research methods (or avoiding the precariousness of a one-legged stool). *Psychology & Marketing, 16,* 291–304.

Hall, C., & White, S. (2005). Looking inside professional practice. *Qualitative Social Work, 4*(4), 379–390.

Harding, S. (1986). *The science question in feminism.* Ithaca, NY: Cornell University Press.

Harding, S. (1987). *Feminism and methodology.* Bloomington, IN: Indiana University Press.

Hawkins, R. L., & Abrams, C. (2007). Disappearing acts: The social networks of formerly homeless individuals with co-occurring disorders. *Social Science & Medicine, 65,* 2031–2042.

Hessler, R. M., Downing, J., Beltz, C., Pellicio, A., Powell, M., & Vale, W. (2003). Qualitative research on adolescent risk using email: A methodological assessment. *Qualitative Sociology, 26*(1), 111–124.

Hertz, R., & Imber, J. B. (Eds.). (1995). *Studying elites using qualitative methods.* Thousand Oaks, CA: Sage.

Hirsch, J., Higgins, J., Bentley, M. E., & Nathanson, C. A. (2002). Social constructions of sexuality: Martial infidelity and sexually-transmitted disease—HIV risk in a Mexican migrant community. *American Journal of Public Health, 92,* 1127–1237.

Hirsch, J., Higgins, M., Bentley, M. E., & Nathanson, C. (2007). The inevitability of infidelity: Sexual reputation, social geographies and HIV marital risk in rural Mexico. *American Journal of Public Health, 97*(6): 986–996.

Hochschild, A., & Machung, A. (1989). *The second shift: Inside the two job marriage.* New York: Avon.

Hohman, A., & Shear, M. K. (2002). Community-based intervention research: Coping with the "noise" of real life in study design. *American Journal of Psychiatry, 159,* 201–207.

Hong, Y., Mitchell, S. G., Peterson , J. A., Latkin, C. A., Tobin, K., & Gann, D. (2005). Ethnographic process evaluation: Piloting an HIV prevention program among injection drug users. *International Journal of Qualitative Methods, 4*(1), Article 1.

Hsieh, H., & Shannon, S. E. (2005). Three approaches to qualitative content analysis. *Qualitative Health Research, 15*(9), 1277–1288.

Humphries, L. (1970). *Tearoom trade: Impersonal sex in public places.* Chicago: Aldine.

Hyde, C. (1994). Reflections on a journey: A research story. In C. K. Riessman (Ed.), *Qualitative studies in social work research* (pp. 169–189). Thousand Oaks, CA: Sage.

Hyden, M., & Overlien, C. (2004). "Doing" narrative analysis. In D. K. Padgett (Ed.), *The qualitative research experience* (pp. 250–268). Pacific Grove, CA: Thomson Learning.

Illingworth, N. (2001). The Internet matters: Exploring the use of the Internet as a research tool. *Sociological Research On-Line, 6*(2), U96–U112. Retrieved October 20, 2007, from http://www.socresonline.org.uk/6/2/illingworth.html

Inui, T. S., & Frankel, R. M. (1991). Evaluating the quality of qualitative research. *Journal of General Internal Medicine, 6,* 485–487.

Irwin, L. G., & Johnson, J. (2005). Interviewing young children: Explicating our practices and dilemmas. *Qualitative Health Research, 15*(6), 821–831.

Israel, B. A., Eng, E., Schulz, A. J., & Parker. E. A. (Eds.). (2005). *Methods in community-based participatory research for health.* San Francisco: Jossey-Bass.

Iversen, R. R. (2008). "Getting out" in ethnography: A seldom-told story. *Qualitative Social Work.*

Iversen, R., & Armstrong, A. L. (2006). *Jobs aren't enough: Toward a new economic mobility for low-income families*. Philadelphia, PA: Temple University Press.

Janesick, V. J. (2000). The choreography of qualitative research designs: Minuets, improvisations and crystallization. In N. K. Denzin & Y. S. Lincoln (Eds.), *Handbook of qualitative research* (pp. 379–400). Thousand Oaks, CA: Sage.

Jessor, R., Colby, A., & Schweder, R. (Eds.). (1996). *Ethnography and human development*. Chicago: University of Chicago Press.

Johnson, P. J., & Onwuegbuzie, J. A. (2004). Mixed methods research: A research paradigm whose time has come. *Educational Researcher, 33*(7), 14–26.

Johnstone, P. L. (2004). Mixed methods, mixed methodology health services research in practice. *Qualitative Health Research, 14*(2), 259–271.

Jones, L., & Wells, K. (2007). Strategies for academic and clinician engagement in community-based partnered research. *Journal of the American Medical Association, 297*(4), 407–410.

Katz, J. (2006). Ethical escape routes for underground anthropologists. *American Ethnologist, 33*(4), 499–506.

Kelle, U., & Erzberger, C. (2004). Qualitative and quantitative methods: Not in opposition. In U. Flick, E. von Kardorff, & I. Steinke, (Eds.), *A companion to qualitative research* (pp. 172–175). London: Sage.

Kelling, G. L., & Coles, C. M. (1996). *Fixing broken windows: Restoring social order and reducing crime in our communities*. New York: The Free Press.

Kemmis, S., & McTaggart, R. (2000). Participatory action research. In N. Denzin & Y. Lincoln (Eds.), *Handbook of Qualitative Research* (2nd ed., pp. 579–605). Thousand Oaks, CA: Sage.

Kerner, J. F., Yedidia, M., Padgett, D., Muth, B., Washington, K. S., Tefft, M., Yabroff, K., R., Makariou, E., Freeman, H., & Mandelblatt, J. S. (2003). Realizing the promise of breast cancer screening: Clinical follow-up after abnormal screening among Black women. *Preventive Medicine, 37*, 92–101.

Kidd, P. S., & Parshall, M. B. (2000). Getting the focus and the group: Enhancing analytical rigor in focus group research. *Qualitative Health Research, 10*(3), 293–308.

Kincheloe, J. L., & McLaren, P. (2000). Rethinking critical theory and qualitative research. In N. K. Denzin & Y. S. Lincoln (Eds.), *Handbook of qualitative research* (2nd ed., pp. 279–314). Thousand Oaks, CA: Sage.

Klinenberg, E. (2002). *Heat wave: A social autopsy of disaster in Chicago*. Chicago: University of Chicago Press.

Knoblauch, H. (2005, September). Focused Ethnography [30 paragraphs]. *Forum Qualitative Sozialforschung/Forum: Qualitative Social Research, 6*(3), Article 44. Retrieved July 20, 2007, from http://www.qualitative-research.net/fqs-texte/3-05/05-3-44-e.htm

Kotkin, S. (2002, September 7). A world war among professors: A clash between number crunchers and specialists in a single region. *The New York Times*, B9–B11.

Krueger, R. A. (1994). *Focus groups: A practical guide for applied research* (2nd ed.). Thousand Oaks, CA: Sage.

Kuhn, T. (1970). *The structure of scientific revolutions*. Chicago: University of Chicago Press.

Kvale, S. (1996). *InterViews: An introduction to qualitative research interviewing.* Thousand Oaks, CA: Sage.

Labov, W., & Waletzky, J. (1967). Narrative analysis: Oral versions of personal experience. In J. Helm (Ed.), *Essays on the verbal and visual arts* (pp. 12–44). Seattle: University of Washington Press.

Ladson-Billings, G. (2000). Racialized discourses and ethnic epistemologies. In N. K. Denzin & Y. S. (Eds.), *Handbook of qualitative research* (pp. 258–278). Thousand Oaks, CA: Sage.

Lakoff, G., & Johnson, M. (1980). *Metaphors we live by.* Chicago: University of Chicago Press.

Laing, R. D. (1965). *The divided self: An existential study in sanity and madness.* London: Pelican Press.

LaPiere, R. T. (1934). Attitudes vs. actions. *Social Forces, 13,* 230–237.

Lazarsfeld, P. F., & Barton, A. (1955). Some functions of qualitative data analysis in sociological research. *Sociologica, 1,* 324–361.

LeCompte, M. D., & Goetz, J. P. (1984). Problems of reliability and validity in ethnographic research. *Review of Educational Research, 52,* 31–60.

LeCompte, M. D., & Schensul, J. J. (1999). *Analyzing and interpreting ethnographic data.* Walnut Creek, CA: Altamira Press.

Leininger, M. (1994). Evaluation criteria and critique of qualitative research studies. In J. M. Morse (Ed.), *Critical issues in qualitative research methods* (pp. 95–115). Thousand Oaks, CA: Sage.

Levin, M., & Greenwood, D. (2001). Pragmatic action research and the struggle to transform universities into learning communities. In P. Reason & H. Bradbury (Eds.), *Handbook of action research* (pp. 103–113). London: Sage.

Levy, R. I., & Hollan, D. W. (2000). Person-centered interviewing and observation. In H. R. Bernard (Ed.), *Handbook of methods in cultural anthropology* (pp. 333–364). Walnut Creek, CA: Altamira Press.

Lewin, K. (1946). Action research and minority problems. *Journal of Social Issues, 4,* 34–46.

Liebow, E. (1967). *Talley's Corner: A study of Negro street corner men.* Boston: Little, Brown.

Liebow, E. (1993). *Tell them who I am: The lives of homeless women.* New York: Penguin.

Lietz, C. A., Langer, C. L., & Furman, R. (2006). Establishing trustworthiness in qualitative research in social work: Implications from a study regarding spirituality. *Qualitative Social Work, 5*(4), 441–458.

Lincoln, Y. S. (1995). Emerging criteria for qualitative and interpretive research. *Qualitative Inquiry, 3,* 275–289.

Lincoln, Y. S., & Guba, E. G. (1985). *Naturalistic inquiry.* Beverly Hills, CA: Sage.

Lincoln, Y. S., & Guba, E. G. (2000). Paradigmatic controversies, contradictions, and emerging confluences. In N. K. Denzin & Y. S. Lincoln (Eds.), *Handbook of qualitative research.* (pp. 163–188). Thousand Oaks, CA: Sage.

Link, B. G., & Phelan, J. (1995). Social conditions as fundamental causes of disease. *Journal of Health and Social Behavior, 35,* 80–94.

Locke L., Spirduso, W., & Silverman, S. (1993). Preparation of proposals for qualitative research: Different assumptions. In L. Locke, W. Spirduso, &

S. Silverman (Eds.), *Proposals that work: A guide for planning dissertations and grant proposals* (3rd ed., pp. 96–118). Newbury Park, CA: Sage.

Lofland, J. (2002). Analytic ethnography. In A. M. Huberman & M. B. Miles (Eds.), *The qualitative researcher's companion* (pp. 137–170). Thousand Oaks, CA: Sage.

Lofland, J., & Lofland, L. (1995). *Analyzing social settings: A guide to qualitative observation and analysis* (3rd ed.). Belmont, CA: Wadsworth.

Luders, C. (2004). Field observation and ethnography. In U. Flick, E. von Kardorff, & I. Steinke (Eds.), *A companion to qualitative research* (pp. 222–230). London: Sage.

Lynd, R. S., & Lynd, H. M. (1937). *Middletown in transition: A study in cultural conflicts.* New York: Harcourt Brace.

Lynd, R. S., & Lynd, H. M. (1956). *Middletown: A study in modern American culture.* New York: Harcourt Brace.

MacClean, L. M., Meyer, M., & Estable, A. (2004). Improving accuracy of transcripts in qualitative research. *Qualitative Health Research, 14*(1), 113–123.

MacGregor, T. E., Rodger, S., Cummings, A. L., & Leschied, A. W. (2006). The needs of foster parents: A qualitative study of motivation, support and retention. *Qualitative Social Work, 5*(3), 351–368.

Madison, D. S. (2005). *Critical ethnography: Methods, ethics, and performance.* Thousand Oaks, CA: Sage.

Magill, M. (2006). The future of evidence in evidence-based practice. *Journal of Social Work, 6*(20), 101–115.

Malinoswki, B. (1922). *Argonauts of the Western Pacific.* London: Routledge.

Malone, R. E., Yerger, V. E., McGruder, C., & Froelicher, E. (2006). "It's like Tuskegee in reverse": A case study of ethical tensions in institutional review board review of community-based participatory research. *American Journal of Public Health, 96,* 1914–1919.

Mancini, M. A. (2005). "Making sense of it all": Consumer providers' theories about factors facilitating and impeding recovery from psychiatric disabilities. *Psychiatric Rehabilitation Journal, 29*(1), 48–55.

Mancini, M. A. (2007). The role of self-efficacy in recovery from serious psychiatric disabilities: A qualitative study with fifteen psychiatric survivors. *Qualitative Social Work, 6*(1), 49–74.

Manderson, L., & Aaby, P. (1992). An epidemic in the field? Rapid assessment procedures and health research. *Social Science & Medicine, 35,* 839–850.

Manderson, L., Bennett, E., & Andajani-Sutjaho, S. (2006). The social dynamics of the interview: Age, class and gender. *Qualitative Health Research, 16*(10), 1317–1334.

Manderson, L., Kelaher, M., & Woelz-Stirling, N. (2001). Developing qualitative databases for multiple users. *Qualitative Health Research, 11*(2), 149–160.

Manicas, P. T., & Secord, P. F. (1982). Implications for psychology of the new philosophy of science. *American Psychologist, 38,* 390–413.

Manwar, A., Johnson, B. D., & Dunlap, E. (1994). Qualitative data analysis with Hypertext: A case of New York City crack dealers. *Qualitative Sociology, 17,* 283–292.

Marcus, G. E. (1994). What comes (just) after "post"? The case of ethnography. In N. K. Denzin & Y. S. Lincoln (Eds.), *Handbook of qualitative research* (pp. 563–574). Thousand Oaks, CA: Sage.

Markham, A. N. (2005). The methods, politics, and ethics of representation in online ethnography. In N. K. Denzin & Y. S. Lincoln (Eds.), *Handbook of qualitative research* (3rd ed., pp. 793–820). Thousand Oaks, CA: Sage.

Marshall, C., & Rossman, G. B. (2006). *Designing qualitative research* (4th ed.). Thousand Oaks, CA: Sage.

Mathew, R. (2008). *Evolving traditions: South Asians and arranged marriages.* Youngstown, NY: Cambria Press.

Maxwell, J. (2002). Understanding and validity in qualitative research. In A. M. Huberman & M. B. Miles (Eds.), *The qualitative researcher's companion* (pp. 37–62). Thousand Oaks, CA: Sage.

Mayring, P. (2004). Qualitative content analysis. In U. Flick, E. von Kardorff, & I. Steinke (Eds.), A companion to qualitative research. (pp. 266–270). London: Sage.

McCall, M. (2000). Performance ethnography: A brief history and some advice. In N. K. Denzin & Y. S. Lincoln (Eds.), *Handbook of qualitative research* (pp. 421–434). Thousand Oaks, CA: Sage.

McCoyd J. L., & Kerson, T. S. (2006). Conducting intensive interviews via email: A serendipitous comparative opportunity. *Qualitative Social Work, 5*(3), 389–406.

McCracken, G. (1988). *The long interview.* Newbury Park, CA: Sage.

McDonald, S. (2005). Studying actions in context: A qualitative shadowing method for organizational research. *Qualitative Research, 5*(4), 455–473.

McKibbon, K., & Gadd, C. (2004). A quantitative analysis of qualitative studies in clinical journals for the 2000 publishing year. *BMC Medical Informatics and Decision Making, 4*(1), 11–20.

Mead, M. (1928). *Coming of age in Samoa.* New York: New American Library.

Menand, L. (2001). *The metaphysical club: A story of ideas in America.* New York: Farrar, Straus, & Giroux.

Merton, R. K., Fiske, M., & Kendall, P. (1956). *The focused interview.* Glencoe, IL: Free Press.

Miles, M. B., & Huberman, A. M. (Eds.). (1994). *Qualitative data analysis: An expanded sourcebook* (2nd ed.). Thousand Oaks, CA: Sage.

Miles, M. B., & Weitzman, E. A. (1994). Choosing computer programs for qualitative data analysis. In M. B. Miles & A. M. Huberman (Eds.), *Qualitative data analysis: An expanded sourcebook* (2nd ed.). Thousand Oaks, CA: Sage.

Miller, D., & Slater, D. (2000). *The Internet: An ethnographic approach.* New York: Berg.

Miller, S. I., & Fredericks, M. (2002). Naturalistic inquiry and reliabilism: A compatible epistemological grounding. *Qualitative Health Research, 12,* 982–989.

Miller, S. I., & Fredericks, M. (2006). Mixed-methods and evaluation research: trends and issues. *Qualitative Health Research, 16,* 567–579.

Mills, J., Bonner, A., & Francis, K. (2006). The development of constructivist grounded theory. *International Journal of Qualitative Methods, 5*(1), Article 3.

Minkler, M., & Wallerstein, N. (2003). *Community-based participatory research for health.* San Francisco: Jossey-Bass.

Mishler, E. (1986). *Research interviewing: Context and narrative.* Cambridge, MA: Harvard University Press.

Mizrahi, T., & Abramson, J. S. (1994). Collaboration between social workers and physicians: An emerging typology. In E. Sherman & W. J. Reid (Eds.), *Qualitative research in social work* (pp. 135–151). New York: Columbia University Press.

Morgan, D. L. (1997). *Focus groups as qualitative research.* Thousand Oaks, CA: Sage.

Morgan, D. L. (2007). Paradigms lost and pragmatism regained. *Journal of Mixed Methods Research, 1*(2), 48–76.

Morrow, S. (2005). Quality and trustworthiness in qualitative research in counseling psychology. *Journal of Counseling Psychology, 52*(2), 250–260.

Morrow, S. L., & Smith, M. L. (1995). Constructions of survival and coping by women who have survived childhood sexual abuse. *Journal of Counseling Psychology, 42*(1), 24–33.

Morse, J. M. (1991). Approaches to qualitative-quantitative methodological triangulation. *Nursing Research, 40,* 120–123.

Morse, J. M. (1994). Designing funded qualitative research. In N. K. Denzin & Y. L. Lincoln (Eds.), *Handbook of qualitative research* (pp. 220–235). Thousand Oaks, CA: Sage.

Morse, J. M. (1995). The significance of saturation. *Qualitative Health Research, 5,* 147–149.

Morse, J. (2005). Evolving trends in qualitative research: Advances in mixed-method design. *Qualitative Health Research, 15*(5), 583–585.

Morse, J. M. (2006). The politics of evidence. *Qualitative Health Research, 16*(3), 395–404.

Morse, J. M. (2007) Qualitative researchers don't count. *Qualitative Health Research, 17*(3), 287.

Morse, J. M. (2007). Reasons for rejection, reasons for acceptance. *Qualitative Health Research, 17*(9), 1163–1164.

Munhall, P. L. (1994). *Qualitative research proposals and reports: A guide.* New York: National League for Nursing Press.

Moustakas, C. (1994). *Phenomenological research methods.* Thousand Oaks, CA: Sage.

Nader, L. (1969). Up the anthropologist: Perspectives gained from studying up. In D. Hymes (Ed.), *Reinventing anthropology* (pp. 284–311). New York: Random House.

National Association of Deans and Directors of Schools of Social Work Task Force on Administrative Research Infrastructures Within Social Work Education Programs. (1997). *Challenges and opportunities for promoting federally funded research in social work programs.* Washington, DC: Institute for the Advancement of Social Work Research.

Nelson, G., Ochocka, J., Griffin, K., & Lord, J. (1998). "Nothing about me, without me": Participatory action research with self-help/mutual aid organizations. *American Journal of Community Psychology, 26*(6), 881–913.

Newman, K., Fox, C., Roth, W., & Mehta, J. (2004). *Rampage: The social roots of school shootings.* New York: Basic Books.

Oakley, A. (1981). Interviewing women: A contradiction in terms. In H. Roberts (Ed.), *Doing feminist research* (pp. 30–61). London: Routledge & Kegan Paul.

Olesen, V. L. (2000). Feminisms and qualitative research at and into the millennium. In N. K. Denzin & Y. S. Lincoln (Eds.), *Handbook of qualitative research* (pp. 215–256). Thousand Oaks, CA: Sage.

Onken, S. J., Craig, C. M., Ridgway, P., Ralph, R. O. & Cook, J. A. (2004). An Analysis of the Definitions and Elements of Recovery: A Review of the Literature. Pre-Conference Paper prepared for the National Consensus Conference on Mental Health Recovery and Systems Transformation, Rockville, MD.

Packer, G. (2006, December 18). Knowing the enemy: Can social scientists redefine the war on terror? *The New Yorker*, 32–40.

Padgett, D. K. (Ed.). (2004a). *The qualitative research experience*. Belmont, CA: Thomson.

Padgett, D. K. (2004b). Spreading the word: Writing up and disseminating qualitative research. In D. K. Padgett (Ed.), *The qualitative research experience* (pp. 285–296). Belmont, CA: Thomson.

Padgett, D. K. (2004c). Mixed methods, serendipity and concatenation. In D. K. Padgett (Ed.), *The qualitative research experience* (pp. 269–281). Belmont, CA: Thomson.

Padgett, D. K. (2005). Qualitative methods in evaluation. In D. Royse, B. T. Thyer, D. K. Padgett, & T. K. Logan, *Program evaluation* (4th ed., pp. 48–61). Pacific Grove, CA: Wadsworth Publishers.

Padgett, D. K. (2007). There's no place like (a) home: Ontological Security in the third decade of the homelessness crisis. *Social Science & Medicine, 64,* 1925–1936.

Padgett, D. K., Conte, S., & Benjamin R. (2004). Peer debriefing and support groups. In D. K. Padgett (Ed.), *The qualitative research experience* (pp. 225–235). Belmont, CA: Thomson.

Padgett, D. K., Gulcur, L., & Tsemberis, S. (2006). Housing first services for the psychiatrically disabled homeless with co-occurring substance abuse. *Research on Social Work Practice, 16,* 74–83.

Padgett, D. K., Hawkins, R. L., Abrams, C., & Davis, A. (2006). In their own words: Trauma and substance abuse in the lives of formerly homeless women with serious mental illness. *American Journal of Orthopsychiatry, 76*(1), 461–467.

Padgett, D. K., Henwood, B., Abrams, C., & Davis, A. (2008). Engagement and retention in care among formerly homeless adults with serious mental illness: Voices from the margins. *Psychiatric Rehabilitation Journal, 31*(3), 226–233.

Padgett, D. K., Mathew, R., & Conte, S. (2004). Peer debriefing and support groups. In D. K. Padgett (Ed.), *The qualitative research experience* (pp. 156–169). Pacific Grove, CA: Thomson Learning.

Padgett, D., Patrick, C., Burns, B. J., & Schlesinger, H. J. (1994). Ethnicity and use of outpatient mental health services in a national insured population. *American Journal of Public Health, 84,* 222–226.

Padgett, D. K., Yedidia, M., Kerner, J., & Mandelblatt, J. (2001). The emotional consequences of false positive mammography: African-American women's reactions in their own words. *Women and Health, 33,* 1–14.

Patton, M. Q. (2002). *Qualitative research and evaluation methods* (3rd ed.). Thousand Oaks, CA: Sage.

Perreault, M., Pawliuk, N., Veilleux, R., & Rousseau, M. (2006). Qualitative assessment of mental health service satisfaction: Strengths and limitations of a self-administered measure. *Community Mental Health Journal, 42*(3), 233–242.

Polkinghorne, D. E. (1988). *Narrative knowing and the human sciences*. Albany: State University of New York Press.

Powdermaker, H. (1966). *Stranger and, friend: The way of an anthropologist*. New York: W. W. Norton.

Punch, M. (1994). Politics and ethics in qualitative research. In N. K. Denzin & Y. S. Lincoln (Eds.), *Handbook of qualitative research* (pp. 83–97). Thousand Oaks, CA: Sage.

Rabinow, P., & Sullivan, W. M. (Eds.). (1979). *Interpretive social science: A reader*. Berkeley: University of California Press.

Ragin, C. C. (1987). *The comparative method. Moving beyond qualitative and quantitative strategies*. Berkeley, CA: Univ. of California Press.

Ragin, C. C., & Becker, H. S. (1992). *What is a case? Exploring the foundations of social inquiry*. Cambridge: Cambridge University Press.

Rallis, S. F., & Rossman, G. B. (2003). Mixed methods in evaluation contexts: A pragmatic framework. In A. Tashakkori & C. Teddlie (Eds.), *Handbook of mixed methods in social and behavioral research* (pp. 491–512). Thousand Oaks, CA: Sage.

Reason, P., & Bradbury, H. (2001). *Handbook of action research*. Thousand Oaks, CA: Sage.

Reinharz, R. (1992). *Feminist methods in social research*. New York: Oxford University Press.

Rennie, D. L., Watson, K. D., & Monteiro, A. M. (2002). The rise of qualitative research in psychology. *Canadian Psychology, 43*, 179–189.

Richardson, L. (2000). Writing: A method of inquiry. In N. K. Denzin & Y. S. Lincoln (Eds.), *Handbook of qualitative research* (2nd ed., pp. 923–938). Thousand Oaks, CA: Sage.

Ridgway, P. (2001). Re-storying psychiatric disability: Learning from first person recovery narratives. *Psychiatric Rehabilitation Journal, (24)*4, 335–343.

Riessman, C. K. (1990). *Divorce talk: Women and men make sense of personal relationships*. Rutgers, NJ: Rutgers University Press.

Riessman, C. K. (1993). *Narrative analysis*. Newbury Park, CA: Sage.

Riessman, C. K. (Ed.). (1994). *Qualitative studies in social work research*. Thousand Oaks, CA: Sage.

Riessman, C. K., & Quinney, L. (2005). Narrative in social work: A critical review. *Qualitative Social Work, 4*(4), 391–412.

Rodwell, M. K. (1998). *Social work constructivist research*. New York: Garland Publishing.

Rolfe, G. (2006). Validity, trustworthiness and rigour: Quality and the idea of qualitative research. *Journal of Advanced Nursing, 53*(3), 304–310.

Rorty, R. (1998). *Truth and progress: Philosophical papers III*. Cambridge: Cambridge University Press.

Rosaldo, R. (1989). *Culture and truth: The remaking of social analysis*. Boston: Beacon.

Rosario, P. (2007). Research as resistance: Critical, indigenous and anti-oppressive approaches. *Qualitative Social Work, 6*(1), 121–125.

Ruckdeschel, R., Earnshaw, P., & Firrek, A. (1994). The qualitative case study and evaluation: Issues, methods, and examples. In E. Sherman & W. J. Reid (Eds.), *Qualitative research in social work* (pp. 251–264). New York: Columbia University Press.

Ryan, G. W. & Bernard, H. R. (2000). Data management and analysis methods. In N. K. Denzin and Y. S. Lincoln (Eds.), *Handbook of qualitative research* (pp. 769–802). Thousand Oaks, CA: Sage.

Ryan, G. W. & Bernard, H. R. (2003). Techniques to identify themes. *Field Methods, 15*(1), 85–109.

Sacks, H., & Garfinkel, H. (1970). On formal structures of practical action. In J. C. McKinney & E. A. Tiryakian (Eds.), *Theoretical sociology* (pp. 338–366). New York: Appleton-Century-Crofts.

Saleebey, D. (2005). *The strengths perspective in social work practice* (4th ed.). Boston: Allyn & Bacon.

Salmon, A. (2007). Walking the talk: How participatory interview methods can democratize research. *Qualitative Health Research, 17*(7), 982–994.

Sandelowski, M. (1993). Rigor, or rigor mortis: The problem of rigor in qualitative research revisited. *Advances in Nursing Science, 16*, 1–8.

Sandelowski, M. (2000). Combining qualitative and quantitative sampling, data collection, and analysis techniques in mixed methods studies. *Research in Nursing & Health, 23*, 246–255.

Sandelowski, M. (2002). Re-embodying qualitative inquiry. *Qualitative Health Research, 12*(1), 104–115.

Sandelowski, M., & Barroso, J. (2002). Reading qualitative studies. *International Journal of Qualitative Methods, 1*(1), Article 5.

Sandelowski, M., & Barroso, J. (2003). Classifying the findings in qualitative studies. *Qualitative Health Research, 13*(7), 905–923.

Sandelowski, M., & Jones, L. C. (1995). "Healing fictions": Stories of choosing in the aftermath of the detection of fetal anomalies. *Social Science and Medicine, 42*, 353–361.

Sands, R. G. (2004). Narrative analysis: A feminist approach. In D. K. Padgett (Ed.), *The qualitative research experience* (pp. 48–62). Belmont, CA: Thomson.

Sanjek, R. (1990). *Fieldnotes: The making of anthropology.* Albany: State University of New York Press.

Schein, E. H. (1987). *The clinical perspective in fieldwork.* Newbury Park, CA: Sage.

Scheper-Hughes, N. (1979). *Saints, scholars, and schizophrenics: Mental illness in rural Ireland.* Berkeley, CA: University of California Press.

Scheper-Hughes, N. (1996). Small wars and invisible genocides. *Social Science and Medicine, 43*(5), 889–900.

Scheper-Hughes, N. (2000). Ire in Ireland. *Ethnography, 1*(1), 117–140.

Schofield, J. (2002). Increasing the generalizability of qualitative research. In A. M. Huberman & M. B. Miles (Eds.), *The qualitative researcher's companion* (pp. 171–203). Thousand Oaks, CA: Sage.

Schön, D. A. (1983). *The reflective practitioner: How professionals think in action.* New York: Basic Books.

Schutz, A. (1967). *The phenomenology of the social world.* Evanston, IL: Northwestern University Press.

Schwandt, T. A. (1994). Constructivist, interpretivist approaches to human inquiry. In N. K. Denzin & Y. S. Lincoln (Eds.), *Handbook of qualitative research* (pp. 118–137). Thousand Oaks, CA: Sage.

Schwandt, T. A., & Halpern, E. S. (1988). *Linking auditing and meta-evaluation: Enhancing quality in applied research.* Newbury Park, CA: Sage.

Schweder, R. A. (2006). Protecting human subjects and preserving human freedom: Prospects at the University of Chicago. *American Ethnologist, 33*(4), 507–518.

Scrimshaw, S. C, Carballo, M., Ramos, L., & Blair, B. A. (1991). The AIDS Rapid Anthropological Assessment Procedures: A tool for health education planning and evaluation. *Health Education Quarterly, 18*(1), 111–123.

Scrimshaw, S., & Gleason, G. R. (1992). *Rapid assessment procedures: Qualitative methodologies for planning and evaluation of health-related programs.* Boston, MA: International Nutrition Foundation for Developing Countries (INFDC).

Scriven, M. (1967). The methodology of evaluation. *AERA Monograph Series in Curriculum Evaluation, 1,* 39–83.

Seidman, I. (2006). *Interviewing as qualitative research.* New York: Teachers' College Press.

Shibusawa, T., & Lukens, E. (2004). Analyzing qualitative data in a cross-language context: A collaborative model. In D. K. Padgett (Ed.), *The qualitative research experience* (pp. 175–186). Belmont, CA: Thomson.

Shibusawa, T., & Padgett, D. K. (in press). Out of sync: A life course perspective on aging among formerly homeless adults with serious mental illness. *Journal of Aging Studies.*

Silverman, D. (2006). *Interpreting qualitative data* (3rd ed.). Thousand Oaks, CA: Sage.

Slevin, E., & Sines, D. (2000) Enhancing the truthfulness, consistency and transferability of a qualitative study: Utilising a manifold of approaches. *Nurse Researcher, 7*(2), 79–89.

Smith, C., & Short, P. M. (2001). Integrating technology to improve the efficiency of qualitative data analysis: A note on methods. *Qualitative Sociology, 24*(3), 401–407.

Snow, D. A. (2002). On the presumed crisis in ethnographic representation: Observations from a sociological and interactionist standpoint. *Journal of Contemporary Ethnography, 31*(4), 498–507.

Snow, D. A., & Anderson, L. (1991). Researching the homeless: The characteristic features and virtues of the case study. In J. R. Feagin, A. M. Orum, & G. Sjoberg (Eds.), *A case for the case study* (pp. 148–173). Chapel Hill: University of North Carolina Press.

Spradley, J. P. (1979). *The ethnographic interview.* New York: Holt, Rinehart & Winston.

Stack, C. B. (1974). *All our kin: Strategies for survival in a black community.* New York: Harper Colophon.

Stake, R. E. (1995). *The art of case study research.* Thousand Oaks, CA: Sage.

Stake, R. E. (2005). *Multiple case study analysis.* New York: Guilford Press.

Stange, K. C., Miller, W. L., Crabtree, B. F., O'Connor, P. J., & Zyzanski, S. J. (1994). Integrating qualitative and quantitative research methods. *Family Medicine, 21,* 448–451.

Steinmetz, A. M. (1991). Doing. In M. Ely, M. Anzul, T. Friedman, D. Garner, & A. M. Steinmetz, *Doing qualitative research: Circles within circles* (pp. 41–68). London: Falmer.

Strauss, A., & Corbin, J. (1990). *Basics of qualitative research: Grounded theory procedures and techniques.* Newbury Park, CA: Sage.

Strauss, A., & Corbin, J. (1994). Grounded theory methodology: An overview. In N. K. Denzin & Y. S. Lincoln (Eds.), *Handbook of qualitative research* (pp. 273–285). Thousand Oaks, CA: Sage.

Stringer, E. T. (2007) *Action research: A handbook for practitioners* (3rd ed.). Thousand Oaks, CA: Sage.

Susser, M. (1997). Authors and authorship: Reform or abolition? *American Journal of Public Health, 87,* 1091–1092.

Swigonski, M. E. (1994). The logic of feminist standpoint theory for social work research. *Social Work, 39,* 387–393.

Szreter, S., & Woolcock, M. (2004). Health by association? Social capital, social theory, and the political economy of public health. *International Journal of Epidemiology, 33,* 1–18.

Tandon, R. (1996). The historical roots and contemporary tendencies in participatory research: Implications for health care. In K. de Koning & M. Martin (Eds.), *Participatory research in health: Issues and experiences* (pp. 19–26). London: Zed.

Tannen, D. (1990). *You just don't understand: Women and men in conversation.* New York: William Morrow and Company.

Tannen, D. (2006). *You're wearing that? Understanding mothers and daughters in conversation.* New York: Ballantine Books.

Tashakkori, A., & Creswell, J. W. (2007). The new era of mixed methods. *Journal of Mixed Methods Research, 1*(1), 3–7.

Tashakkori, A., & Teddlie, C. (Eds.). (2003). *Handbook of mixed methods in social and behavioral research.* Thousand Oaks, CA: Sage.

Taylor, S. J. (1987). Observing abuse: Professional ethics and personal morality in field research. *Qualitative Sociology, 10,* 288–302.

Taylor, S. J., & Bogdan, R. (1984). *Introduction to qualitative research: The search for meanings* (2nd ed.). New York: John Wiley.

Tedlock, B. (2000). Ethnographic and ethnographic representation. In N. K. Denzin & Y. S. Lincoln (Eds.), *Handbook of qualitative research* (pp. 455–486). Thousand Oaks, CA: Sage.

ten Have, P. (1999). *Doing conversation analysis.* London: Sage.

Teram, E., Schachter, C. L., & Stalker, C. A. (2005). The case for integrating grounded theory with participatory action research: Empowering clients to inform professional practice. *Qualitative Health Research, 15*(8), 1129–1140.

Tesch, R. (1990). *Qualitative research: Analysis types and software tools.* London: Falmer.

Thomas, J. (1993). *Doing critical ethnography.* Newbury Park, CA: Sage.

Thorne, S. (1998). Ethical and representational issues in qualitative secondary analysis. *Qualitative Health Research, 8*(4), 547–555.

Thorne, S. (2000). Data analysis in qualitative research. *Evidence-Based Nursing, 3,* 68–70.

Thorne, S., Jensen, L., Kearny, M. H., Noblit, G., & Sandelowski, M. (2004). Qualitative metasynthesis: Reflections on methodological orientation and ideological agenda. *Qualitative Health Research, 14*(10), 1342–1365.

Tjora, A. H. (2006). Writing small discoveries: An exploration of fresh observers' observations. *Qualitative Research, 6*(4), 429–451.

Travers, M. (2006). Post-modernism and qualitative research. *Qualitative Research, 6*(2), 267–273.

Twinn, S. (1997). An exploratory study examining the influence of translation on the validity and reliability of qualitative data in nursing research. *Journal of Advanced Nursing, 26,* 418–423.

Uehara, E. (2001). Understanding the dynamics of illness and help-seeking: Event structure analysis and a Cambodian American narrative of "spirit invasion." *Social Science and Medicine, 52,* 519–536.

Ungar, M. (2006). "Too ambitious": What happens when funders under-estimate the strength of qualitative research design. *Qualitative Social Work, 5*(2), 261–277.

Van Maanen, J. (1988). *Tales of the field: On writing ethnography.* Chicago: University of Chicago Press.

van Manen, M. (Ed.). (2002). *Writing in the dark: Phenomenological studies in interpretive inquiry.* London, Canada: Althouse.

van Manen, M. (2006). Writing qualitatively, or the demands of writing. *Qualitative Health Research, 16,* 713–722.

Wackerbarth, S. B., Streams, M. E., & Smith, M. K. (2002). Capturing the insights of family caregivers: Survey item generation with a coupled focus group/interview process. *Qualitative Health Research, 12*(8), 1141–1154.

Wahab, S. (2003). Creating knowledge collaboratively with female sex workers: Insights from a qualitative, feminist, and participatory study. *Qualitative Inquiry, 9*(4), 625–642.

Waldrop, D. (2004). Ethical issues in qualitative research with high-risk populations. In D. K. Padgett (Ed.), *The qualitative research experience* (pp. 236–249). Belmont, CA: Thomson.

Walker, A. J., & Allen, K. R. (1991). Relationships between caregiving daughters and their elderly mothers. *The Gerontologist, 31,* 389–396.

Walker, D., & Myrick, F. (2006). Grounded theory: An exploration of process and procedures. *Qualitative Health Research, 16*(4), 547–559.

Wang, C., & Burris, M. A. (1997). Photovoice: Concept, methodology and use for participatory needs assessment. *Health Education & Behavior, 24*(3), 369–387.

Wang, C. C., Morrel-Samuels, S., Hutchinson, P., Bell, L., & Pestronk, R. M. (2004). Flint photovoice: Community building among youths, adults and policymakers. *American Journal of Public Health, 94*(6), 911–914.

Wang, C. C., & Redwood-Jones, Y. A. (2001). Photovoice ethics: Perspectives from Flint photovoice. *Health Education and Behavior, 28*(5), 560–572.

Weiss, R. S. (1994). *Learning from strangers: The art and method of qualitative interview studies.* New York: Free Press.

Weitzman, E., & Miles, M. (1995). *Computer programs for qualitative data analysis: A software sourcebook.* Thousand Oaks, CA: Sage.

West, C. (1989). *The American evasion of philosophy: A genealogy of pragmatism.* Madison, WI: University of Wisconsin Press.

Weston, C., Gandell, T., Beauchamp, J., McAlpine, N., Wiseman, C., & Beauchamp, C. (2001). Analyzing interview data: The development and evolution of a coding system. *Qualitative Sociology, 24*(3), 381–400.

White, M., & Epston, D. (1990). *Narrative means to therapeutic ends.* New York: Norton.

Whittemore, R., Chase, S. K., Mandle, C. (2001). Validity in qualitative research. *Qualitative Health Research, 11*(4), 522–527.

Whyte, W. F. (1955). *Street corner society* (2nd ed.). Chicago: University of Chicago Press.

Williams, C. C., & Collins, A. A. (2002). The social construction of disability in schizophrenia. *Qualitative Health Research, 12*(3), 297–309.

Wilson, H. S., & Hutchison, S. (1991). Triangulation of qualitative methods: Heideggerian hermeneutics and grounded theory. *Qualitative Health Research, 1*, 263–276.

Wimpenny P. & Gass, J. (2000). Interviewing in phenomenology and grounded theory: Is there a difference? *Journal of Advanced Nursing, 31*(6), 1485–1492.

Wolcott, H. F. (2001). *Writing up qualitative research* (2nd ed.). Thousand Oaks, CA: Sage.

Wolf, M. M. (1978). Social validity: The case for subjective measurement or how applied behavior analysis is finding its heart. *Journal of Applied Behavior Analysis, 11*, 203–214.

Yin, R. K. (2003). *Case study research: Design and methods* (3rd ed.). Thousand Oaks, CA: Sage.

Yin, R. K. (Ed.). (2004). *The case study anthology.* Thousand Oaks, CA: Sage.

Yip, K. (2006). Self-reflection in reflective practice: A note of caution. *British Journal of Social Work, 36*, 777–788.

Zola, I. K. (1983). *Missing pieces: A chronicle of living with a disability.* Philadelphia: Temple University Press.

Index

About the Author

Deborah K. Padgett, a professor at New York University School of Social Work, received her doctorate in anthropology and completed post-doctoral training programs in public health and psychiatric epidemiology at Columbia University and Duke University. A mental health services researcher, Dr. Padgett has published extensively on the health/mental health needs and service use of underserved ethnic groups, women, and the homeless. In addition to previous NIH grants, she is currently Principal Investigator of an all-qualitative R01 grant from NIMH to study recovery and the service delivery system for homeless adults with co-occurring mental and substance use disorders in New York City.

In addition to this text, Dr. Padgett is the editor of a reader in qualitative methods, *The Qualitative Research Experience* (2004) and *The Handbook of Ethnicity, Aging, and Mental Health* (1995), and coauthor of *Program Evaluation,* 4th edition (2004). Her expertise in qualitative methods has led to contributions to NIH Training Institutes and grant reviews. Dr. Padgett has also been an active mentor of other researchers and has served on numerous journal editorial boards. Currently, she is teaching courses on socio-behavioral health and qualitative/field methods in New York University's Global Public Health program.

Dr. Padgett has been active in the Society for Social Work and Research (SSWR) since its inception and served as SSWR Board Member (2002–2007) and President (2004–2006). She received an unprecedented honor in 2006 when SSWR announced the Deborah K. Padgett Early Career Fellowship in recognition of her contributions.